Our Love Is Here to Stay

OUR
Love
IS HERE TO STAY

TONY & LOIS
EVANS

Multnomah® Publishers *Sisters, Oregon*

OUR LOVE IS HERE TO STAY
published by Multnomah Publishers, Inc.

© 2004 by Tony and Lois Evans
This book is a revised and expanded edition of the authors' previously published *Seasons of Love*
International Standard Book Number: 1-59052-131-5

Cover design by The DesignWorks Group

Italics in Scripture are the authors' emphasis.
Unless otherwise indicated, Scripture quotations are from:
New American Standard Bible® © 1960, 1977, 1995
by the Lockman Foundation. Used by permission.
Other Scripture quotations are from:
The Holy Bible, New King James Version (NKJV) © 1984 by Thomas Nelson, Inc.
Holy Bible, New Living Translation (NLT)
© 1996. Used by permission of Tyndale House Publishers, Inc. All rights reserved.
The New Testament in Modern English, Revised Edition (Phillips) © 1958, 1960, 1972 by J. B. Phillips
The Holy Bible, *English Standard Version* (ESV)
© 2001 by Crossway Bibles, a division of Good News Publishers. Used by permission. All rights reserved.
The Holy Bible, New International Version (NIV) © 1973, 1984 by International Bible Society,
used by permission of Zondervan Publishing House

Multnomah is a trademark of Multnomah Publishers, Inc.,
and is registered in the U.S. Patent and Trademark Office.
The colophon is a trademark of Multnomah Publishers, Inc.

Printed in the United States of America

For information:
MULTNOMAH PUBLISHERS, INC. • P. O. BOX 1720 • SISTERS, OR 97759

Library of Congress Cataloging-in-Publication Data

Evans, Anthony T.
    Our love is here to stay / Tony and Lois Evans.
        p. cm.
    Rev. and expanded ed of: Seasons of love. c1998.
    ISBN 1-59052-131-5
    1. Spouses—Prayer-books and devotions—English. I. Evans, Lois, 1949- II Evans, Anthony T.
Seasons of love. III. Title.

BV4596.M3E928 2004
242'.644—dc22

                                                    2004015653

04 05 06 07 08 09 10—10 9 8 7 6 5 4 3 2 1 0

We gratefully dedicate this book
to our parents,
James Basil and Annie Eleen Cannings
and
Arthur Sherman and Evelyn Lucille Evans.
Thank you for modeling to us
the love, commitment, dedication,
faithfulness, and grace of a God-centered marriage.

*T*he thesis of this book is that since God created the institution of marriage, He's the one who has to make it work!

As of this writing, we have been married thirty-four years. During this time we have had to face and communicate our way through financial struggles, job and ministry pressures, personality differences, child-rearing trials, and myriad other challenges that are the common lot of married couples.

Sometimes people ask us how we have made it thus far. Our answer is always the same: "He who began a good work in [us] will perfect it" (Philippians 1:6). God does not begin things He does not plan to finish, and marriage is one of those things. *Our love is here to stay!*

Thirty-four years ago we promised to weather the good and the bad and to do it together. There was no provision for circumstances, no matter how difficult, to overrule that commitment.

Yet it is not just our human tenacity that has allowed us to weather the challenges the years have brought our way. The key is that Jesus Christ and His Word are the foundation of our lives. He is the centerpiece of our marriage relationship. He occupies the throne of our lives, and as such He is the One who makes the joys and pleasures of this wonderful union called marriage so meaningful to us.

Over these years, God has given us many truths that have undergirded our relationship. *Our Love Is Here to Stay* is our way of sharing some of these truths with you so that, with the mighty help of the Holy Spirit, you will be able to experience the blessing of His presence in your home.

Our prayers are that the two of you will get together for a few minutes each day to meet with God, and that the daily principles shared in this book will help you grow in your relationship with each other and with God. We have both written from our hearts in these pages: Some devotionals are authored by Tony, and some by Lois. Some days, the readings will focus on the husband and father in the home; other days, the wife and mother will be the focus. As you read together, you will be able to encourage one another. As the Book says: "Let us consider how to stimulate one another to love and good deeds" (Hebrews 10:24).

If you will join regularly as a couple, with sincerity of heart, to meet with the Author of your relationship, we can assure you that your marriage and home life will begin to experience His powerful hand.

It is our hope that God will use these daily devotionals to help you enhance the spiritual, emotional, and personal development of your marriage relationship. Then you too will be able to look with confidence into the future and say, "Our love is here to stay!"

Tony and Lois Evans

Winter

WHEN ALL ELSE FAILS...

Be subject to one another in the fear of Christ.

EPHESIANS 5:21

Have you heard the story of the husband whose wife catches a cold each successive year of their marriage? Here's how it progresses:

Year 1: "Sugar dumpling, this cold is making you mighty uncomfortable. Won't you let your lover boy take his baby to the doctor to get rid of that nasty cough?"

Year 2: "Darling, that cold seems to be getting worse. Call Dr. Miller."

Year 3: "You'd better lie down, dear, and rest with that cold before the baby wakes up."

Year 4: "Be sensible now and take care of that cold before it gets any worse."

Year 5: "You'll be all right. Just take some aspirin. By the way, how about ironing these pants for me to wear today?"

Year 6: "Would you do something about that cough instead of barking like a seal?"

Year 7: "Woman, do something about that cold before you give me pneumonia!"

It's true...if we're not careful, we can move from concern for our spouse to concern only or ourselves. But things don't have to fall apart after the honeymoon. Commit yourselves to spending time each day together in God's Word. Open the "instruction manual" and find out how this beautiful thing called marriage is supposed to work. Ask God to restore that "Year 1" sense of excitement to your marriage. That's just what He's waiting to do.

THE IMPORTANCE OF OUR ATTITUDE

*I have learned to be content in
whatever circumstances I am.*

PHILIPPIANS 4:11

Over the years, I've been an illustration in more of Tony's sermons than I can count. That's part of being a pastor's wife! Sometimes he exaggerates a little, but he has called me on one particular trait I have to admit to. I tend to be obsessive-compulsive. Things have to be a particular way and done at a particular time, or I begin to struggle with my attitude. (I have a feeling I'm not the only person who is like this.)

For people like us, learning to have a proper attitude when things aren't going our way is an adjustment that takes the daily help of the Holy Spirit. As Christians, we have the God-given power to adjust to whatever circumstances we find ourselves in. That's what is says in the Book! Yes, those adjustments require a growth process—and leaning hard on Christ. But the apostle Paul reminds us it can be done.

Each partner brings a set of expectations and needs into a marriage. We naturally want to get our desired goals accomplished, get our needs met, and receive the attention we need. And when it doesn't happen…we react.

But God wants us to react *supernaturally*, not naturally. He wants us to develop biblical attitudes. And with His help, we can do it. We really can.

PUTTING CHRIST'S POWER TO WORK

I can do all things through
Him who strengthens me.

PHILIPPIANS 4:13

*S*ome Christian couples sit in the pew on Sunday morning singing that their God is "so high you can't get over Him, so low you can't get under Him, so wide you can't get around Him"…but they don't believe He can put their marriage back together.

Given our weak humanity, it isn't hard to understand why marriages struggle to survive the pressures of the twenty-first century. But here's the good news: We don't have to rely on our own finite power to hold things together. With Christ as our Enabler, we can do all things because He has promised to give us the strength.

If I had the athletic ability of home-run king Henry Aaron, I could hit a lot of home runs. If I had the musical ability of Mozart, I could create beautiful music. If I had the mind of Albert Einstein, I could solve difficult equations.

I don't have those abilities in the physical realm, but spiritually I have all the ability I need to accomplish whatever God asks me to do. And since God's command is that a husband and wife commit themselves to each other for life, every Christian couple has the ability to accomplish God's will for their marriage.

God made marriage, and He can make it work. Claim that power for your marriage, beginning today.

HOW TO HAVE A
"MISSIONARY MARRIAGE"

*This mystery is great; but I am speaking
with reference to Christ and the church.*

EPHESIANS 5:32

In this life, men and women are married to one another.

But when we are gathered together in heaven, there will be no marriage (Mark 12:25). Instead, every member of the church will be wed to Christ. Knowing that marriage is a model of the eternal union of the believer and Christ in heaven gives us a very special reason for improving the quality of our marriages.

Everyone agrees that a good marriage is more pleasant than an unhappy one. But equally important, because marriage is designed to be a model of the heavenly union between Christ and believers, your marriage may be the tool the Holy Spirit uses to win someone to Christ.

Or your marriage may cause another person to turn away from God's offer of salvation.

That in itself should be reason enough for us to learn to be godly mates and live the abundant life in the context of a growing, Christ-centered marriage.

We never know exactly who may be watching our lives. But we know that many unbelievers keep a close eye on Christians, trying to decide whether these followers of Jesus have anything going for themselves that's worth finding out about.

Make your marriage a brightly burning light for Christ, and somebody else will be drawn to the flame.

ORIGINAL JOB DESCRIPTION

The LORD God took the man and put him into the garden of Eden to cultivate it and keep it.

GENESIS 2:15

*B*efore the temptation and fall of man, Adam walked and talked with God the way two friends might visit on a summer evening. During those talks, they discussed work.

God had a job description in mind for the first man. He was to tend and cultivate the Garden of Eden—a pleasant task before weeds came on the scene!

Remember, Adam was still single at this point. In other words, God gave Adam a job *before* He gave him a helper and family.

It's clear from the order of events in Genesis 2 that God wants a husband to work and be responsible, to be the provider for his family.

Things have become a whole lot more complicated in our day, with many women in the workplace, sometimes earning more money than their husbands.

But the biblical priority has not changed. God has still given the man the primary responsibility to provide for his family. In fact, Paul said in 1 Timothy 5:8 that a man who refuses to do this is worse than an unbeliever.

When a Christian man makes his wife and family feel well cared for and protected, regardless of the size of his salary, he demonstrates that he is serious about being a husband and father who pleases God.

A SUITABLE HELPER

Then the LORD God said,
"It is not good for the man to be alone;
I will make him a helper suitable for him."

GENESIS 2:18

Creating a mate for Adam was God's idea, not Adam's. Genesis 2:18 reminds us that all of God's plans are perfect.

The problem is not marriage. It's the people who are bound together in a relationship that make it good or bad. As one man said, "I thought my marriage would be ideal. But now it's become an ordeal, and I want a new deal."

One of the most important things a husband must learn is how to cherish his wife as the life helper God created her to be. God made Eve to correspond perfectly to Adam. She was just what he needed to complement and complete him.

The word *helper* means "one who is brought alongside to assist." Throughout the Bible, women were given one basic responsibility: to help. But when Adam and Eve fell, marriage fell with them. From that point on, the roles of husband and wife would be complicated by our sinfulness. One "fruit" of the fall is that instead of being helpers in the home, many women have been forced to become mother, father, and breadwinner because there is no husband present.

But in a home where the husband is committed to love and lead, his wife is free to become a helper. And when that happens, a husband has the best friend he can ever have in his corner.

A HUSBAND'S GREATEST NEED

The wife must see to it that she respects her husband.

EPHESIANS 5:33

*D*id you know that God never commanded wives to love their husbands?

Certainly, God expects such love. Paul told Titus that older women should "encourage the young women to love their husbands" (Titus 2:4). But God's basic command is for wives to *respect* their husbands.

There's no denying that men have strong egos...with a great need for recognition. Just as women have a need to be loved, men have a need to be respected. That is why Peter tells wives not to use their tongues to turn disobedient husbands around, but rather to use reverence (1 Peter 3:1–2).

When a man's wife gives him respect, he is more likely to return that respect with the love and security she seeks.

Sarah called Abraham "lord," recognizing his position as head of the home and as a demonstration of sincere respect (1 Peter 3:6). That pleased Abraham, but more important, it pleased God.

In fact, God honored Sarah so much that He gave her a child when she was ninety! And He will honor your submission as well.

Many men don't receive respect at their jobs or in the world, where they're looked at as inferior no matter what their age. There needs to be a place where they know they are respected.

That place, in God's wise plan, should be the home.

WHAT MAKES A MAN?

The LORD God commanded the man, saying,
"From any tree of the garden you may eat freely;
but from the tree of the knowledge
of good and evil you shall not eat."

GENESIS 2:16—17

When God called Adam on the carpet for his sin, he tried to pin the blame on God Himself. *"It was the woman You gave me who caused this mess!"* (see Genesis 3:12).

But God wasn't buying it. Adam knew very well what God had commanded. God issued this command before He ever created Eve. So although Eve sinned first, Adam was the one God went looking for.

The conversation God had with Adam points to a weakness in many homes today. Too many Christian husbands don't really know what God has said about their responsibility to their wives and families.

Many men in our culture tend to draw their identity not from God's Word, but from their friends at work, the athletes they admire, or the images on television.

But God's definition of manhood is in direct conflict with the culture's idea of what makes a man. Biblical manhood is the ability to put divine truth into action at home and on the job. No amount of strength, good looks, or liquid assets can improve a man's performance from God's perspective.

Husband, if God is going to hold you accountable for what happens under your roof, you'd better get into the Book and find out what He has said. Then teach it to your family…and start leading.

There is nothing more manly than that.

THE PERFECT EXAMPLE OF SUBMISSION

Being found in appearance as a man,
[Jesus] humbled Himself by
becoming obedient to the point of death,
even death on a cross.

PHILIPPIANS 2:8

My mother had many struggles to overcome, raising eight children, putting many of her dreams and goals on hold. She submitted to God's will for her life. I would often hear her say, *"For His name's sake."* My mother was not in a marriage and raising a family for herself, but for His name's sake. What a role model!

In Philippians 2:5–11, Paul tells us that Jesus was and is God Himself, equal in essence to the Father. But to accomplish our salvation, Jesus voluntarily laid aside the independent use of His deity and placed Himself under the absolute authority of His Father.

Jesus joyfully submitted to the Father's will, even though it meant going to the cross. When I consider what He did for me, I realize that the submission He asks of me is not only possible, but can be done with joy.

It also helps me to remember that submission in marriage is not one-sided. As the leader in our home, Tony is called to submit to Christ as his head (1 Corinthians 11:3).

But the Bible says we as Christian wives are to submit to our husbands "as to the Lord" (Ephesians 5:22; 1 Peter 3:1–6). I can submit to Jesus without reservation...and I can trust Him to honor my submission to Tony.

CELEBRATE THE DIFFERENCE

*"She shall be called Woman,
because she was taken out of Man."*

GENESIS 2:23

*H*ave you heard it…or said it? "We're just not compatible. We're as different as night and day."

In light of God's design for marriage, this is one of the most obvious statements a husband or wife could make. *Of course* you're different!

I don't hear a young man complaining about the differences between men and women when he gets ready to walk down the aisle and marry the young lady who has captured his heart. He's ecstatic that she isn't just like him!

The reason a husband and wife need each other is *because* they are different. One of the sweetest blessings God has given me is a woman who has a personality totally different from mine. I'm an outgoing, exuberant, public personality, while Lois is sedate and serene.

Because our personalities are in contrast, when I'm too outgoing, her reserve pulls me back. And when she is too reserved, my enthusiasm pulls her forward. Occasionally this causes friction, but those are minor distractions. Our goal remains to make our God-given differences work for us instead of against us.

When God brought Eve to Adam, he recognized immediately how distinctly different she was from him—and he was excited about those differences. Adam also knew that Eve was part of him—she made him complete and drove away his loneliness.

The Creator knew what He was doing.

Oooo-weee!

The LORD God fashioned into a woman
the rib which He had taken from the man,
and brought her to the man.

GENESIS 2:22

To prepare Adam for marriage, God put him to work naming the animals. Before long, Adam noticed that for every ram there was a ewe; for every rooster, a hen. But there was no one for Adam. He began to experience the need for a partner.

Then the Lord put him to sleep, opened his side, removed a rib, and closed up the flesh. While Adam slept, God made a woman from his rib. The word *fashioned* in Hebrew means "to build." And no one knows how to build like God!

Having created Eve, God brought her to Adam. When Adam woke and saw her, he said words that are literally translated, "This is now." That seems like a strange thing to say, until we understand that the spirit behind Adam's declaration is joyous astonishment. This phrase could be translated, "Oooo-weee!" Here was the solution to Adam's need.

My Christian brother, that woman God gave you isn't just a nice addition to your life. You *need* her, and she has a right to supersede all other loves and relationships in your life, except your love for Christ.

Manhood is not the ability to make it alone. God planned for a man to be made complete through a lifetime of faithful dedication to a specific woman. This is manhood as our wise Creator designed it.

A WOMAN'S EMOTIONAL WIRING

Be kind to one another, tender-hearted,
forgiving each other.

EPHESIANS 4:32

God made a woman to be a responder. He made her a little softer, a little warmer, a little more intricately fashioned.

In other words, when a husband shows his wife the exclusive, self-sacrificing love the Bible talks about, she will respond to that love. So the very thing a husband wants he receives by giving and serving, not by demanding.

God does not want a wife to love her husband and respond to him because he demands it; God wants her to respond because he overloads her emotional circuits with loving care, because he wears her out with love and attention.

I tell many men who come to me for marital counseling, "Stop pushing so hard and start loving a little harder." If a husband lets his wife know she is loved and makes her feel secure, he won't have to worry about their relationship. She will be right there, responding to his needs.

For many husbands, loving like this will require an apology and a new start. "I haven't loved you the way I am supposed to love you, and I know that it has affected our relationship. But I'm going to change. I'm going to love you deeply the way you need to be loved."

It is a commitment worth making…a thousand times over.

GET EXCITED ABOUT OPPOSITION!

Consider it all joy, my brethren,
when you encounter various trials,
knowing that the testing of your faith produces endurance.

JAMES 1:2–3

I enjoy a good game of basketball. I'm unstoppable…when I play alone. When there's no opposition, I can make any play and hit any shot.

But some years ago, I had an opportunity to go one-on-one with a star member of the Dallas Mavericks basketball team. Suddenly, I wasn't playing so well!

But that's the way the game of basketball is designed to be played. Having to face an opponent and learn how to cooperate with teammates to overcome the opposition should make me a better player, not a poorer one.

It's the same in marriage. Life's trials aren't designed to destroy your union. On the contrary, it's in learning how to face and overcome opposition and tough times *together* that a couple grows closer to each other and to God.

Until you face opposition as a couple, you will never really know how strong your marriage is. Until you have to work together to overcome an opponent, you will never know how good your teamwork might be.

Sure, the enemy will take aim at your marriage. From day one, his goal has been the destruction of marriage and family. But God has a wonderful way of turning Satan's attacks into faith-building trials. So the next time you and your spouse bump into opposition, get excited. God is about to grow your marriage!

STAYING OUT OF DEBT

Know well the condition of your flocks,
and pay attention to your herds.

PROVERBS 27:23

The writer of Proverbs urges us to know our financial situation well, to pay attention to where we are. Couples can fall into debt when they stop giving heed to what they are doing financially.

People fall into debt for one or more of four basic reasons:

1. They're ignorant of God's principles of finance. They don't know what God has said about money and debt, so they don't know how to put His Word into practice. They wind up doing "what everyone else is doing" and fall into financial bondage.

2. They have given in to greed. Self-indulgence, impulse spending, and a desire to have more—no matter what the cost—is a surefire formula for debt. The Bible calls these things greed, which leads to unwise decisions out of a desire for more.

3. They have planned poorly. It's amazing how many couples I talk to have no answer when I ask them about their financial plan for living within their budget. When people fail to plan, they plan to fail.

4. They are the victims of a financial catastrophe—something that is beyond their control.

Are you in debt right now? Identifying the cause of your debt is the first step toward doing something about it.

RESTORE THE LUSTER

Therefore remember from where you have fallen,
and repent and do the deeds you did at first.

REVELATION 2:5

*C*an marriages that have lost their luster be revived? The
answer is a resounding *yes!* As long as both of you are still breathing,
there is real hope. The formula for restoring a marriage parallels the
formula Jesus Christ gave to the church at Ephesus.

This church had been reduced to loveless rituals, but Christ
offered the members a way to revive their first love for Him: *remember, repent,* and *return.* Let's apply this to marriage.

First, a couple needs to *remember,* to reflect on the early days of
their friendship and marriage, when love ruled their lives. Can you
remember how you treated one another? Spoke to one another?
Built up one another?

Second, the formula calls for *repentance.* To confess that you are
wrong is tough, especially when words are not enough. To repent
means to change direction. In this case, the right direction is probably the early stage of your marriage, when your relationship with
one another took precedence over your careers, friends, and even
your own interests.

Finally, a couple needs to *return* to the "works" they did at first.
That means recapturing something of that earlier relationship.

You can't return to the past, but you can bring the works of the
past into the present and the future simply by redoing them in a
consistent, loving fashion.

POSTING A GUARD

The peace of God, which surpasses all comprehension, will guard your hearts and your minds in Christ Jesus.

PHILIPPIANS 4:7

Francis Schaeffer once said that the true spiritual battle—and the loss of victory—is always in the thought world.

We can really only concentrate on one thing at a time. When I am plagued by negative, destructive thoughts, I've found it's possible to replace them with positive, uplifting ones. I know this isn't always easy—especially for people who have established a pattern of pessimism—but it is possible. All things are possible with God.

Uninterrupted time in the Word is one of the best cures for gloom I can think of. Store God's Word in your heart and mind through reading, memorizing, and quoting Scriptures such as Jeremiah 29:11, Romans 8:28, and Philippians 4:6, 13.

Also, develop a regular meeting time with a prayer partner so you can encourage one another. Share some good time over lunch or doing an activity you both enjoy.

When you read Philippians 4, it's obvious that the changing circumstances of Paul's life did not affect his inner contentment. Paul didn't have self-sufficiency; he had divine sufficiency—a calm acceptance of life's pressures. He allowed the peace of Christ to "do sentry duty" around his heart and mind, which is what today's verse literally means.

Our thoughts are like measles—catching. What type of thoughts and attitudes are your spouse and children catching from you?

PICKING UP THAT ROCK

"Ask, and it will be given to you; seek,
and you will find; knock, and it will be opened to you."

MATTHEW 7:7

A little boy was trying to pick up a large rock, but couldn't budge it.

His father, watching the struggle, decided this was a good time for a lesson. "Go ahead, son," he urged. "Pick up that rock."

"I can't, Dad. It's too heavy."

"Sure you can, son. Pick up the rock."

The boy grabbed the rock again, puffing and straining, but he couldn't move it. "It's too heavy, Dad."

"Son, the reason you can't pick up the rock is because you're not using all your strength."

This really puzzled the boy, so he grunted and groaned some more. Finally he said in frustration, "But Daddy, I *am* using all my strength!"

"No, you're not," came the reply. "You haven't asked me to help you." And with that, the father leaned over and picked up the rock.

I think I know where that same rock is, because I've tried to pick it up a few times myself! How about you? Are you huffing and puffing, grunting and groaning in frustration, trying to move a boulder in your life when Jesus is standing there saying, "You haven't asked Me to help yet"?

Why do we struggle so much when God is waiting to show His power in our lives—power and help far, far beyond anything we can ask or imagine (Ephesians 3:20)?

ADDING A POSITIVE
TO YOUR NEGATIVE

Words from the mouth of a wise man are gracious.

ECCLESIASTES 10:12

I don't like being around negative people because they might rub off on me.

Now don't get me wrong. If there's a need or a complaint, I want to face it and get it resolved. But there's a difference between a person who has something negative to bring up and a negative person.

Negative people see only what's wrong, never what's right. And negative people typically never have a solution to the problem they're so upset about.

In Ephesians 4:25–32, Paul told the liars, thieves, and bad-mouthers among these believers to quit lying, stealing, and tearing people down with their words. But he also offered solutions: work for your money, speak the truth, and make sure your words are healing, not damaging.

Negativism is lethal, especially in a marriage. If all a mate hears is what's wrong, what doesn't work, and why nothing ever looks good, the negative partner is mixing up a recipe for trouble.

If you see a problem in your marriage, your observation may be valid. But what solutions are you offering? Where's your plan to help turn things around? In what ways are you affirming things that are right?

A positive spirit says, "Here's the problem, and here's how I want to help us solve it."

TILL DEBT DO US PART

*Godliness actually is a means of great gain
when accompanied by contentment.*

1 TIMOTHY 6:6

The pressure of debt is squeezing many marriages today, and
the results can be disastrous.

Someone has said that when it comes to money, there are three
categories of people: the "have's," the "have not's," and the "have not
paid for what they have's."

Among Christian couples today we have more than our share of
people in the third category, those who are in debt up to their ears
and see no way out. I'd like to suggest a fourth category: the "content with what they have's."

The Bible teaches that taking on more financial obligations
than you can handle is a sign that something is wrong spiritually.
Carrying debt that cannot be repaid is abnormal for a Christian.

Money is tainted: 'taint mine, 'taint yours. Everything we have
belongs to God. He has promised to meet our needs. Until we can
be content with His provision, debt will continue to be a noose
around the neck of our marriages.

Is debt a problem in your house? Start getting a handle on it
today. Ask God to give you contentment. He will!

Don't let money ruin your marriage!

A MATTER OF HONOR

"Offer to God a sacrifice of thanksgiving,
and pay your vows to the Most High."

PSALM 50:14

*L*ois and I made a vow when we got married and established our home: At no time would any money come into our home for which God did not get the minimum tithe of 10 percent—and He would get His portion *first*.

Today's verse is a powerful reminder that God is the source of our blessings and that we owe our thanks to Him for what we have. A vow is simply a promise you make to God, to honor Him in some way. In our case, it was a vow to honor God with all of our finances.

What happens when you honor God? That's the subject of the next verse in Psalm 50. Here's the promise God makes: "Call upon Me in the day of trouble; I shall rescue you, and you will honor Me" (v. 15). When you honor God, when you make His glory and His work your priority, He becomes your greatest helper in your time of need, whether it's a financial crisis or a spiritual need.

"If you give Me what's Mine," God says, "if you bring Me into the equation by honoring Me, then I will hear you when you have need of Me and call upon Me."

No, God doesn't make deals. But He does honor those who honor Him. Count on it!

BELIEVING THE WRONG MESSAGE

The wicked borrows and does not pay back.

PSALM 37:21

As far as the Bible is concerned, debt is a spiritual issue before it is a financial issue.

It is a violation of God's Word to take on debts that you do not take proper responsibility for. That not only means repaying the obligation, but repaying it in a timely way. How we handle our money is a matter of our character, not just our checkbook.

Ecclesiastes 5:5 says it is better not to take a vow than to take a vow and not pay it. That has a direct application to our finances.

Why do so many Christian couples get themselves into debts that they can't repay? I think it's a problem of believing the wrong message. See, everybody out there has a product and a marketing plan to sell you that product. These people want to convince you that you deserve, want to have, and ought to buy what they're selling.

But God's Word tells us not to take on obligations we can't take care of with the resources He has given us. So the question is, whom are you and your mate going to believe?

My encouragement to you is to believe God. I'm talking about believing His Word when He says that He knows your needs before you even ask Him.

Go to God first with your needs…and wait for His supply.

HE'S STRONG WHEN I AM WEAK

*[Jesus] has said to me, "My grace is sufficient for you,
for power is perfected in weakness."*

2 CORINTHIANS 12:9

*Y*our attitude affects your thinking…which in turn affects your feelings…which in turn affects your actions.

In other words, your attitude determines your whole perspective on life—how you deal with the challenges or problems God sends your way. Or whether you even try.

A dear Christian sister once asked me to speak to her group. She was very gracious, and didn't pressure me at all to say yes.

I decided to accept. And further, I made up my mind to stretch out on my Jesus and prepare something new.

But when the time came to prepare, my spirit began to balk. "You didn't have to accept this engagement. You can't do this. You don't have a thing to say on that subject."

Did I ever develop an attitude! I not only talked to myself, I began to answer back: "You're right, I can't do this. I don't have the time. I'll call someone to come and take my place."

This was my struggle—and my thinking had to change. So I told Satan no, and told the Lord, "Yes, in Your power I'm going to give this preparation all the gusto I have."

My attitude of fear, uncertainty, and doubt began to melt away. God gave me a message and—when the time came—the power to deliver it.

WHAT'S YOUR PLAN?

*"A nobleman went to a distant country...and he called
ten of his slaves and gave them ten minas and said to them,
'Do business with this until I come back.'"*

LUKE 19:12–13

The parable Jesus told in Luke 19:11–27 is about doing king-dom business with the King's resources. A big part of that kingdom responsibility is what we do with the money God allows us to manage for Him.

The nobleman in the parable had a plan. He divided his money among his servants and told them to do business with it. The nobleman, of course, is God, who has left us with resources to manage as His stewards.

When the nobleman returned, he had words of praise for the servants who had a plan of their own and put his money to good use. His only rebuke was for the servant who had no plan. He simply hid the money away in a handkerchief.

One of the reasons we're in such financial messes as couples and families is that we have failed to put a God-honoring plan in place to manage our money. The world has set our financial agenda, so God is not able to bless us according to His principles.

If you follow everyone else's way of handling your money, then don't be surprised if you wind up in the mess everyone else is in!

Having a budget—a thoughtful financial plan—that includes your giving to the Lord is a great way to stay out of the debt trap.

DON'T ROB GOD

"Bring the whole tithe into the storehouse...
and test Me now in this," says the LORD of hosts,
"if I will not open for you the windows of heaven."

MALACHI 3:10

*P*eople in trouble or in need make all kinds of promises about giving to the Lord. But when it comes time to follow through on the promises, there is no action.

The Bible calls that robbing God. That's strong language, but that's what the Lord told Judah through the prophet Malachi. Some believers rob God month after month, year after year, and then wonder why things aren't going too well for them financially.

But the person or the couple who is robbing God—withholding the portion that is due Him—needs to know that prayer alone won't help. Having the pastor call won't do the job. Even the bank won't be able to help.

The reason is that when you rob God, He puts holes in your pockets or purse. Even if you get a raise or a promotion, it doesn't help because the washing machine is going to break down, the roof is going to leak, and the car is going to act up.

That's the bad news. But the good news is that if we will be faithful in giving God the first fruits of our income, He will be freed up to bless us.

If you feel like you're putting your money in a bag with holes, ask God to show you how to sew up the holes.

COMMUNICATION DOESN'T JUST HAPPEN

*You are Christ's body,
and individually members of it.*

1 CORINTHIANS 12:27

As believers in Jesus Christ, we are all members of His body. That means we're vitally connected to each other. Eye to hand. Brain to toe. Lungs to heart. A healthy human body functions because it has a communication system.

Now think about your marriage. Jesus said that when a man and woman are joined in matrimony, "they are no longer two, but one flesh" (Matthew 19:6). That means to survive and thrive, you need to communicate with each other.

Too many couples think good communication will "just happen." But it takes *work,* because a marriage brings together two different people with different personalities, and two different sets of experiences and assumptions.

Man of the house…do you know how you can improve your communication skills almost overnight? Work as hard to communicate with your wife now as you did when you were trying to win her.

Back then, you jumped to turn off the TV if she called and wanted to talk. You had no problem finding cards that said what was on your heart. The flowers and candy were frequent. You talked about your plans and dreams.

Why stop now? Kill the ball game, look your wife in the eyes, and tell her you want to talk. You'll be on your way!

TELLING THE TRUTH

Speak truth each one of you with his neighbor,
for we are members of one another.

EPHESIANS 4:25

*I*f you want to improve communication in your marriage, here's a bedrock commitment you need to make: tell the truth.

Now, I don't mean say everything that comes to your mind, regardless of the consequences. That's not truth telling; that's just running off at the mouth.

Truth is that which corresponds to reality. It's the right word spoken at the right time. It's what needs to be said when it needs to be heard. That means telling the truth can be painful, but if so, it's pain that is intended to bring healing.

Whenever you hear a wife say, "I really can't tell my husband the truth. He doesn't want to hear it. He just shuts me out," you know there is a marriage in trouble.

Whenever you hear a husband say, "Every time I tell my wife the truth about something that's not pleasant, she blows a fuse or gives me the cold shoulder," you can mark that marriage down as a troubled one.

As husbands and wives, we must set aside our defensiveness and quick retorts. We must create an environment in our marriages that makes it conducive for our spouse to tell the truth.

When we do, good things happen. Lines of communication get opened up. And God brings blessing, because He not only loves the truth, He *is* the Truth.

HOW TO BE GOOD AND ANGRY

Be angry, and yet do not sin.

EPHESIANS 4:26

*I*f you ever find yourself angry, you're in good company. God gets mad, too. The Bible says that God is angry at wicked people every day. Jesus Christ became so angry with the money changers and merchants misusing God's house of worship that He made a whip and drove them from the temple.

Anger is a normal human emotion. God built it into us so that when we see sin and wrong happening in our world, we will be stirred to do something about it.

But we know that when it is mishandled or expressed inappropriately, anger can become sinful—and terribly destructive. When does anger cross the line from legitimate to lethal?

- *When it makes plans to hurt the one who made you angry.* Now you've gone beyond being upset to seeking revenge. Only God is qualified to judge a situation and exact punishment. "Vengeance is Mine, I will repay," God says (Romans 12:19).
- *When you attack the person and not the problem.* One man said, "When my wife and I have an argument, she gets historical."

    His friend said, "Don't you mean hysterical?"
    "No," he replied, "I mean *historical*. She goes back to the beginning and brings up everything I ever did."

That's not dealing with the issue at hand, that's a personal attack, and it becomes displeasing to God.

DON'T GO TO BED MAD — 1

Do not let the sun go down on your anger.

EPHESIANS 4:26

Anger unleashed wrongfully is hard to overcome.

According to Proverbs 18:19, "A brother offended is harder to be won than a strong city." How many times have you wished you could take back what you said or did?

Some people say, "I just explode and then it's all over." Well, so does a shotgun. But when the smoke clears, a shotgun blast leaves some serious damage behind.

But it isn't healthy to stuff it, either, pretending like nothing is wrong, letting it build up or fester. The key, according to the Bible, is to learn the proper timing to express and deal with anger.

Ephesians 4:26 gives us the parameters: Before sunset! Before bedtime!

It's an issue of obedience. God is pleased when we obey His Word and refuse to go to bed mad.

For that matter, harboring anger doesn't get us anywhere! When you and your spouse, or you and your children, go to bed without resolving the problem—or at least agreeing to address it—this thing grows overnight. So the next day, you wake up with the same stuff to face, only now it's grown to twice its size.

Scripture couldn't be more clear: Don't give your enemy such a foothold in your heart and in your home!

DON'T GO TO BED MAD — 2

Be angry, and yet do not sin.

EPHESIANS 4:26

*S*ometimes Ephesians 4:26 gets taught and applied too glibly.

Paul isn't necessarily saying that no matter what happens in a day, we just need to kiss and make up and resolve everything before we go to bed.

There are some conflicts that simply can't be fixed that quickly. Let's say a serious conflict occurs between a couple, or between the parents and a child, at 5:00 in the afternoon. Everyone involved is angry, and there are important—sometimes complicated—issues to be talked about and resolved.

In cases like that, it's probably not realistic to think things can all be happily resolved by bedtime. One man said, "The Bible says not to go to bed angry. My wife and I haven't been to sleep in three weeks."

That's not the idea. But neither is going to bed mad! Instead, *don't let the sun go down without addressing the issue.* That may involve settling things if it's a marital spat or concerns a child who doesn't like a rule.

But if the problem is really serious, obeying the Bible may involve agreeing to deal with it tomorrow. The point is that the issue that caused the anger won't be ignored or swept under the rug. It's on the family agenda, and with God's help and wisdom, it *will* be resolved.

DON'T GO TO BED MAD — 3

Do not give the devil an opportunity.

EPHESIANS 4:27

*D*on't let your anger just build up day after day. That's the bottom-line message of Ephesians 4:26–27.

When you do, you invite the devil to jump right into the middle of the situation. You are giving him access to your heart and mind, and while you're sleeping he's building a workshop in your subconscious.

Another way to translate the word *opportunity* is "foothold." How you handle anger can give Satan a grip, a place to stand in your life.

Now if you are a believer in Jesus Christ, Satan cannot touch you in terms of your eternal destiny. You are secure in Christ. But he can certainly mess up your daily walk with Christ, your marriage, and your family when you give him an opening into your heart through unresolved anger.

The problem is that Satan is never satisfied with just a little corner of your life. What he does with that foothold is start building what the Bible calls a fortress or a stronghold (see 2 Corinthians 10:4). When Satan gets a grip through your anger problem, he multiplies that until you've got all kinds of problems.

The best way to prevent this is to shut the devil out before he gets a foot in the door. Resolve anger, deal with the issues, and enjoy God's peace.

LEAVING AND CLEAVING — 1

For this reason a man shall leave his father and his mother,
and be joined to his wife; and they shall become one flesh.

GENESIS 2:24

*Y*ou and I can't improve on God's idea for anything—and that goes double for marriage!

I want to look at the beauty and simplicity of God's basic plan for marriage: leave, cleave, and become one.

Notice the reason for the closeness of the marriage union. A man is to join himself totally to his wife "for this cause," because woman was taken out of man (Genesis 2:23). Woman came from man's flesh, and a man and his wife are to become one flesh again.

Jesus underscored the importance of God's original plan for marriage when some Pharisees came to Him, trying to get Jesus to paint Himself into a corner on the issue of marriage and divorce (see Matthew 19:3–6). God intended for woman and man to be joined together in a relationship that required leaving and cleaving.

The tragedy today is that a lot of people have these words read at their weddings, yet they don't really understand what's involved here. Too many young women who get married have not really left mama emotionally. The same thing can be said of a young man who finds it hard to leave the security of his home ("nest") to accept responsibility for his own household.

But even given these problems, leaving and cleaving is still the divine ideal. The One who created marriage knows best how to make it work.

LEAVING AND CLEAVING — 2

*The man said, "This is now bone of my bones,
and flesh of my flesh; she shall be called Woman,
because she was taken out of Man."*

GENESIS 2:23

The first step in making a marriage is for the man to leave his father and mother. That means more than renting your own place. It means a husband must be willing to subjugate all his previous relationships to his marriage.

That includes not only Mama and Daddy, but his friends and his own interests as well. A man who thinks that marriage won't change his activities and hangout time with all of his buddies doesn't understand what marriage is all about.

My brother, is your wife a nice addition to your life, or is she your *life*?

See, you must be willing to break with anything or anyone to show your wife that there is nothing more important to you than loving her and spending time with her. That may cost you something you had planned to do this weekend.

But God asks us men to leave because a husband and wife are one flesh, and because one of a woman's greatest needs in marriage is a sense of security.

Your wife needs to know she's number one to you! When a man can make that commitment and keep it, he will begin to understand what marriage is all about.

A secure wife is free to love and please her husband, motivating him to love her all the more!

LEAVING AND CLEAVING — 3

*"[A husband and wife] are
no longer two, but one flesh."*

M A T T H E W   19:6

*C*leave means to stick to something like glue, or to attach oneself in a viselike grip. But cleaving involves much more than a physical coupling of two bodies. It means a totality of union with a whole person.

If we're not careful, too often our "Let me love you" words to our spouse actually mean, "Let me please me." I believe God addressed this word to the husbands because we men are particularly vulnerable to this error.

Our whole culture teaches men to use women for their own pleasure. So it's easy sometimes for a man to bring that mindset into marriage—where it is devastating. And of course, wives can become self-centered, too.

But that's the devil's plan, not God's. To cleave to your spouse means you have made a total commitment to your partner—not only to the other person's body, but to her heart, mind, and soul as well.

My brother, to cleave to your wife means that you work hard at pleasing her, not yourself. She needs to know that nothing will ever cause you to pull away from her and tear that love relationship.

Wife, cleaving to your husband includes respecting and supporting him in his efforts to lead the marriage and the family.

Cleaving is costly, but the reward is an intimacy of life that rivals anything on earth!

LEAVING AND CLEAVING — 4

The wife does not have authority over her own body,
but the husband does; and likewise also the husband
does not have authority over his own body, but the wife does.

1 CORINTHIANS 7:4

*P*aul set down a fundamental principle of marriage for us as
believers. A husband and wife are no longer two bodies, but one—
so each partner has equal authority over the one body that makes up
their marriage.

It takes a lifetime to become totally "one flesh" in marriage.
That is why marriage is "till death do us part."

Obviously, "one flesh" includes sexual faithfulness. It also
involves a sensitivity to your partner. Paul said, "No one ever hated
his own flesh, but nourishes and cherishes it" (Ephesians 5:29). Two
people who are truly one flesh will be incredibly sensitive to each
other's needs and desires.

This is why Paul says each member of a marriage has authority
over the partner's body. A husband and wife are to meet each other's
needs.

But the concept goes far beyond the physical. I believe God has
made the husband responsible to help his wife remove the blemishes
in her life, just as Jesus Christ loves and cleanses the church of which
He is the head (see Ephesians 5:25–27). A man can only fulfill that
important and demanding role in his marriage when he is truly one
flesh and one spirit with his wife.

In Genesis 2:24, God promises to take two people and make
them one…when they do it His way.

CLIMATE CONTROL — 1

Your wife shall be like a fruitful vine within your house.

PSALM 128:3

*T*oday's verse give us a fascinating look at the responsive nature of women and how it affects the home.

A person who fears the Lord and walks in His ways (Psalm 128:1–2) will find his wife blossoming like a fruitful grapevine. In a favorable climate, grapevines need no coaxing to grow. Given the right environment, they will grow and produce grapes from which wine (a drink symbolizing celebration and happiness in biblical times) is made.

But grapevines need the right care and attention and even pruning to make them fully productive. It's much the same in marriage. The husband is responsible for creating a climate in which his wife can grow and flourish.

A woman is a wonderfully complex being who cannot be expected to flourish just because her husband marries her and situates her in a house. There's a lot more to a growing, satisfying marriage than two people legally joined and living under the same roof.

The husband needs to be the climate setter and climate adjuster when necessary. And when he gets that temperature control set right, he can expect a joyful response from his wife. But to create the right climate, a husband must be at home enough—*and attentive enough while he is at home*—to maintain an ideal temperature.

CLIMATE CONTROL—2

Your wife shall be like a fruitful vine within your house...thus
shall the man be blessed who fears the LORD.

PSALM 128:3–4

The west wall of a house in which I once lived was covered with a vine. Each summer, the rain and sunlight caused that vine to grow with incredible speed. It had to be trimmed and then trimmed again. It delighted us with its exuberant growth, because it was in the right place with just enough of everything it needed to flourish.

So it is with a wife who finds her husband providing the right climate. She will delight her husband with her love, providing him with the joy he needs and desires. The better and more constant the climate, the better, faster, and more consistent the wife's growth will be. And as she grows and is fulfilled, her husband will benefit from her growth.

The husband who is rarely at home frustrates his wife and damages her self-confidence. And when he is home, a husband must be ready to give his time and attention to his wife so he can know what she needs in order to grow and flourish.

What's the temperature in your marriage? Ask God to help you adjust that thermostat to the right setting. Paul wrote: "Husbands, love your wives and do not be harsh with them" (Colossians 3:19, NIV). In other words, if you want a summer wife, don't bring home winter weather.

LOVE YOURSELF,
LOVE YOUR WIFE — 1

Husbands ought also to love their
own wives as their own bodies.

EPHESIANS 5:28

*T*he apostle Paul gave us husbands an easy-to-understand guideline for providing the kind of nurturing love that our wives need and deserve.

Simply stated, a man should do for his wife only those things that he would like to have done for himself. Most men don't slap their own bodies around, even when their bodies displease them. Most men don't ignore their own basic needs.

Many of us keep a watchful eye on the hairline, the waistline, and any other line that might suggest we're losing our youthful vitality! In fact, if the truth were known, most of us men pay as much or more attention to the physical than the women we accuse of being overly sensitive about their appearance.

And when a man does accidentally hurt himself—cutting himself while shaving, for example—he takes great care to stop the bleeding and ease his discomfort.

In the same way, if a man causes his wife emotional pain, he ought to tenderly treat her wound to the best of his ability.

Apart from this kind of loving care that recognizes a wife's emotional makeup, Peter says that men's prayers will be hindered (1 Peter 3:7). That is, God determines whether He will communicate with a husband based on that husband's willingness to treat his wife in a sensitive and loving way.

LOVE YOURSELF,
LOVE YOUR WIFE — 2

He who loves his own wife loves himself.

EPHESIANS 5:28

When we husbands ignore, neglect, or undervalue our wives, a dark cloud comes over our whole household. When we cause our wives emotional pain, both of us suffer. After all, it's not like a husband gets any benefit from failing to nurture his wife.

Paul adds another motivation in Ephesians 5 for husbands to care for their wives. We men are called to nurture and cherish our wives *the way Christ does the church.* And we know that Christ loved the church, even when that love took Him to the cross.

Since a husband and wife are one in Christ, joined together by God, to be at odds with one another is to be in sin. And sin always breaks fellowship with God as well as fellowship between people.

But a husband can restore fellowship and intimacy in his marriage by treating his wife with the same kind of love he has received from Jesus Christ.

Let's see…what kind of love is *that?* Patient. Constant. Faithful. Forgiving. Selfless. Encouraging. Healing. Redeeming. That list, of course, goes on and on. That's why we need to lean on Him to love as He wants us to love.

One final thought for husbands: If you want to learn how your wife wants to be treated, *ask* her! Most women are very capable of articulating their needs and desires.

AVOIDING THE SQUEEZE

Do not be conformed to this world,
but be transformed by the renewing of your mind.

ROMANS 12:2

Everything we do, good or bad, begins with a thought. It may then become a desire and finally an act of the will, but it all starts in the brain.

If the mind, then, is the gate to the emotions and the will, we are wise to put guards at that gate!

Ever heard of GIGO? It's an old computer acronym that stands for "garbage in, garbage out." In other words, if you put bad information into your mind, you'll get bad information out of it.

If you allow movies, television, magazines, or novels to program your mind, then what you are putting in will eventually come out. And that might be dangerous to your marriage—and your spiritual life.

The question is whether these things are impairing your ability to think for yourself—and to think biblically.

We need to reject the world's attempts to form us or manipulate us, both as individuals and as a married couple. We need to keep in mind that the things of this world are temporary, while the things of God are eternal. We sometimes give far more value to this world than it deserves. Let's make sure our minds—and our hearts—aren't being squeezed into the world's mode of thinking.

THE KEY TO REAL POWER

A cord of three strands is not quickly broken.

ECCLESIASTES 4:12, NIV

The Trinity is made up of three coequal Persons who are in essence one: God the Father, God the Son, and God the Holy Spirit.

Christian marriage is designed to be an earthly, although admittedly imperfect, replica of the divine Trinity. It consists of three persons who are one: a man, a woman, and Jesus Christ. Jesus is the third component that is missing from so many marriages.

As Christians, we are to have marriages that reflect Christ's dynamic presence in our home. It is His resurrection power operating in the lives of a believing couple that gives them the ability and power to establish a loving marriage.

Could it be that your marriage has not tasted of this power because one or the other of you, or perhaps both of you, have never received Christ as your Savior and Lord?

If you have, you have resurrection power at your fingertips. But if you have never truly trusted Christ, I have good news for you today. God sent His Son to earth to die on the cross as a substitute for your sin. Whenever men or women respond to Christ in faith, trusting Him alone as Savior, He not only forgives them but empowers them to live new lives. And when Christ makes you new, He includes your marriage in that new life.

HE IS ABUNDANTLY ABLE

*Now to Him who is able to do far more
abundantly beyond all that we ask or think,
according to the power that works within us,
to Him be the glory in the church.*

EPHESIANS 3:20–21

$\mathcal{D}$o you get the idea that Paul believes God is able to do anything that may be needed in your life or marriage?

This is one of the Bible's greatest statements of God's power. God is able—*abundantly able!* It doesn't matter what you put after that, because once you bring God into the formula you have set aside all the normal expectations and limitations that human beings set up.

It doesn't matter what problem or challenge you are facing in your marriage or family today; God is able. If there is a wall of some sort between your and your spouse, God is able to help you tear that wall down. If a wayward child is giving you problems and disrupting your home, God is able to call that child back to Himself and restore peace in your home.

I can say that God is able because I read it in the Bible, which is the infallible, errorless Word of God. But I can also say it because God has proven Himself able in my life and ministry since the day I committed my life to Him. Anything that has been accomplished in my life can be explained by the fact that God is abundantly able to do anything and everything.

What are you up against today? God is able!

IT'S OKAY TO BE DIFFERENT

*This I say...that you walk no longer
just as the Gentiles also walk.*

EPHESIANS 4:17

I remember that growing up, I was always the one left out at
school because I was a Christian. The pressure to conform was so
strong!

Sometimes when I was a girl, I got tired of being known as a
Christian. So I would fuss to my mother, and she would always
share verses such as Ephesians 4:17 with me. Or she would remind
me that the Christian life isn't supposed to be easy (see 2 Timothy
3:12).

Of course, I didn't want to hear that. But what stabilizing truths
these have become for my life. We need to develop the mind-set as
believers that we are *supposed* to be different. Let's face it: You and I
won't always fit in because most people will think we don't live in
the real world.

Christian wives can really feel the pressure to fit in; the world
has such high expectations of women these days. To be a biblical
wife and mother can subject you to pressure, sometimes even from
other Christians!

Being different, not weird, because you belong to Christ is not
always easy. But it becomes easier as you put the Scripture into practice and grow and develop in the Lord. You may not be very
popular, but then, you weren't promised popularity on this earth.

A THIMBLE, OR A RESERVOIR?

"I will not let you go unless you bless me."

GENESIS 32:26

*I*f you were to fill a thimble with water from the Pacific Ocean, that thimble would be full of genuine Pacific Ocean water. There just wouldn't be very much of it in relation to what's available.

It's the same if you took a bucketful. Once you fill it to the rim, you'll get no more water—even though the ocean has a lot more to give.

But what if you dug a reservoir? Well, the deeper you dig your reservoir, the more the ocean will fill it. But you can't dig deep enough to exhaust the ocean's supply.

The same is true with God. So many Christians are happy with a little bit of God. Others may say, "I don't want a thimbleful of God. I want a bucketful." So they fill their bucket and go on their way, leaving behind the vast resources and power of God.

Still others decide to dig a reservoir and fill it—and begin to realize something of His limitless power.

If you're satisfied with a little bit of God, that's all the experience of God you are ever going to get. We need to quit being satisfied with ordinary Christian lives, with average marriages. Let's reach out to take hold of God, and discover the One who can fill not only our reservoir, but the universe, with Himself.

FIXING THE BROKEN PLACES

Keep fervent in your love for one another,
because love covers a multitude of sins.

1 PETER 4:8

The ugly scar on my leg tells the story of an old football injury. My leg had a multitude of broken pieces, but the surgeon knew exactly what he was doing.

He made the right incision at the right place at the right time, screwing on a metal plate to hold the broken pieces together. The result is that today, my formerly shattered right leg is stronger than my left leg that has never been broken.

Love can do the same thing for broken people. Now don't misunderstand—Peter's statement does not mean we can skip sin or just pretend that everything is okay. He's not talking about a cover-up. Sin always has to be dealt with.

The idea here is that love does not broadcast the other person's sins. Neither does love hold a person's sin against him, refusing him another chance.

Instead, love "bears all things" (1 Corinthians 13:7) by forgiving the sinner, because we know we are forgiven people ourselves. Love can also heal by helping the offender grow stronger and put away old habits and life patterns.

What better place to practice the healing, forgiving ministry of love than in your home? Godly love can put the broken pieces back together and fix a steel plate over the weak area, making it stronger than it was before.

ARE YOU AN IMPLODER OR A BUILDER?

Let no unwholesome word proceed from your mouth, but only such a word as is good for edification according to the need of the moment, so that it may give grace to those who hear.

EPHESIANS 4:29

A few years ago, a historic building in downtown Dallas was imploded after all efforts to salvage it had failed.

It was an impressive sight watching this multistory building quiver and then collapse in a matter of seconds. All it took was for the workmen to weaken some key support beams and plant some charges in strategic places.

Sadly, it's possible to "implode" our mate's spirit with a few careless words spoken in anger or from a spirit of revenge. "Unwholesome" words can eat away a person's spirit and self-worth because the word *unwholesome* here means "rotten." It was used of rotten fruit, rotten vegetables—even decomposed bodies.

Paul is saying that kind of speech belongs in the garbage can with yesterday's leftovers. It belongs in the graveyard.

We may live in a "trash talking" culture, but you don't have to bring that rotten mess home!

Instead of tearing your mate or kids down with your words, make it your commitment to build them up. That's exactly what it means to edify others. We build people up when we speak appropriate, grace-producing words—even in correction or rebuke.

The difference between the right word and the wrong word spoken in "the heat of the moment" is the difference between lightning and a lightning bug—in other words, all the difference in the world!

THINKING LIKE CHRIST — 1

*"All things that I have heard from My Father
I have made known to you."*

JOHN 15:15

Have you ever thought about what it means when the Bible
says, "We have the mind of Christ" (1 Corinthians 2:16)?

That is a staggering reality! This means that we have the ability
to think God's thoughts after Him. It means that we have the
capacity to think about things the way Jesus Christ would think
about them. Paul called it having the same attitude as Christ
(Philippians 2:5).

Since we have the mind of Christ, we don't have to think the
way we used to think. We don't have to see people the way we used
to see them. And we don't have to approach life with the same attitudes we used to exhibit.

Think what would happen to our marriages if we as Christians
began to respond to our spouses with the mind and attitude of Jesus!
So much delicious spiritual fruit would begin to grow and mature in
our lives that our relationship as a couple would take on a whole
new flavor.

And the benefits don't stop there. A husband and wife relating
to each other with a Christlike spirit become a father and mother
able to bless their children with godly guidance. Such a home
becomes a beacon in any neighborhood, attracting unhappy, searching men and women to its radiant light.

THINKING LIKE CHRIST — 2

Be transformed by the renewing of your mind.

ROMANS 12:2

*E*ven with the mind of Christ at our disposal, we are still very imperfect people who can easily lapse back into old ways of thinking. But Scripture is clear: It is more than possible for us to think and live with renewed minds.

So how can we learn to exercise the mind and attitude of Christ that is already ours? Here are some ingredients you can begin using today:

Meditate on God's Word (Psalm 1:2–3).
Seek God's will (Matthew 26:39).
Bear the burdens of others (Galatians 6:2).
Resist the devil (Matthew 4:1–11; James 4:7).
Learn to control your mental focus (Philippians 4:8).
Celebrate your identity in Christ (Romans 6:4).
Be careful how you view life (Romans 8:6).
Look for God's purpose in everything (Romans 8:28).
Seek His strength in your weakness (2 Corinthians 12:9).

How does this work in moment by moment? Paul offers the strongest clue in 2 Corinthians 10:5, when he says, "We are taking every thought captive to the obedience of Christ." By the power of the indwelling Holy Spirit, we begin to run every thought, every speculation, and every flight of imagination through a "Christ filter," stopping destructive, bitter, hateful, lustful thoughts before they can ever take root.

The result? When Christ's mind dominates our minds, then we will be truly in our right minds!

HOW TO BE CONTENT
WHERE YOU ARE

But godliness with contentment is great gain.

1 TIMOTHY 6:6, NIV

*B*iblical stewardship is more than just the check you drop in the offering plate on Sunday. It involves the part you keep for yourself, too.

That's what Paul tells us in 1 Timothy 6:6–7, a powerful passage on greed and stewardship. One reason we can be content with what we have (and don't have) is that when we leave this place, our wallets stay here (v. 7). All of our stuff stays put when we go to heaven.

I don't mean it's wrong to want to better oneself. But if we cannot be content with where we are until God takes us where we want to be, we are greedy. So many Christian couples are knocking themselves out just like the world to get ahead and pile up the toys. What's missing?

Well, I think what's missing too is the first part of the equation in today's verse: *godliness* plus contentment equals gain. What is godliness anyway? It's focusing my mind and heart so completely on being like Jesus Christ in how I think and what I do that when people look at me, they get a clear picture of what Christ is like.

We can't follow Christ wholeheartedly and chase the pot of gold at the end of the rainbow at the same time.

TURNING YOUR TRIALS INTO TRIUMPHS — 1

*"In this world you will have trouble. But take heart!
I have overcome the world."*

JOHN 16:33, NIV

*I*f you're not in the middle of a trial right now, just hang around. The next one is probably on the way.

Jesus Himself assured us that trials will come! No one, and I mean none of us, can dodge trials. Someone has said you're always either in the middle of a trial, just coming out of one, or just heading into one. So we need to find out what resources God has given us to deal with trials.

What is a trial, anyway? It's an adverse circumstance that God allows or even brings about in the lives of His children to deepen our faith in Him.

My concern is not so much where your trials come from, but what you do when they show up. How you respond to cataclysmic circumstances has a lot to do with what shape you're in when you come out on the other side. The good news is that you're not out there alone. No matter what the source of your trial, Jesus has the situation well in hand. He has already overcome *anything* you and your mate could possibly face in this world.

Peter tells us, don't be caught by surprise when the hard times come (1 Peter 4:12). Just make sure you have your emergency plan in place: *Run to Jesus as fast as you can!*

TURNING YOUR TRIALS
INTO TRIUMPHS — 2

"Do not let your heart be troubled."

JOHN 14:1

*W*here do trials come from? From any of a number of directions. Sometimes they come simply because we live in a sin-cursed world and the curse rubs off on us. So we become the victim of a crime or accident or illness that crashes into our individual lives, puts our marriage to the test, or strains our family to the limit.

Sometimes trials are the result of our own sin. We yield to a temptation that leads to a set of circumstances that are tough to deal with. At other times, God may send us a trial to teach us a specific lesson. And don't forget that the enemy can attack us with trials for the purpose of bringing about our spiritual defeat.

The best place to learn how to deal with trials is right in the middle of one. That's why Jesus told His disciples to get into a boat and row out to the middle of the Sea of Galilee (Matthew 14:22). He knew very well that a huge storm was coming, but He wanted the Twelve to learn the encouraging truth that He had total authority over their trials. He wants us to get that message, too.

Trials are not designed to sink your boat, but to help you improve your navigation skills.

THIS WORLD IS "NUTHIN'"

*"What does it profit a man to gain the whole world,
and forfeit his soul?"*

MARK 8:36

In a magazine interview, former heavyweight boxing champ Muhammad Ali told how it used to be when he was the champ.

At one point in the story he made this statement: "I had the world, and it wasn't nuthin'."

That's the message the Bible wants us to get! This world is "nuthin'" compared to what God has in store for us. That's why Paul reminds believers who are rich not to get the big head or fall in love with their wealth (see 1 Timothy 6:17–19).

Paul also tells us not to "fix [our] hope" on money. That is, don't get locked into it so that it controls you and quenches your desire for godliness. Riches, he reminds us, are so uncertain. And you don't want to be hugging too tight on something that could disappear tomorrow.

Instead, we're to fixate on the God who gives us these things to enjoy, because He will never leave us or let us down. God is not a tight-fisted miser who hoards His blessings. When we are pleasing to Him, He delights in giving us good things to enjoy.

God places His resources in your hands so you might use them to do good, help others, and bring Him glory. And as you do, you are laying up for yourself treasure in heaven.

WHAT IT TAKES TO BE A WINNER — 1

Do you not know that those who run in a race all run,
but only one receives the prize?

1 CORINTHIANS 9:24

A concert pianist was once asked, "How did you come to play the piano so well?"

"By planning to neglect anything that did not contribute to it," she answered. Now this pianist was not saying that other things were wrong. They just didn't contribute to her goal of being the best at her chosen craft, so she left them off.

There is nothing wrong with wanting to be the best. There is nothing wrong with wanting to be a winner. We just need to make sure we're competing in the right game to win the right prize. The only prize worth giving our lives to is Jesus' commendation, "Well done, good and faithful servant."

So let me ask you, what's your passion as individuals and as a couple? What is it that makes you look forward to getting out of bed tomorrow?

My passion is to be a winner for God. I want to close my eyes every night knowing that I did my best for Him as a pastor, father, and husband. I'm running the Christian race to win, not just place or show!

If you're feeling really brave today, ask your mate whether you are living like a winner in your marriage.

WHAT IT TAKES TO BE A WINNER — 2

Run in such a way that you may win.

1 CORINTHIANS 9:24

A winner breaks from the pack, intent on winning the race. The apostle Paul wasn't satisfied just to be back in the pack of runners.

See, the problem is a lot of us want to walk or jog the Christian race. But if it's a race, the idea is to run at top form so you can get to the finish line as soon as possible.

But if we're going to run to win, we need to make some decisions. "Everyone who competes in the games exercises self-control in all things," Paul says (1 Corinthians 9:25).

He was talking about the Isthmian Games, an event held every two years, similar to the Olympics. The athletes trained for many months. Everything they did was measured against the goal of winning their event.

If you wanted to win a wreath, you had to exercise a lot of self-control. Why? Because you can't live any way you want and still be a winner!

Ancient athletes were willing to discipline their bodies for months to win a garland of greenery, placed on their heads at the winner's stand.

The problem was that this garland would soon fade to brown and die. How much more should we be willing to discipline ourselves to win the eternal prize of God's approval in time and eternity?

WHAT IT TAKES TO BE A WINNER — 3

Let us also lay aside every weight...
and let us run with endurance the race that is set before us.

HEBREWS 12:1, ESV

When it comes to winning the race for God, talk won't get the job done. We're so used to "trash talking" athletes today that we forget games aren't won in front of microphones. *Saying* you're going to win has never made anybody a winner.

Some believers aren't running as winners because they get hung up on side issues and lose sight of the prize.

Committed athletes want to win the gold so much that it controls their very lives. Sleeping and eating habits change. Relationships change. Everything changes because the serious athlete has his eye on the prize.

Our commitment to Christ needs to guide our decisions, too. For instance, if you're committed to making your marriage all that God wants it to be, you won't have to struggle very long deciding whether you should pick up the TV remote for the evening or spend time talking with your mate.

Once you get the larger goal in sight, it will help you get rid of the things that weigh you down, and pursue those daily decisions that will get you to the finish line.

Paul said, "One thing I do" (Philippians 3:13), not "Many things I play around with." Is that true for you and your mate? What must you let go of to get closer to God and to one another?

NOT PERFECT, JUST AUTHENTIC—1

"Let your statement be, 'Yes, yes' or 'No, no';
anything beyond these is of evil."

MATTHEW 5:37

Authenticity is a big buzzword these days. Everybody seems to be talking about the need to be authentic in our dealings and relationships.

But there's nothing new about the concept of authenticity. Jesus spoke about it in the Sermon on the Mount. Today's verse captures the heart of what it means to be an authentic person.

As believers, we should be the kind of people whose everyday speech is totally reliable. When we say yes, that's what we mean. The same is true when we say no. Our spouses, children, and coworkers shouldn't have to wonder whether we're telling the truth or will stand behind what we say.

There's no better place to learn authenticity than at home. It's hard to fool those you live with. Your family will usually know if what you are doing and saying on the outside matches who you are on the inside.

We may be able to wear a mask with other people, but the mask doesn't work at home. That's why it's so important that you as a couple hold each other accountable for your words and actions.

It isn't fun being reminded of exaggerations, inconsistencies, or neglected promises. But God gave us the gift of each other—two imperfect people—to help us become the men and women He wants us to be.

NOT PERFECT, JUST AUTHENTIC — 2

When Jesus saw Nathanael approaching, he said of him,
"Here is a true Israelite, in whom there is nothing false."

JOHN 1:47, NIV

How wonderful it would be if Jesus could look into our lives and say what He said to Nathanael: "This is a true man, a true woman. There's nothing false or deceitful in this person at all."

Only He can bring that sort of consistent character into our lives. Why? Because Jesus Himself is the perfect model of authenticity. He was the perfect Son of God, so it was impossible that He could be anything but totally truthful. The apostle Peter, who knew Jesus as well as anyone on earth, testified that no "deceit" was ever found in Jesus' mouth at any time (1 Peter 2:22).

You may say, "But, Tony, I can't be perfect like Jesus." That's true. Neither can I. But authenticity doesn't demand perfection.

In fact, one of the traits of authentic people is that they are the first to admit they aren't perfect. So when they blow it, they don't pass over the mistake or excuse it. They call it what it is.

Even Nathanael wasn't perfect. But he had an undivided heart. He was free of guile or deceit. With Nathanael, what you saw was what you got. Could the same be said of you and me today?

Pray that God will help you be the kind of person whose heart and mouth are on the same channel!

A PLAN...OR A SCHEME? — 1

A faithful man will abound with blessings,
but he who makes haste to be rich will not go unpunished.

PROVERBS 28:20

*D*o you have a financial plan in place that God can bless?

I'm not necessarily talking about your investments. I mean a plan that gives God His rightful place in your finances, and allows you to take care of needs without having to live in debt.

I'm also talking about a plan that includes discipline, so that one or the other of you don't try to pursue your every want and desire.

The Bible teaches that wise management pleases God. If you don't have a plan God can bless, you won't get the full benefit of what you earn. He may even take away what you have, because you're messing over what He gave you.

The exiles who returned to Jerusalem found themselves in a similar situation. Because they had neglected to put the Lord first in their lives and in their plans, He could no longer bless their work. God told them:

"You have planted much, but have harvested little. You eat, but never have enough. You drink, but never have your fill...You earn wages, only to put them in a purse with holes in it" (Haggai 1:6, NIV).

Every dime you bring home was given to you by God. And while only a portion goes directly to His storehouse, the local church, all of your money is to be managed for His glory.

A PLAN...OR A SCHEME?—2

*But those who want to get rich fall into temptation
and a snare and many foolish and harmful desires
which plunge men into ruin and destruction.*

1 TIMOTHY 6:9

There are many people today who don't want to manage their money; they want to *luck* their way into wealth. And the primary way a lot of God's people are trying to do this it through "get-rich-quick" games like the lottery.

Let me spell it out. The lottery is a pagan, unrighteous way of trying to make progress. The lottery is born out of a hellish desire to get rich quick. When you buy into this kind of scheme, you have left God's path for dealing with your finances or trying to overcome debt or other financial problems.

Proverbs 28:22 tells us, "A man with an evil eye hastens after wealth and does not know that want will come upon him." God opposes any scheme that is designed to help you get rich overnight, because that means you don't have to work for what you have.

To get rich overnight does not require any faithfulness or productivity. Every time you go into a gas station or store and buy a lottery ticket, you are saying, "God, I don't trust You. I've got to luck my way to success."

When you do that, you miss God's activity in your life and forfeit His power. God wants you to have a plan, not a scheme.

BRICKS OR CATHEDRALS?

Here is what I have seen to be good and fitting:
to eat, to drink and enjoy oneself in all one's
labor in which he toils.

ECCLESIASTES 5:18

A man was walking down the street one day and passed a construction project. He asked one of the workers, "What are you doing?"

The man answered, "I'm laying bricks."

Another laborer was working a few feet away, so the man asked him, "What are you doing?"

The second man said, "I'm building a cathedral."

Some men lay bricks, while others build cathedrals. The difference is in your perspective on work. Are you content to lay bricks, or do you want to build a cathedral?

The Bible has a lot to say on this subject, because God is big on work, particularly for men, because of our leadership role as providers for our families. It's unfortunate that we live in a world where people are finding ways to get out of work, or to be illegitimate in their work, because work is a gift from God.

You won't hear that many places these days, but it's true. Work existed before sin existed. So if you only look at work as part of the curse that came because of Adam's sin, you've missed it. Work was always a part of God's plan. Genesis 1 brings this out because it shows us God Himself at work in Creation.

Have you thanked God for your work lately? Ask for His help to be and do your best.

CHOOSE FOR YOURSELF — 1

*The serpent was more crafty than any beast of the field
which the LORD God had made. And he said to the woman,
"Indeed, has God said...?"*

GENESIS 3:1

The first conversation between a human being and Satan was about God. Satan didn't come to Eve to talk about shopping, money, health, or sex.

He said, "I want to talk about God," because Satan's agenda is always getting people to rebel against Him.

The real issue in Eden wasn't whether Eve would eat a piece of fruit. The issue was, whom would she obey? That's the issue for all of us. As individuals, as a married couple, you have to decide under whose authority you will place yourself. Who will be Lord of your life? Of your home?

When Adam and Eve ate the fruit, they were saying in essence, "Satan, you are lord of our lives. We submit to your authority."

Notice that Satan waited until he could tempt Adam and Eve together. He knew that if he could get this husband and wife to yield to him, he would have access to their offspring. And tragically, his strategy worked.

Adam's and Eve's first son, Cain, murdered his brother, Abel. And it went downhill from there!

Satan's goal has always been to destroy the family, driving a wedge between them and God. As husband and wife, as father and mother, you can frustrate the plans of hell by bowing to the Lordship of Christ, and giving him first place in your home.

CHOOSE FOR YOURSELF — 2

"Choose for yourselves today whom you will serve...
but as for me and my house, we will serve the LORD."

JOSHUA 24:15

The issue for mankind from the beginning has been whom we will serve, God or Satan. Satan wants to bring as many people as possible under his control, because Satan is at war with God—and now we are at war with Satan.

Sometimes people wonder why God didn't just annihilate Satan after his rebellion. That's a complex question, but one reason seems to be that God is giving every person an opportunity to choose, the way Satan had an opportunity to choose. Joshua said to the people of his day, "Choose for yourselves today whom you will serve" (Joshua 24:15).

That was the question Job faced. In all of his suffering, would Job obey God or curse Him?

It was the issue the twelve disciples faced, at a time when many other followers of Christ turned and left Him. Jesus asked them, "Do you want to go away as well?" (John 6:67, ESV).

We all face that decision. When you accept Jesus Christ as your Savior and place yourself under His Lordship, you reverse the choice Adam and Eve made in the Garden of Eden.

We need to reaffirm Jesus' Lordship in our personal and family lives every day. Tell Him you want Him to be Lord of your life—of your marriage— today.

How to Be a Problem to Satan

*[Christ] is also head of the body, the church; and He is the
beginning, the firstborn from the dead, so that He Himself
will come to have first place in everything.*

COLOSSIANS 1:18

When you come to Christ, you leave Satan's kingdom and
come over to God's kingdom.

That makes you a problem to Satan. When you commit your
life to Jesus Christ, not only has Satan lost you, he loses anyone you
touch. If we men learn how to be godly husbands and fathers, Satan
may lose our whole offspring. If we learn how to be witnesses for
Christ, Satan may lose some of our friends or family.

Satan wants to stop you. He can't touch your salvation, so he
attempts to destroy the effectiveness of your faith. Satan can keep
you so tired that you don't have the energy to serve God. He will
keep you too entertained or too distracted or too busy or too whatever to do much for the Lord.

The only answer to Satan's attacks is a total commitment of
everything you are and do to the Lord Jesus Christ. Christ deserves
our all because "all things have been created through Him and for
Him," and "He is before all things, and in Him all things hold
together" (see Colossians 1:16–17).

The simple fact is that no area of our lives lies outside of Jesus
Christ's control. You cannot keep any area of your life to yourself
because all things were created by Christ and for Christ. He deserves
it all.

ARGUING BY GOD'S RULES — 1

Let your speech always be with grace,
as though seasoned with salt, so that you
will know how you should respond to each person.

COLOSSIANS 4:6

Here's a resolution for you to make as a couple today. Resolve that you won't waste your disagreements!

What I mean by that is, agree together that you won't allow your arguments to simply deteriorate into hurtful words, accusations, or name-calling. Promise each other that you won't argue *unless each side presents at least one possible solution to the problem.*

You may be thinking, *That's a lot of work. I'd rather just get what I have to say off my chest.* It may be a lot of work to bend over backward in an attempt to communicate fairly and avoid hurting your spouse. But one thing is certain. When you bend over backward, you never have to worry about falling on your face.

Yes, it takes work to disagree agreeably with each other. But consider the possible alternatives: screaming and hollering, angry words and thoughts, put-downs, or a frosty silence.

These don't have to happen if you follow God's rules for your speech, rules such as "Let no unwholesome word proceed from your mouth," and "Let all bitterness and wrath and anger…be put away from you" (Ephesians 4:29, 31).

By putting the brakes on your tongue and taking time to really think through the issues of married life, you're laying a foundation for years and years of joyful companionship.

ARGUING BY GOD'S RULES — 2

*Let your speech always be with grace,
as though seasoned with salt, so that you will know
how you should respond to each person.*

COLOSSIANS 4:6

*I*nstead of letting our words get out of control in an argument, the Bible counsels us to season our words with salt. Salt is a preservative that keeps rottenness from setting in. If you'll salt down your words before you say them, you'll preserve your relationship and avoid the kind of words that can spoil a love relationship.

Besides, rotten words grieve the Holy Spirit (Ephesians 4:30). And a grieved Holy Spirit is like corrosion on a battery's terminals. When your battery gets corroded, you lose access to the power. The Holy Spirit is the power of the Christian life. If you use rotten and unwholesome words around your house, don't be surprised if you have no power in your spiritual life.

So if you have been using this kind of language with your mate, you owe him or her an apology. If you've been using this kind of language with your children, you owe them an apology, too.

Maybe you didn't know you could use God's rules for healthy communication even when you're disagreeing with one another. But the fact is, that's when you need God's rules the most!

Get down on your knees together today and ask God to help you be kind and tenderhearted toward one another (Ephesians 4:32), even when you're arguing!

A DOMESTIC PEACE INITIATIVE

Forgive us our debts, as we also
have forgiven our debtors.

MATTHEW 6:12

There's an invisible wall running through the middle of many homes, dividing husband from wife. Neither crosses over, except to argue. Or maybe there's no communication at all—just a sullen, silent truce because neither party is willing to compromise.

It's time to dismantle that wall and make peace. You say, "But we don't love each other anymore. We sleep in different beds." Okay, *then love your neighbor!*

"Well, we're not neighbors, we're enemies." *Then love your enemy.* It doesn't matter how you slice the bologna, the Bible has you covered.

Here's a key to keeping the peace. Each of you has to be gracious enough to wipe the mental slate clean. The Bible calls this forgiveness.

That's a hard thing to do, especially if you've been hurt. I'm not suggesting you forget the past ever happened. The Bible doesn't focus on forgetting a wrong, but on refusing to hold that wrong against the other person—just as we wouldn't want God to hold our sins against us.

Jesus taught that our forgiveness from God depends on our willingness to forgive. This isn't the forgiveness of salvation, but the forgiveness that maintains intimate fellowship, and opens the way for God's blessings.

As long as the two of you can forgive each other, you've got a powerful tool for blessing. Don't let anything mess with that.

DOING THE RIGHT THINGS

*God is faithful, who will not allow
you to be tempted beyond what you are able.*

1 CORINTHIANS 10:13

How does a woman find the time and energy to support her husband, fulfill her own duties, and still maintain her first love for the Lord?

One thing God has taught me over the years is to let *Him* set my priorities. I've seen it time and again. When I'm doing the things God wants me to do, I can get everything done in the time I have, and do so with energy and joy.

But when I try to do only what *I* want to do, or what others demand that I do, then my joy is gone and I don't have the stamina I need to get it all done.

God seeks to accomplish His agenda in our lives. The more time we spend in His presence, then, seeking and learning His will, the more productive we will become in what He wants us to accomplish. The more we pursue Him, the clearer His will becomes to us.

God promises He will not give us more to handle than we can bear. The problem comes when *we* take on more than we can bear. No one can do it all! We don't need to worry about all the things we *could* be doing. Let's just concentrate on those things God has called us to do.

NOURISHING THOSE LITTLE SPROUTS

*Your children [will be] like olive
plants around your table.*

PSALM 128:3

*I*n a classic psalm that describes the family that pleases the
Lord, the psalmist likens children to olive plants.

Olive trees were very important in biblical days. Olive oil was
used for cooking, medicine, and many other things.

Notice that these are olive *plants*, not yet full-grown trees. They
need extra care and attention as they grow and develop.

What a great picture of the way we should be tending and nurturing our children. They are little "shoots," little starts off the big
plant that need to be cultivated and cared for.

You know how it is with young plants. You have to make sure
they're watered and packed in good soil. The idea is that our children are filled with potential that needs to be developed and brought
to full growth.

But Dad and Mom, you won't know how well your children are
growing up around your table unless *you* are at that table, too!

I'm convinced there are a lot of boys who would go the right
way if they only had the right man at home challenging them in the
right way. The same needs to be said about girls and their mothers.

Dad, you're the thermostat of the home. It's up to you primarily
to set and maintain the right temperature for little olive plants to
grow.

FAMILIES THAT MAKE AN IMPACT

The LORD bless you from Zion....
Indeed, may you see your children's children.

PSALM 128:5–6

This great psalm makes it clear that a God-pleasing family is maintained within the community of believers.

Zion was Israel's place of worship. Hebrews 12:22 uses Zion to refer to our place of worship, too. If you want the blessing of Zion to rest on your family, see to it that your family is a vital part of your local church.

One problem today is that we have too many church "hitchhikers." The problem with a hitchhiker is that he doesn't invest in the car or buy the gas. He just wants a free ride.

Our churches are also plagued by "McChristians." They want drive-through Christianity. No getting out, no going inside, no commitment, no sacrifice, no inconvenience. Just drive by, order what you want, and leave the rest for someone else.

But that's not what God wants for our families, because He knows that godly families can't survive and thrive in isolation. We need the nurture of the assembled body of Christ.

And when our families are properly nurtured in the body of Christ, they are ready to turn around and make a powerful impact on the community.

If we can get our homes and our churches right, our neighborhoods will have peace and our cities will be better places to live.

GROWING INTO GRACE

Grow in the grace and knowledge of our
Lord and Savior Jesus Christ.

2 PETER 3:18

*T*here are some places in the world you simply have to experience. Postcards or movies cannot do them justice.

As you approach the Taj Mahal, in India, you really can't see it very well. All you see is a white building in the distance with an entrance like a keyhole.

As you go through that entrance you encounter another opening, and the view expands. But when you pass through the last opening, you are staggered by what you see. The beauty of that palace is beyond description.

That's what it's like as we try to comprehend God's grace. Peer at grace from a distance, and it's just another theological concept. Nice, but hardly overwhelming. But the closer you get, the more mind-boggling God's grace becomes. If you ever get a handle on grace, it will revolutionize your spiritual life—and even your marriage.

The theme of grace dominates the New Testament. But in order to appreciate the potency of grace, you must grow spiritually so that more of God's marvelous grace becomes yours.

That's why Peter tells us to grow in grace. We are to grow in our understanding and application of grace. We serve God because of the grace He extended to us at salvation. The Christian life is loving, accepting, forgiving grace from beginning to end—much like marriage!

CRACKS IN THE WALL

*"If the foundations are destroyed,
what can the righteous do?"*

PSALM 11:3

A few years ago, an ugly crack appeared in our bedroom wall. So I called a painter, who patched and repainted the wall. It looked great.

But about a month later the crack reappeared, uglier than ever. I called the painter back and asked him to fix my problem. Not long after that, the crack came back *again*—and brought lots of other cracks with it. So I called a different painter.

The new man looked at my wall and shocked me by saying, "I'm sorry, sir. I can't help you. You don't have a problem with cracks in your wall. Your problem is a shifting foundation on your house. Until you stabilize your foundation, you'll always have cracks in your wall."

What a perfect metaphor for the family. Until we stabilize the foundation, we'll forever be repairing cracks—struggling with problems that keep coming back.

What are you doing to stabilize the spiritual foundation of your home?

As individuals, you need to keep your own walk with the Lord strong. Then as a couple, make sure you're taking time to pray together for yourselves and your family. Don't let Satan chip away at the foundation!

It's the basic stuff that keeps a family strong: prayer, God's Word, worshiping together. Do the basics right, and a lot of other things will take care of themselves.

BECOMING GOD'S IMITATORS

Be imitators of me, just as I also am of Christ.

1 CORINTHIANS 11:1

*I*s anybody imitating you?

That's part of what's supposed to be happening if we are to obey Jesus' command to "make disciples" (Matthew 28:19). Disciples learn from the people discipling them, just like students learn from their teachers, and children imitate their parents.

Paul was the preeminent discipler. He could urge the believers in Corinth to follow him because he was following the Lord. There's nothing wrong with following someone if that person is following Christ.

The real danger for most of us is not that we will suddenly plunge off the deep end and lapse into gross sin or toss our faith aside. That could happen, of course, and we must always be on guard.

But I think a more prevalent danger is that we will continue to take in the truth and simply sit comfortably on it until we are so spiritually bloated we can't move.

We must exercise, *using* what we are learning to change our own lives and help bring other people along in the faith. Discipleship is designed to keep the fat off by allowing us to burn spiritual calories as we put into practice the truth of God.

As a spouse and parent, you probably already have people imitating you! Better ask God to help you make sure your example is a worthy one to follow.

GOD'S SENSE OF HUMOR

"I know the plans that I have for you," declares the LORD,
"plans…to give you a future and a hope."

JEREMIAH 29:11

I had always wanted to get married and share in ministry with my husband, but I had one exception to that desire. I told the Lord that I *never* wanted to be a pastor's wife!

Well, God has a sense of humor! I married Tony in 1970, we went off to seminary a while later, and in 1976 we started the Oak Cliff Bible Fellowship with ten people in our home. I was now officially a pastor's wife!

Obviously, God's plans for my life were different from mine. And in those early years of Tony's ministry, I struggled with this.

Certainly if God had called Tony to be a pastor, then He *was* calling me to be a pastor's wife. I said yes to that call because I had committed myself to Tony in marriage.

But God proved His plans were best. Because I was in His will, He gave me the ability to get the job done without compromising my priorities of home and family.

Is God unfolding a plan in your life or in your marriage right now that isn't the blueprint you had in mind? Look at today's verse again. You may not know all God is doing, but isn't it wonderful to realize that *He* knows the plans He is bringing to pass for you?

HOW TO BE CONTENT

*"Blessed are those who hear the word
of God and observe it."*

LUKE 11:28

Blessed is one of the most fascinating words in the New
Testament.

This word literally means "happy"—but more than just
circumstantially-driven happiness. That is, there was more involved
in blessedness than just being happy because things are going well.

Jesus uses this word to say that you can be blessed if you will
hear and heed His Word. He is saying it is your opportunity, even
while you are on earth, to have the contentment of God on your
life. This is the peace and happiness that remain no matter what the
world hands out to you.

You can be as "relaxed" as God is when you are obeying Him,
because He will lift you above the everyday stuff that swirls all
around you.

Jesus' most extensive use of the word *blessed* was in the
Beatitudes, part of the Sermon on the Mount (Matthew 5:3–12) in
which the Lord spelled out the ways that His disciples could experience His blessedness. And while He spoke to His disciples, a great
crowd of people "eavesdropped."

We might say that Jesus was inviting the people in the crowd to
become kingdom people and enjoy His blessedness. In the same
way, people around us should be able to look at us, see our divine
contentment, and want it for themselves.

NO NEED TO BLUSH

*Do you not know that your bodies
are members of Christ?*

1 CORINTHIANS 6:15

God's Word speaks freely and openly about the subject of sex. God doesn't have to blush or pull down the shades when the issue comes up. Why? Because He created us. He made us male and female. And since sex is God's idea, He reserves the right to tell us how it should function.

Paul discusses our sexuality and the proper functioning of sex in 1 Corinthians 6:15–7:9, an extended passage that introduces us to a number of key principles related to sex and marriage.

The church at Corinth was in the midst of a very pagan, sex-saturated city. Corinth was the Las Vegas of the day. It was "the Strip." When it came to sex, this city's motto was, "Anything goes."

People allowed their bodies to belong to whoever wanted them. And many of the Corinthian believers came out of that background. So they needed a new message concerning their bodies.

In today's verse, Paul put the message in the form of a question. As believers, the Corinthians needed to know that they belonged to Christ—body, soul, and spirit. Therefore, they could not do whatever they wanted in the area of sex.

The fact is that each member of a marriage, and every believer, belongs first to Christ. When you understand that, your commitment to marital faithfulness takes on a new dynamic.

A STARTING POINT FOR BIBLICAL MANHOOD

I want you to understand that
Christ is the head of every man.

1 CORINTHIANS 11:3

*T*oday's verse makes a foundational statement about the way
God intends the world to function. Paul says that God has designed
creation to function by means of a hierarchy—a chain of command.

Even the Trinity operates under a chain of command. First
Corinthians 11:3 goes on to say that God is the head of Christ. This
doesn't mean Christ is inferior to the Father, because the Son is
equal in essence to the Father. Instead, it's a matter of the management of creation. God the Father calls the shots, and Christ the Son
is obedient to the Father.

When Christ was on earth, He never made a decision or a plan
that was not in keeping with His Father's will.

For believers, authority flows from God the Father to Christ,
and then from Christ to the man. So the starting point for a biblical
definition of manhood is that we as men are to function under the
authority of Jesus Christ.

That means He calls the shots in our personal lives, our careers,
and our families. A real man is not some mythical, rugged individu-
alist, out there on his own. A real man is one under divine authority.

Christian brother, does Jesus Christ call the shots in your life? If
not, then don't complain that your wife rejects your calling the shots
for her.

A SEASON FOR EVERYTHING

*There is a time for everything, and
a season for every activity under heaven.*

ECCLESIASTES 3:1, NIV

To keep life's priorities in their proper place, we must remember that everything has a season. God doesn't want us to do it all *now*.

When our children were young, I would sometimes get frustrated that I wasn't using my administrative abilities outside the home. But it just wasn't my season for that yet. God's first priority for me was to concentrate on my kids.

People didn't always understand that. I can remember women getting upset because I declined their invitations to speak at their churches or other events.

But as my children grew older and started going to school, God began to open up new doors and gave me desires that matched those open doors. The season God had for me was changing, and I began to use my gifting in new ways.

No matter how much you may wish to change the season you are in today, don't try to rush God's plan. If you try to change seasons on your own, you will remove yourself from God's will and lose your peace, productivity, and power. Relish the season God has you in, and wait with patient expectation for the change of seasons that will surely come.

Whatever season we are in, God wants us to wait on Him and trust that He always has our best at heart.

DOING WHAT GOD DOES

God saw all that He had made,
and behold, it was very good.

GENESIS 1:31

God enjoyed His creation work. We know this because every time He made something, He congratulated Himself. "That's good."

God felt good about what He had accomplished.

You're supposed to feel good when you work, too. It's the feeling an accountant gets when the numbers come out right…or an athlete when he scores…or a business executive when he closes the deal. When you can say about your work, "That's good," you're imitating God. That's how it was meant to be.

You were made to be a producer, because you were created in the image of a God who works. That's why one of the first things God did when He created Adam was to give him a job (Genesis 2:15).

Please note that sin had not yet spoiled the scene, so Adam's job as overseer and manager of Eden had nothing to do with the curse. God gave him the authority to do something creative by naming the animals (Genesis 2:18–19).

In John 5:17, Jesus said, "My Father is working until now, and I Myself am working." That's God's attitude toward work. You were not put here just to watch what someone else is doing, but to help cultivate, manage, and shape God's creation. What an awesome honor! You get to do what God does.

GOD'S GRACE PLAN—1

*He predestined us to adoption as sons through Jesus Christ...
to the praise of the glory of His grace,
which He freely bestowed on us in the Beloved.*

EPHESIANS 1:5—6

*E*verything God has done, does today, and will ever do for us is grounded in His grace. Grace is the inexhaustible supply of God's goodness, by which He does for us that which we could never do for ourselves.

What could we not do for ourselves? Well, we could not save ourselves. But the death of Christ on the cross freed up the grace of God by dealing with the issue of sin. God's grace toward us could not be activated until sin was addressed.

So God saved you by grace. He also keeps you day by day in His grace. And it is grace by which God gives you the power to pull off what He wants you to do. It's all by grace.

But if you do not understand the all-encompassing nature of God's grace, you can quickly fall into the old trap of trying to earn His favor by the good things you do for Him. But anything we try to do to "help God's grace along" is an insult.

And when we consider the overwhelming, never ending river of grace that flows our way, we would do well to remember our Lord's words to His disciples: "Freely you received, freely give" (Matthew 10:8).

It's time to spread a little of that grace around under our own roof.

GOD'S GRACE PLAN — 2

*For of His fullness we have all received,
and grace upon grace.*

JOHN 1:16

God's whole plan for us from start to finish is a grace plan. And it's such a big plan that according to Ephesians 2:7, God is going to put us on display for all eternity as the prime example of what His grace can do, "so that in the ages to come He might show the surpassing riches of His grace in kindness toward us in Christ Jesus."

God's grace is so inexhaustible, and His grace plan for us is so huge, that one million years from now, the Niagara Falls of His wonderful grace will still be flowing with no letup. God will never run out of grace!

Now let me make an application to your marriage. If God's only plan for dealing with you as individual believers is to deal with you in grace, how do you suppose He wants you to treat each other? With grace!

In other words, you are never more like Jesus Christ than when you treat your mate with the same grace you have received from God.

Because we are human, we will never be perfect in the way we dispense grace. But marriage gives us a built-in training ground to help us learn to respond…as He responds to us.

ARE YOU FAITHFUL WITH YOUR MONEY?

So if you have not been trustworthy in handling worldly wealth, who will trust you with true riches?

LUKE 16:11, NIV

*J*esus knew that money is a very accurate measure of a believer's spiritual temperature. Someone has calculated that of Jesus' thirty-eight parables, sixteen of them use the issue of wealth as a measure of a person's spiritual maturity. In fact, one out of every ten verses in the New Testament makes reference to material possessions.

The Bible contains about five hundred verses on prayer, a little fewer than five hundred verses on faith, and more than a thousand verses on money and finance.

This was a big deal to Jesus and the apostles. They understood that our spiritual condition is often most clearly revealed in our attitude toward our possessions.

In Luke 16:1–13, He told the story of a faithless manager to highlight our need for faithfulness. In the parable, the manager was untrustworthy in the handling of his master's finances. Jesus used the story to teach us that handling our finances is a "practice run," so to speak, for the kingdom responsibility that God wants to assign us.

But if we blow it in the way we use our money, we're not giving God any reason to trust us with the "true riches," which are spiritual. If, on the other hand, we use our money for eternal purposes, we'll have true treasure waiting for us in heaven.

PLEASURE THAT LASTS

You will make known to me the path of life;
In Your presence is fullness of joy;
In Your right hand there are pleasures forever.

PSALM 16:11

*L*ots of people today live for temporary pleasure. To them, work and everything else is just filler between the parties.

But today's most avid pleasure seekers pale in comparison to King Solomon, the wealthiest and wisest man who ever lived. Later in his life, Solomon lost his sense of purpose. In an attempt to recapture it, he turned first to pleasure, as he admitted in Ecclesiastes 2:1–11. He thought if he could "party hearty," he would find the sense of purpose he sought.

Read these verses and you will notice three key words: me, myself, and I. Solomon began living for these three people, and didn't deny himself any pleasure his heart could imagine (2:10).

Did earthly pleasure fill the emptiness in Solomon's soul? Here is his answer. "All was vanity and striving after wind" (Ecclesiastes 2:11).

Talk about futility. Try to grab a fistful of wind, and you'll have the essence of what Solomon is saying. There's nothing there.

If you are banking on the world's pleasure to fill you up, you're going to be left empty. But once you find *real*, satisfying pleasure in a dynamic relationship with God, you'll find "the path of life"!

Since God's desire to lead you is greater than your desire to be led, ask Him to guide your footsteps—and follow where He leads.

A "THEOLOGY" OF SEX — 1

May the God of peace Himself sanctify you entirely;
and may your spirit and soul and body be preserved complete.

1 THESSALONIANS 5:23

When the apostle Paul addresses the issue of sex in
1 Corinthians 6:12–19, what grabs my attention is the fact that he
essentially uses a Trinitarian argument.

In other words, when you read these verses you'll encounter
God the Father, Jesus Christ, and the Holy Spirit. So while we may
think of sex as a pretty "earthy" subject, Paul is saying that *what happens on earth is not the whole story.* The holy, divine Trinity in heaven
is intimately concerned with the issue of how you handle your sexuality and what you do with your body.

Sex is a holy subject, since God is involved in it, and His presence sanctifies it. So Paul doesn't simply argue, "Immorality isn't
nice. You ought not do it." Instead, he says, "This thing is bigger
than you and your spouse. It has theological implications."

Paul's argument in 1 Corinthians 6 is that sexual purity is
demanded because of God the Father (vv. 12–14), it's expected
because of God the Son (vv. 15–16), and it's possible because of
God the Spirit (vv. 17–19).

That's a powerful reason to strive for purity and faithfulness in
this critical area of life. And that's some powerful help to keep you
on that path.

A "THEOLOGY" OF SEX — 2

Let marriage be held in honor among all,
and let the marriage bed be undefiled,
for God will judge the sexually immoral and adulterous.

HEBREWS 13:4, ESV

*M*any people who falter sexually do so because they lose sight of God's perspective on sex, limiting themselves to the human dimension. So whenever you hear someone say, "But I'm only human," that's a human-centered argument. It reflects man's way of thinking, not God's.

When Paul wrote to the Corinthians on this subject, he wasn't shy about reminding them of their recent past. Even though some of them used to be "fornicators" and "adulterers" (1 Corinthians 6:9), they were no longer like that because they had been sanctified (v. 11).

So Paul says, "Don't give me that 'I'm only human' argument. You may have been 'only human' at one point, but now you have God the Father, God the Son, and God the Holy Spirit to help you."

When you got saved, something divine happened to you—to *all* of you. God redeemed your body as well as your soul and spirit. And He is in the process of sanctifying your body, setting it apart for His use. If you or your spouse lose sight of the "theology of sex"— the fact that God is deeply concerned about your marriage and your sexuality—then you won't have His power to help you with the decisions of day-to-day living.

TOO PERFECT?

An excellent wife, who can find?
For her worth is far above jewels.

PROVERBS 31:10

The woman described in Proverbs 31 embodies the spiritual qualities and gifts that would enable any woman to fulfill any role God might call her to take.

Demonstrating a fervent love for the Lord, she continued to love, support, serve her husband and family. And yet at the same time, she developed to the full the abilities and gifts God gave her as an active woman in her community.

I'm fully aware that many women today think the Proverbs 31 woman is almost too perfect, too much of an ideal. These women would argue that no one can match the standards portrayed by this paragon of virtue, strength, and humility.

But I don't believe God put this profile in the Bible to frustrate women because we feel like we can't measure up to the ideal. I believe God is inviting us, in the power of His Holy Spirit, to strive toward this portrait of a godly woman, wife, mother, and business-woman.

In case you are wondering where to begin today, I invite you to look at Proverbs 31:30: "A woman who fears the LORD, she shall be praised." Here is the key to this woman's life, or any woman's life. When our walk with the Lord is in its proper place of priority, He helps us balance and prioritize all other responsibilities.

ABSOLUTE NECESSITIES: WORSHIP

*The true worshipers will worship the Father
in spirit and truth; for such people the
Father seeks to be His worshipers.*

JOHN 4:23

hat an astounding verse!

Imagine: the great God of the universe is looking for people to worship Him!

The second chapter of Acts tells us that believers in the early church went to the temple every day, "praising God" continually (vv. 46–47).

Worship is the furnace of the spiritual life. Worship is the celebration of God for who He is and what He has done. The issue in worship is not necessarily what you get out of it, but what God gets out of it.

Praising God, worshiping Him, and celebrating Him for who He is and what He has done are the ways to get God's attention. God responds to our worship. In fact, God invites us to worship Him. As we have learned in today's verse, He has taken the initiative.

You will be surprised at the way the Spirit of God will ignite your Christian lives, both as individuals and as a couple, when worship becomes not an event, but an experience; not a program, but a way of life. That includes both public and private worship, because both are crucial for a growing disciple of Jesus Christ.

If you want God's power in your life and your marriage, then worship must be part of your daily operation.

ABSOLUTE NECESSITIES:
FELLOWSHIP — 1

*They were continually devoting
themselves...to fellowship.*

ACTS 2:42

*B*iblical fellowship is so much more than coffee and dough-
nuts in Sunday school, or a potluck meal in the fellowship hall. It is
the sharing of our very lives with other believers. You cannot become
a disciple of Jesus Christ independently of others.

That's why the church is so important. It is the "fireplace"
where one log touches another and the fire is maintained. The members of the church at Jerusalem not only shared their lives with one
another, they even shared their possessions as needs arose (Acts
2:44–45).

If you are getting dull in your spiritual life, you need to be in
proximity to others who are on fire so their fire can ignite you. If
you are losing your spiritual fire and you're alone, you're going to
become ashes.

So the question is, are we connected with other believers who
desire to be on fire, too? Does your church have small group meet-
ings during the week? (That's where the action is!) There was simply
no such thing as a nonchurched Christian in the New Testament.

As couples, we need to be in the company of other couples who
love the Lord and face the same challenges and opportunities that
we do. This is more than an "extra" in our Christian lives. It's an
absolute necessity.

ABSOLUTE NECESSITIES: FELLOWSHIP — 2

But encourage one another day after day...that none of you will be hardened by the deceitfulness of sin.

HEBREWS 3:13

We need each other because the best of us can become spiritually dull and flat sometimes, and want to throw in the towel. The best of us sometimes fall flat on our faces. "Let him who thinks he stands take heed lest he fall" (1 Corinthians 10:12, NKJV), because falling is right around the corner.

Back in generations past, Sunday was a much more important day in Christian homes. People came together for worship, and then made time to be with one another or share a meal together.

Perhaps there was a deeper felt-need for God in those days. Sunday seemed like a joyful oasis in the week, while Mondays were often painful, with heartaches, headaches, and pressures. It's really no different today, is it? We *need* the reinforcement of fellowship experienced on Sunday, or whenever Christians gather.

Fellowship in the Bible was designed to show us that we can't make it on your own. In fact, the book of Hebrews urges us to "encourage one another day after day" (3:13).

One of the wonderful things about being married is that you have built-in daily fellowship! Make sure the two of you are working hard on your relationship, and are "stimulat[ing] one another to love and good deeds" (Hebrews 10:24).

ABSOLUTE NECESSITIES: SCRIPTURE

The word of God is living and active and sharper
than any two-edged sword.

HEBREWS 4:12

*I*f you've got a messed-up mind, you're going to have a messed-up life. The body reflects the thought processes of the mind, and many of us have come into the Christian life with warped minds, contaminated by an ungodly system.

Our minds need to be renewed (Romans 12:2). Only then will our lives be transformed. I've discovered that when you try to change people's actions without changing their thinking, you only do a temporary, patchwork job.

If you want to fix what you do, you must first fix how you think about what you do. A transformed mind comes through the study and practice of the Bible. Many of us have habits in our lives that we want to get rid of. But we say, "I can't," because we've been brainwashed by the enemy to believe we will never have victory in this area.

But God's Word can change that, if we will feed on it regularly. If you are going to become a disciple, you must have a dynamic experience with the Bible. When it comes to spiritual education, we have a divine Teacher, the Holy Spirit. Jesus said the Spirit would remind us of all that He taught (John 14:26).

This indwelling Spirit loves to make God's Word come alive. He is eager to set your heart on fire!

ABSOLUTE NECESSITIES: BEING A WITNESS

He who is wise wins souls.

PROVERBS 11:30

The most obvious event of the church's witness in Acts 2 was Peter's great Pentecost sermon. This is the same Peter who, just a few weeks earlier, was too scared to admit he even knew Jesus.

What was the difference? The Holy Spirit had taken control of Peter, and he was about to take off and soar in his spiritual life. He became a bold and faithful witness for Jesus Christ.

You say, "But Tony, I'm not bold. I'm a private person."

Maybe so, but when something very exciting happens in your life, you *will* talk about it without much prompting. Anyone who is so "private" that he or she never opens up about anything that matters has to be a pretty boring person.

One reason some of us Christians don't share Christ is because we've lost our excitement about Him. When He is exciting to you, you can't keep Him to yourself.

The believers who received the Spirit on Pentecost became witnesses. The result of their witness and Peter's sermon on that day was the addition of three thousand new believers to the church.

Now that's a witness! And please notice that these three thousand people did not come because of some evangelistic program. They came because God's people were overwhelmed by the experience and presence of God's Spirit. They were excited about Jesus.

DOING IT ALL

"Many daughters have done nobly,
but you excel them all."

PROVERBS 31:29

The feminist movement of the last thirty-plus years has given us a lot of angry and frustrated women. They are determined to prove to themselves and everyone else—particularly to men—that they can do anything a man can do, and do it better.

Modern-day feminists, however, have nothing on the woman of Proverbs 31. She did all of the things suggested by this song, and clearly did them right.

But it wasn't out of anger or frustration, or to "prove" something. And it wasn't because she was a "superwoman" who didn't need anyone else. Instead, what we see in Proverbs 31 is a woman who accomplished more than most feminists will ever accomplish, yet with unswerving devotion to the Lord in the setting of a loving home and family.

The message to women is this: God's Word gives us true liberty without getting us sidetracked into divisive politics or the fierce competition between the sexes.

With all the duties and demands that wives and mothers face these days, you may not feel like a queen in your home. But the writer of Proverbs wants you to know that any woman who can meet life's challenges, while keeping her love for God strong, deserves the honor paid to a queen (Proverbs 31:10). Christian brother, have you honored your wife today?

Spring

BLESSED POVERTY

"Blessed are the poor in spirit,
for theirs is the kingdom of heaven."

MATTHEW 5:3

*J*esus began the Sermon on the Mount by pronouncing blessed-ness, or happiness, on those who reflect the attitude of the kingdom of God and the character of the King.

This first Beatitude has nothing to do with economics, of course. Jesus isn't primarily concerned with how many cars you have or what kind of clothes you wear.

Neither is the Lord talking about a "Poor me" syndrome—how low you can hang your head because you feel so worthless and humble.

Instead, those who are poor in spirit are people who recognize their total dependence on God. They are husbands and wives who understand that they cannot be the marriage partner they need to be apart from God. They are fathers and mothers who understand that effective parenting is impossible unless they cry out to God for help.

How poor in spirit does Jesus really expect us to be? The word He used for poor means "beggar." Beggars were common in His day, and from what we can tell, not ashamed to beg for their living.

Beggars know they can't make it on their own, so they're not hesitant to cry out for help. God wants us to make the same discovery about our lives and our marriages.

On the streets of God's kingdom, it's the beggars who are happy!

CONSULT THE LIFE-MAKER

You will seek Me and find Me when you search
for Me with all your heart.

JEREMIAH 29:13

What do so many of us men do with our lives? We do like I did one year with the bicycle I bought my son for Christmas. It came with one of those thick assembly manuals written by someone for whom English is a second language.

I *hate* taking the time to read those things. So, like any intelligent, self-respecting American man, I figured, "Hey, I've got a doctoral degree. I can certainly put a bike together without any help."

Eight hours later, I had nothing but the handlebars on. Lois came to the door of the garage with a novel suggestion. "Honey, why don't you just read the directions?"

In my frustration and futility, with my pride crushed, I finally did just that. I humbled myself, and let the creator of the bike tell me how to put it together. Forty-five minutes later, the bike was assembled.

The Life-Maker knows more about putting life together than you or I ever will know. We need to humble ourselves and say, "Lord, I don't know how to put life together by myself. It has too many pieces. Show me the purpose You have for me."

Life starts making sense when you begin your search for purpose in the right place—by seeking the face and the heart of God.

No Chains

All things are lawful for me, but not all things are profitable.
All things are lawful for me,
but I will not be mastered by anything.

1 CORINTHIANS 6:12

*P*aul gives us a timeless truth principle that we can apply to any activity we may engage in, as individuals or as married couples.

One reason this principle is so valuable is because of our tendency to carry even good things too far—even letting them take control of us. But God never intended these good, legitimate activities to enslave us.

Even though an activity may be lawful, it should never boss you around. Even though an activity or appetite may be okay, it was not given to master you.

In 1 Corinthians 6:13, Paul gives us two examples of what he is talking about. The first is food. It's lawful to eat—praise God! But it's not okay to let food dominate your life until your appetite is out of control. Food is a temporary reality, so don't let it become your focus.

The second example is sex. God gave you sexual desires. They are healthy and normal. And it's healthy and normal to seek their fulfillment within your marriage.

But Paul says we are not to be *mastered* by our sexual desires. He did not give us our bodies so we could practice immorality, or insist that our mates meet our sexual demands regardless. Don't let something legitimate get out of hand, or it will slap chains on you.

NO MORE RAMBOS

*Hear, O sons, the instruction of a father,
and give attention that you may gain understanding.*

PROVERBS 4:1

*T*oday's children are sometimes called a lost generation. But the fact is that our children, especially our boys, are the *product* of a lost generation. They're being raised in an environment that does not model biblical manhood or hold them accountable to that standard.

The male model of recent years is the Rambo-type superman who can slay dozens and never go down, who carries out his one-man vendetta and never sheds a tear.

We now have a generation of boys and young men who have this mentality. They're quick to deal out violence, and that's scary enough. But what's even more scary is that they can deal out violence and feel nothing. They seem to be beyond normal human sensitivity. That didn't just happen. These kids were nurtured on a culture of violence.

They've been bombarded by popular entertainment and peer groups that have reshaped their thinking. Without healthy male examples, they're growing up with no concept of true manhood.

The effect on young girls is just as devastating. We have a generation of girls who don't know how to identify the right kind of man, because they haven't seen any!

We men need to recapture our homes for Christ. If you're ready, He'll help you! Ask God to help you draw a line in the sand and declare to the enemy, "Here I stand."

FEEL THE BURN

"Speak, LORD, for Your servant is listening."

1 SAMUEL 3:9

*T*he first time you lift weights or work out, it's not going to be fun. When you come back home, you're going to hurt. It's called *feeling the burn.*

The reason it hurts, of course, is that you are using muscles that aren't used to being exercised. The way to get over the pain is to work those muscles some more and make them ache more. Eventually, you'll get used to the exercise and the pain will be replaced by the feeling you get when your body is in good shape.

You can't go to the gym or health club one week and expect to come out looking like the people on television. That's simply not going to happen.

If you want to be an "in shape" Christian, then you have to be an effective spiritual exerciser. Obedience has to become a way of life.

If you want an adventure, ask the Lord, "What do You want to do with my life? What must I obey so that I will have the fruit of Your blessing on my life and on my family?"

And if you want an even bigger adventure, agree together to begin praying this way as a couple. If you will accept the challenge of obeying Christ in everything, the payoff will be beyond your wildest dreams!

MIRROR, MIRROR ON THE WALL

"Man looks at the outward appearance,
but the LORD looks at the heart."

1 SAMUEL 16:7

*L*et's face it. Even a woman who is blessed with unusual physical beauty will still fall prey to the passing of the years and the inevitable fading of her youthful good looks. Time takes its toll on everyone.

There's nothing wrong with physical attractiveness. Women do not need to apologize for their beauty. There is nothing godly about a woman neglecting her appearance. But the problem comes when outward beauty ceases to be merely one aspect of a woman's life, and becomes the main focus of her heart.

"Charm is deceitful and beauty is vain," says of the writer of Proverbs (31:30). This is not because charm or beauty are inherently sinful. The deceit comes when a woman tries to capitalize on her beauty to get what she wants, or allows her identity to be wrapped up in the way she looks. Beauty was never meant to be a measure of a woman's worth.

The Bible assures us that while man looks on the outward appearance, God looks at the heart (1 Samuel 16:7). So if the subject of physical beauty makes you feel intimidated, don't let it. God isn't holding a beauty contest. By depending on the power of the indwelling Holy Spirit, you can achieve the noble character that He desires. Physical beauty eventually fades, but a godly character grows more beautiful with time.

YOUR PLANTING RESPONSIBILITIES

He who sows sparingly will also reap sparingly,
and he who sows bountifully will also reap bountifully.

2 CORINTHIANS 9:6

*I*f you knew that the man living next door to you was a thief,
would you leave your windows unlocked when you left the house?
Of course not. You don't want him to have access to your goods.

Well, God says that because so many of His people are thieves,
He has locked the windows of heaven so they can't have access to
His blessings.

In Malachi 3:8–10, God accused the Israelites of robbing Him
by withholding their tithes and offerings. Bring Me the whole tithe,
God challenges the people, and I will take the padlock off the windows of heaven (v. 10).

Giving God the portion of their income that He requests is one
of a couple's basic, nonnegotiable "planting" responsibilities in the
handling of their finances. That this is nonnegotiable is obvious
from the fact that God told Israel, "You are cursed with a curse, for
you are robbing Me" (v. 9).

Now when it comes to your taxes, you don't have to worry
about keeping back what belongs to the government. The government takes its share first.

But we can hold back that which is God's because He doesn't
force us to give. The consequences still remain, however. I'm convinced that some Christian couples with financial woes aren't just
poor handlers of money. They're under God's curse because they are
disobeying Him.

LIFE BLESSING OR LIFE SENTENCE?

With good will render service, as to the Lord, and not to men,
knowing that whatever good thing each one does,
this he will receive back from the Lord.

EPHESIANS 6:7–8

When Adam and Eve rebelled against God, it affected their work. When they tried to go their own way, it impacted their economic well-being. One judgment for sin was a curse on work:

> "Cursed is the ground because of you; in toil you will eat of
> it all the days of your life. Both thorns and thistles it shall
> grow for you; and you will eat the plants of the field; by
> the sweat of your face you will eat bread."

GENESIS 3:17–19

We definitely have a problem. God says from now on, creation will *resist* man's work. This is why so many men feel like work is a life sentence rather than a blessing. When you're in a job you don't like, when you feel that your job is meaningless, what you're feeling are the thorns and thistles of the curse. It's part of mankind's fall into sin. When man fell, work fell with him.

That's the bad news. But here's the flip side. In Romans 8:19–25, Paul says creation is awaiting redemption, when Eden's curse will be reversed. Our final redemption is still future, but we don't have to wait for heaven to enjoy our work. When Christ redeemed us, He also redeemed work and filled it with new meaning. We're now working for Him!

THE NEVER ENDING STORY
OF GRACE — 1

Grace and peace be multiplied to you...
seeing that [God's] divine power has granted to us
everything pertaining to life and godliness.

2 PETER 1:2—3

*I*f you two were like Lois and me, you didn't exactly have everything you needed when you first got married.

For most newlyweds, it would be an understatement to say that
they lacked a few of the essentials—like a house and furniture! But
as mind-boggling as it seems, the moment you got saved God put
within you everything you would ever need to become a fully
mature, fully functioning believer. And He did it by His grace,
which Peter says is so big you need a multiplication table to figure it
out, not an adding machine!

A good illustration of the way God equips us in grace is human
birth. When a baby is born, that tiny body contains all the information that baby needs to grow to full maturity. It's all there.

But for that baby to realize its full potential, the baby still has to
eat and grow. The awesome truth of God's grace is that we are complete in Christ. You don't get saved by grace and then move on to
God's really good stuff. Everything He has for you is already yours
through His grace.

But that grace potential is realized as we grow spiritually. It is
growth that brings out what's inside. And we should be satisfied
with nothing less than the multiplication of God's grace in our lives.

THE NEVER ENDING STORY OF GRACE — 2

*But grow in the grace and knowledge of
our Lord and Savior Jesus Christ.*

2 PETER 3:18

*D*o you remember when you were eight or nine years old and wanted to be a teenager? At ten, I remember telling my father, "Daddy, I'm almost a teenager!"

Then I became a teenager and got used to that, so I started looking forward to becoming a man. Then I would say to my father, "Daddy, I'm almost a man." I was always looking forward to what was next. Being able to drive. Being able to vote. Going to college. Getting my own place. Meeting the right woman and getting married.

Eventually, life runs out of new expectations because our lives are finite and limited. But God's grace knows no limits. The story of grace never ends, so you can always look forward to the next chapter. There's no reason that you cannot grow into the fullness of everything that God by His grace has encoded in your spiritual DNA!

In case you haven't figured it out yet, marriage is one of the things God gives you to help bring out your potential and allow you to grow into full maturity.

Give grace to your spouse freely…receive grace from your spouse humbly when you've blown it.

Most of all, drink in the grace of Jesus Christ for daily cleansing and for the strength and wisdom to be the partner God wants you to be.

WHERE ARE YOU PUTTING IT? —1

Do not lay up for yourselves treasures on earth,
where moth and rust destroy and where
thieves break in and steal.

MATTHEW 6:19, NKJV

*Y*ou're probably well acquainted with this familiar verse.
Many of us memorized it when we were kids.

But one danger of childhood memory verses is that we can leave
them back in childhood. Matthew 6:19 is a good example of this
tendency. But we cannot afford to miss the force of Jesus' words
here.

Let me show you why through a short Greek lesson. In the
original language, the words *lay up* and *treasure* are from the same
root. So Jesus is literally saying, "Do not treasure up treasure for
yourselves."

In other words, if we are going to follow Jesus, we cannot give
our hearts to the accumulation of material wealth. Does that mean
Jesus doesn't want your family to have a savings account? Does this
command disqualify you from investing on Wall Street? Is it wrong
to have some money put aside for tough times that may come?

This cannot be what Jesus is saying, because the Bible applauds
saving. The writer of Proverbs urged us to study the ant and the way
it stores up its food, and imitate the ant's wise preparation (Proverbs
6:6–11).

Jesus' intent is not to discourage preparation for the future. The
following two verses, Matthew 6:20–21, make it clear that the Lord's
concern is that we not let earthly accumulation become the focus of
our lives.

WHERE ARE YOU PUTTING IT? — 2

*Command those who are rich in this present world
not to be arrogant nor to put their hope in wealth,
which is so uncertain, but to put their hope in God,
who richly provides us with everything for our enjoyment.*

1 TIMOTHY 6:17, NIV

*J*esus wants us to examine *why* we are accumulating wealth. If it's to prepare for the future, fine. But if we are spending our time stockpiling for earth rather than stockpiling for heaven, we are in trouble.

Jesus knows it is possible for us as couples to get our priorities so out of whack that we fall into the trap of doing everything for ourselves, and nothing for the kingdom of God.

People like that may have fat bank accounts, but their spiritual accounts are bouncing checks because they have stored up things for themselves but not for God.

So how do we make sure our money and other treasures—including time and talents—are producing dividends in heaven? By investing them in God's work down here on earth. The question you need to ask yourselves today is this: In what ways is the kingdom of God benefiting from our wealth...from the investment of our experience and talents in the body of Christ...from the strategic use of our time in sharing Christ and helping His people?

Do a "checkbook checkup" together today, answering the question above. If you don't like the answer, decide how—and when—you're going to make changes.

SAME OLD, SAME OLD

"Do not call to mind the former things,
Or ponder things of the past.
Behold, I will do something new,
Now it will spring forth."

ISAIAH 43:18—19

*L*egions of modern men suffer from what I call the "same old, same old" disease. You ask them how it's going, and they answer, "Oh, you know, same old, same old."

What they mean is, every day they get out of that same old bed and go to that same old bathroom to stare in the mirror at that same old face. They go to that same old closet and thumb through those same old clothes to put on that same old body. They go to that same old kitchen, sit at that same old breakfast table, and eat that same old breakfast cooked by that same old wife (I'm treading dangerous ground here).

Then they go to that same old garage, get in that same old car, and drive down that same old road to that same old office. There they work with those same old people, doing that same old thing, receiving that same old pay. And on it goes.

Are you in a rut right now? A rut is nothing more than a grave that's open on both ends. Don't look around at the walls of your rut, my friend; *look up.* God wants to give you a new sense of purpose and significance. Ask Him to interrupt your routine with His renewed vision for life and living for His kingdom.

HAPPY MOURNERS

*"Blessed are those who mourn,
for they shall be comforted."*

MATTHEW 5:4

The mourning Jesus speaks of is sorrow over our sin. It's what Paul called "the sorrow that is according to the will of God" (2 Corinthians 7:10). You mourn over your sin when it tears you up so much you can't help but cry.

Why don't we see more Christians crying over sin? Because we don't often come to grips with how sinful and messed up we often become. We measure ourselves against the wrong standard, and conclude that we're okay.

We laugh at things that we know aren't right, and tell ourselves, *Well, this isn't nearly as bad as some of the stuff out there.* We do questionable things, and tell ourselves, *God understands.*

But God says, "No, you don't understand. You ought to be crying, not laughing." When Paul saw himself he cried out, "Wretched man that I am!" (Romans 7:24). Paul mourned because he saw his sin. When he compared the character of God with his own life, there was such a discrepancy that he mourned.

The mourning Paul spoke of in 2 Corinthians 7:10 is a godly sorrow that leads to repentance—a change of heart, a change of mind, a change of ways. In other words, true spiritual mourning leads to a solution. The mourner deals with sin, and in that dealing experiences the indescribable comfort of God's forgiveness.

BETTER SEW UP THAT HOLE

"You have sown much, but harvest little...and he who earns, earns wages to put into a purse with holes."

HAGGAI 1:6

Ever felt like your purse or wallet had a hole in it?

It's easy to feel that way as we watch our money. As one guy said, "Yeah, my money talks. It says, 'Good-bye.'"

Haggai was talking to people who had returned to Jerusalem from the Babylonian captivity. Their first priority should have been to rebuild God's temple so the worship of God could be restored.

But after beginning the temple, the people let it sit unfinished while they built lavish houses for themselves.

Here was a clear case of God's people laying up treasure for themselves while ignoring God's priorities. God could not let this insult continue, so He sent a few of His "moths" (see Matthew 6:19) to eat holes in their purses.

There's a fundamental principle here we don't dare miss. If you aren't using your material possessions to further the kingdom of God and reflect His priorities, there's no place you can stash your money where He can't get at it if He chooses to do so.

In other words, when we do not prioritize God's kingdom in our financial stewardship, we are investing in things that have a very short lifespan!

So if your bank account seems to have holes, it's a good idea to check out the "eternal value" of your portfolio.

THE INCREDIBLE VALUE OF TRUST

The heart of her husband trusts in her,
and he will have no lack of gain.

PROVERBS 31:11

*N*o relationship can survive and flourish very long without trust. This is especially true of marriage.

The picture of confident trust in today's verse contrast sharply with the "battle of the sexes" being promoted in our secular culture, which is shredding so many marriages.

Trust is so crucial to a marriage. The opposite of a husband and wife who trust each other is a couple who say and do things that break the confidence between them.

Marriage is such an intimate relationship that a husband and wife gain intimate knowledge that needs to be held in complete trust. This is not because these things are wrong, but because they are private.

A woman in particular understands the power of these things, and she can be tempted to use them against her husband when she is angry. And when a husband breaks his marital trust, it takes a woman of extraordinary character not to retaliate.

Is your marriage marked by absolute trust? I hope so. When a husband knows his wife is a trustworthy person, he can take risks and soar to greater heights in his calling. And when a wife knows her heart is safe in her husband's care, she is free to grow into the person God wants her to be.

THE CENTRALITY OF THE HOLY SPIRIT

"I will ask the Father, and He will give you another Helper, that He may be with you forever; that is the Spirit of truth."

JOHN 14:16–17

*T*he Holy Spirit is at the heart and core of the Christian faith. And yet, there seems to be a great deal of confusion surrounding His Person and work.

I'm convinced that if believers could get a handle on who the Holy Spirit is and what He does, our individual Christian lives—to say nothing of our marriages—would never be the same.

One of the foundational passages for understanding the Person and work of the Holy Spirit is Jesus' upper room discourse (John 13–17). It was here He promised His followers that God the Father would send them "another Helper."

This was not one of the greatest moments in the lives of the disciples. It was a spiritual downtime. Everything was going wrong. Judas had shown himself to be a traitor. Jesus had just told Peter that he would betray Him. Plus, the Jews wanted to get rid of Christ and all of His followers.

Then came the worst blow. Jesus told them He was going away, and that they couldn't follow—yet.

This was the sorrowful, perplexing, tension-filled environment in which Jesus introduced His disciples to the stabilizing ministry of the Spirit.

What problems and tensions are you facing today? You can draw on the same supply of power and strength Jesus promised His disciples—the mighty Holy Spirit of God.

DO YOU HAVE A KINGDOM VISION?

"The LORD has sought out for Himself a
man after His own heart."

1 SAMUEL 13:14

*I*n Jeremiah 5:1, God sends Jeremiah roaming through the streets of Jerusalem trying to find just one man "who does justice, who seeks truth."

Then God makes an astounding promise. If Jeremiah could find even one man like that, God would pardon the people! But the prophet could not find one man of justice and truth, either among the poor or the great (vv. 4–5). So God's judgment fell on the nation.

God is always hunting for faithful men. There are plenty of males, but what He wants is a man after His heart. He wants a man who has a vision of what God could do with him.

Too many of us men have learned about manhood from the wrong sources. We have taken our heroes and models from Hollywood and from the sports world. And we try to import that nonsense into our marriages and families.

We Christian men need a twofold kingdom vision. First, we need to see the agenda God has laid out for men in His Word. Second, we need a clear picture of how God wants us to carry out that agenda in our lives.

God wants to give you a vision. Are you ready? Ezekiel 22:30 tells us God is looking for a man to stand in the gap. Will you be that man?

IT'S ALL JUST BORROWED

Not to us, O LORD, not to us, but to Your name
give glory.... Our God is in the heavens;
He does whatever He pleases.

PSALM 115:1, 3

*G*od didn't create us for *our* pleasure. He created us for
Himself. He's the owner, and you and I are just the managers.

God created man to be a steward of His creation. He said to
Adam, "I want you to oversee My domain, to rule over it for Me. I
put it in your care. It's yours to use and enjoy, but I want you to
manage it the way I would manage it."

Therefore, since the universe is God's place, He does whatever
He pleases with it.

The Bible declares that God owns it all (Psalm 24:1–2). That's
about as clear as it gets. Now unless you and I helped Him create
the world, we really don't own a thing. This is important for us men
in particular to understand and believe, because men are into ownership. That's where we get a big part of our masculine identity.

Remember, my brother, you and I were born with nothing but
our skin on. The only reason we'll be buried in a nice suit is because
somebody else dressed us. And there will be no U-Haul following
the hearse, because everything we have is only borrowed from God.

Start living today as if everything you have is on loan from
God, and you'll save yourself a lot of worry.

LOSING OUR "LOSER'S LIMP"

Walk in the way of good men
and keep to the paths of the righteous.

PROVERBS 2:20

Many men today are suffering from what I call a "loser's limp." This is what happens when a guy is playing baseball and the ball is hit over his head. He knows he should make the play, but he misjudges the ball.

Since he doesn't want anyone else to know he muffed the play, he falls down and gets up limping. The idea is that if it weren't for whatever he tripped over, or the sudden cramp he got in his leg, he would have caught the ball. A loser's limp is a way of camouflaging failure.

Far too many Christian men are camouflaging their failure to be kingdom men. They give excuses. "If it weren't for the way I was raised," "Well, my father left my mother," "If it weren't for this woman God gave me…"

But excuses won't get the job done. We need to realize that just being a male isn't enough to make us faithful kingdom men who are effective for Christ in our homes.

Too many men are still missing in action, and too many women have been thrust into the role of leadership at home. But the good news is that God is still looking for men He can trust and use. How about it, brother? Let's go for His best together!

SOLID INVESTMENT ADVICE

"Store up for yourselves treasures in heaven,
where neither moth nor rust destroys,
and where thieves do not break in or steal."

MATTHEW 6:20

*S*ometimes we are tempted to push statements about heaven off into the distant future—"pie in the sky, by and by." We tend to compartmentalize life into the here and now and the hereafter.

But Jesus didn't operate with that dichotomy. His concern is that we live *today* with heaven in view. His intense desire for us is that we do God's will on earth just as God's will is being done in heaven.

Jesus wants His kingdom to be our primary focus now, so that whether it's our savings account, our home, or whatever, we use it for eternal purposes.

We need to remember that heaven begins on earth. Eternal life begins the minute we accept Christ as our Savior. Heaven is not only our future, it's our present. So the issue isn't *when* we get our treasure, but *where* our treasure is located.

If you are using the time, abilities, and material things God gives you to store up treasure in heaven, there's no question that you are securing your tomorrow.

But you are also securing your today. Why? Because the person who has heaven's view of earth's stuff is the person who gets the most enjoyment out of life. The person who tries to hoard it all down here is the one who loses, both now and in eternity.

ENJOY THE GIFT — 1

*I know that there is nothing better for them than to rejoice and
to do good in one's lifetime; moreover, that every man who eats
and drinks sees good in all his labor—it is the gift of God.*

ECCLESIASTES 3:12–13

*R*ight in the heart of a book written to explore the futility and
meaninglessness of life, Solomon stops and says, "Actually, life is a
gift from God."

That is a great perspective. It's only when we view life as the gift
of God that we begin to find its purpose. It's only as we live in time
from the perspective of eternity that we find life's meaning.

Now if life is God's gift to you, then the fastest way to find your
purpose in life is through thanksgiving. What do you say when
someone brings you a gift? You say, "Thank you," and then you
enjoy the gift. You don't try to take it apart and figure it out.

In other words, if you want to find your purpose, don't go looking for your purpose. Look for the Purpose-Giver. If you want to
find the secret to life, look to the Author of life. That's why the
greatest way to find out who you are is not to look in the mirror,
but to look to God, the One who gave you your identity. Because
when you find Him, you find you.

ENJOY THE GIFT — 2

"I am the Light of the world;
he who follows Me will not walk in the darkness,
but will have the Light of life."

JOHN 8:12

Jesus said, "I came that [you] may have life, and have it abundantly" (John 10:10).

Life is not found in the living, but in the Living One. Jesus agreed with Solomon that life is a gift from God. So you find what you're looking for when you stop looking for it...and let the Giver of life grant it to you.

You may have to think about that for a minute. But when you do, you'll realize what a freeing thing this is. Instead of looking for your purpose within yourself, locate God and you will find yourself.

So what is the purpose of life? The discovery and the enjoyment of God. Try as you might (Solomon did!), you will never find a greater purpose or passion in life. That's why the apostle Paul said he had one goal: "That I may know Him" (Philippians 3:10).

If you know God, you will know your purpose. Not because you went purpose-hunting, but because you went God-hunting.

Pray, "God, I want to know You more than anything. Reveal Yourself to me, and I'll let You reveal me to me." When you do that, you'll know why you are here and where you are going.

You will know you...without even trying.

IT'S NOT THE SAME THING

The body is not for immorality, but for the Lord,
and the Lord is for the body.

1 CORINTHIANS 6:13

Have you ever heard this argument? "Sex is no different than eating. You get hungry, you eat. You get turned on, you have sex. It's the same thing."

But the Bible teaches that any attempt to treat our sexual drives the way we handle other natural appetites is a huge mistake, because the correlation breaks down.

For many people today, indulging their sexual desires has become as ordinary as eating when they are hungry. But Paul says in no uncertain terms that while the stomach is made for food, our bodies are not made for immorality (v. 13).

In other words, morality is not a "drive-through" issue. It is *not* the same as eating—or anything else, for that matter. Eternal issues are at stake when it comes to sexual morality.

Why? Because our bodies were made for the Lord. That is, they are much more than a container for sexual desires. Our bodies are vehicles through which we are to honor and serve God and bring Him glory. What we do with our bodies impacts our spirits, and that impacts eternity.

God wants us to make a clear distinction between fast food and fast sex. He is honored when we exercise control over our desires and keep ourselves pure in His sight.

No Simple Answer

She looks well to the ways of her household,
and does not eat the bread of idleness.

PROVERBS 31:27

*D*oes the Bible permit believing wives and mothers to work outside the home? The answer depends on several factors. For instance, the noble woman of Proverbs 31 was a capable business-woman as well as a wife and mother.

This woman dealt in textiles and real estate, made garments, and engaged in works of charity (v. 20). But it's obvious from this entire passage (Proverbs 31:10–31) that none of her outside activities caused her to neglect her family. They were well fed, well clothed, and ready for every season.

This illustrates a biblical principle governing the choice of outside activities for a wife and mother who seeks to please God: They are permissible as long as they don't take priority over a woman's primary responsibility to be a "[keeper] at home" (Titus 2:5, KJV).

The Bible is clear that a woman's primary focus is to be on her home. But being a worker at home doesn't necessarily mean being a "stayer" at home. God is not telling women to stay home and never venture out for any other commitments. The issue is a woman's priorities and the way her outside activities impact her home.

When I begin to feel stressed out and harassed, it's a clear indication that I'm probably trying to handle more things than God intended me to handle…and it's time to refocus.

TOUGH TIMES, EXCITING TIMES

*My God will supply all your needs according to
His riches in glory in Christ Jesus.*

PHILIPPIANS 4:19

When Tony and I moved to Dallas in the early seventies so he could enter seminary, we had one small child and no extra money.

Though Tony was a full-time student, he still accepted his responsibility to provide for his family. We both knew that our daughter needed me at home, so we made a commitment before the Lord that I would not work outside the home. This meant we would have to get by on whatever Tony could earn working part-time. He brought home $350 a month.

Those were hard times financially—but also exciting times. We saw God meet our needs time and again. I remember one day when there was no money and not much to eat in the house. I was in tears. I couldn't understand why the Lord would put us in that situation.

That morning, Tony asked me how much it would take to meet our needs, and I said five hundred dollars—an awful lot in those days. But together we asked God to supply. Tony said if God did not give him some sign of provision, he would drop out of seminary for a year to work full-time.

But when Tony went to his mailbox at school that day, he found five hundred dollars! I will never forget that experience. God's supply is always more abundant than our need.

Do You Need a New Boss?

Slaves, be obedient to those who are your masters according to
the flesh, with fear and trembling,
in the sincerity of your heart, as to Christ.

Ephesians 6:5

*G*od's will for you, which is "good and acceptable and perfect"
(Romans 12:2), includes your work.

Apart from Christ you can have the best job in the world and
still be empty inside. Work itself can't give you meaning. In fact,
James 4:13–17 says work can become a source of sin when God's
will is excluded.

In those verses, James says that instead of arrogantly making our
business plans, we need to say, "If the Lord wills, we will live and
also do this or that." Otherwise, we're just bragging. And James con-
cludes, "All such boasting is evil."

Work apart from Christ can be a curse. Conversely, it becomes
blessed when you include God's will. The degree to which you inte-
grate God into your work is the degree to which you will find
meaning in what you do every day.

The idea is to take God *with* you to the job. If you don't go to
work tomorrow thinking, "I'm going to work for the Lord," then
you've missed the meaning of work. The quickest way to transform a
bad job is with a new attitude. And the quickest way to get a new
attitude is to change bosses.

You may feel like a slave at work—and you are! But you are
Christ's slave, and that makes all the difference.

BE CAREFUL WHERE YOU PUT IT

Where your treasure is, there your heart will be also.

MATTHEW 6:21

*J*esus warns us to be careful where we invest our time, money, and talents, because our hearts will follow along behind our investment.

Suppose you're sitting in church next Sunday morning and the pastor reads an urgent announcement: Your house is on fire!

Now I doubt that you would stay to hear the rest of the sermon. You would probably get up immediately and rush out to check on your house.

I would do the same thing. Why? Because we invest a lot of ourselves and our treasures in our homes, and a big piece of our hearts are there.

Jesus isn't forbidding us to enjoy and protect the things He has given us. And it's okay with Him if we reap a legitimate return for our work. What He's talking about here is the problem of living for ourselves.

See, when you live for yourself, your real problem isn't the love of money. That's only a symptom. The real problem is your priorities. Because we will come to love what we invest in, Jesus says to make sure that God's kingdom and His righteousness are the focus of our lives.

If God is your focus, He will have your treasure. And whoever has your treasure will get your heart!

A Vision with Staggering Dimensions

"Let Us make man in Our image, according to Our likeness;
and let them rule over the fish of the sea and over the
birds of the sky and over the cattle and over all the earth."

GENESIS 1:26

Adam, along with Eve, was not only to rule the earth, but he was to bear and reproduce the image of God. That's bigger than any man can pull off by himself.

God gave Adam a job, but He gave him a job so he could achieve a bigger goal, a kingdom agenda. Christian brother, if you cannot sit in your chair right now and articulate God's kingdom call on your life, then something's missing.

A vision is the ability to see beyond the immediate and the visible. A kingdom vision is a view of life that's far bigger than just "getting by" day after day. It is a calling that allows you to make an impact for eternity while you're still here in history.

God has called you and me as men to something bigger than life. He has called us to set the pace and lead the way in our homes, in the church, and ultimately in His worldwide kingdom.

WE BELONG TO GOD TWO WAYS

From Him and through Him and to Him are all things.
To Him be the glory forever. Amen.

ROMANS 11:36

*S*uppose I came over to your house and said, "Look, I don't like your furniture. It just doesn't look right. It's got to go. All of this has to be changed."

What are you likely to say to me? "Excuse me, you're in *my* house. I paid for this furniture, and I'm paying this house note. You haven't made one dime's worth of investment in this house. So with all due respect, mind your own business."

We haven't made one dime's worth of investment in God's creation. We haven't added one iota to what He has made. A Christian recognizes God as the absolute owner of everything.

That is Paul's point in today's verse. God created this world for Himself. But if you are a Christian, you not only belong to God because He created you. You also belong to Him because He redeemed you. "Do you not know that...you are not your own? For you have been bought with a price" (1 Corinthians 6:19–20). Therefore, "Whether, then, you eat or drink or whatever you do, do all to the glory of God" (1 Corinthians 10:31).

If you're the creator, you have the right to demand that your creation fulfill your purpose and nobody else's. This is our challenge and our call as a couple: to do things God's way.

STRENGTH UNDER CONTROL

"Blessed are the gentle, for they shall inherit the earth."

MATTHEW 5:5

Many people think of meekness or gentleness as cowering timidity, a synonym for weakness.

The fact that Jesus referred to Himself as gentle (Matthew 11:29) ought to dispel that idea. God's Son is neither cowering nor weak.

Gentle was a word used to describe a wild horse that had been brought under control. A wild horse doesn't do anybody any good. But when that same powerful animal was taken in hand by a skilled trainer and tamed, it would be ready to ride or pull a chariot or whatever. The animal was still as strong as ever, except that now that strength was under control.

That's where we get the definition of gentleness. People who exhibit this quality have put themselves in the hands of a new Master. They're under His control, not going off wild, doing what they want to do. A person of gentleness is one whom God has tamed and put into His service.

Gentleness is the ability to love when you feel like hating, to forgive when you feel like seeking revenge, to submit to the will of God when your flesh resists it.

Why? Because you've been domesticated by heaven. God the Holy Spirit has brought you under His control. And as followers of Jesus, the Gentle One, you will share someday in His ultimate victory.

WHEN THE PROBLEMS DON'T GO AWAY — 1

Be strong in the grace that is in Christ Jesus.

2 TIMOTHY 2:1

*T*he strength you need every day to live the Christian life is found in God's grace.

Some believers think grace is what you need to get saved. And it's true. Grace *is* necessary in salvation, for we are saved by God's grace (Ephesians 2:8). But grace is also what *keeps* us. That's the lesson God's people have always had to learn. And the lesson usually comes in the midst of hardship.

In times of severe temptation and trials, we are encouraged to "draw near with confidence to the throne of grace, so that we may receive mercy and find grace to help in time of need" (Hebrews 4:16).

In the course of everyday life, we often find ourselves over our heads with problems that won't budge and heartaches that won't go away. Any married couple who has children knows what it is to face such hard circumstances and perplexing questions.

One thing God wants to teach us is that even when we are out of answers and out of strength, grace always has a fresh supply. He has all the grace we will ever need, and His grace is totally comprehensive. It touches every area of our personal lives, our marriages, and our families.

Whatever you may be facing today, His grace will see you through.

WHEN THE PROBLEMS
DON'T GO AWAY—2

I give thanks to my God always for you
because of the grace of God that was given you in Christ Jesus.

1 CORINTHIANS 1:4, ESV

*P*aul would learn the lesson of sustaining grace through an affliction that dogged him all his days. He wrote about it in 2 Corinthians 12, where he says he asked God three times to remove this hurtful thing in his life. But God's answer was grace: "He said to me, 'My grace is sufficient for you, for my power is made perfect in weakness'" (v. 9, NIV).

God was saying to Paul that His grace is so comprehensive it's sufficient to deal with the problems that don't go away. Paul's physical problem stayed with him, but grace covered its presence.

Do you ever feel the need for that kind of powerful grace? We all do! The frustration we often feel is, *Why is this happening to us? Why doesn't God just take this away?* The answer could be that your next lesson in grace is wrapped up in that hard circumstance or immovable problem.

Let me tell you, if the two of you have not yet discovered how great God's supply of grace truly is, you have a wonderful surprise coming! God's goodness is staggering, and He's waiting and wanting to give it away to you!

All you have to do is ask God for all the grace you need. It's already there. It just needs to be unveiled, unloaded, and expanded in your life.

THE MODESTY OF A
KINGDOM WOMAN — 1

*I want women to adorn themselves with proper clothing,
modestly and discreetly, not with braided hair and
gold or pearls or costly garments.*

1 TIMOTHY 2:9

*D*epending on how many females are in your house, and what
their ages are at the moment, your family will at some point face the
issue of modesty in dress.

In 1 Timothy 2:9–15, Paul gave detailed instruction regarding
the kinds of adornment and activities that should mark God's kingdom women.

This is a crucial text outlining the agenda that is to characterize
women "making a claim to godliness" (v. 10). The first item on this
agenda is a godly woman's propriety when it comes to her appearance.

The word *adorn* is the verb *kosmeo,* which translates into the
English word *cosmetic.* It means to arrange or put in place. Here
Paul uses the verb form of the same word Peter used when he wrote
to believing women, "Your adornment must not be merely external" (1 Peter 3:3).

God understands that women will spend time arranging themselves, putting everything in order. He knows that women give
special attention to what they wear and how they look. The instruction to kingdom women is not to ignore this area or pretend like it
doesn't matter, but to dress with modesty and good decorum as the
standard.

There ought to an air of dignity and respect about a kingdom
woman—a kind of beauty that doesn't depend on anything external!

THE MODESTY OF A KINGDOM WOMAN — 2

I want women to adorn themselves...
by means of good works,
as is proper for women making a claim to godliness.

1 TIMOTHY 2:9—10

Many of the women coming into the church at places like Ephesus and Corinth were coming out of pagan backgrounds. So they were coming to church dressed like the world. They were in style with the times, but not in style with the kingdom.

The fashion emphasis today—even as it was then—is heavy on immodesty. Too often, to dress fashionably *is* to dress immodestly, especially for girls and younger women. But as kingdom families, your family and mine are called to a different standard.

Paul told Timothy, "Make sure the women in God's family understand that as kingdom women, their need for modesty and propriety in dress may mean they have to take on a different look."

Modesty has to do with not drawing undue attention to yourself or being ostentatious in appearance. The issue is excess. A kingdom woman is called of God not to dress in a way that stimulates inappropriate responses. His mention of gold and pearls and expensive clothes was a way of saying, "Don't look like the women out there on the street. Don't try to dazzle and impress others."

The challenge to kingdom women is not to send the wrong message by the way they dress. Don't let people decide who you are by what they see, unless what they see is a woman of dignity and honor.

THE MODESTY OF A KINGDOM WOMAN — 3

The fruit of the Spirit is…self-control.

GALATIANS 5:22–23

*T*alking about modesty in a woman's apparel can sometimes be like walking through a minefield. No matter where you step, you're likely to set something off!

For some women, setting an example of godly modesty in dress may mean a change of wardrobe. For others, it may just mean a simple alteration here and there.

The word *discreetly* in 1 Timothy 2:9 refers to self-control. It has to do with making a decision based on discipline. In this case it may involve a believing woman saying, "I like that dress, and it looks good on me. But I have to say no because it's not modest."

In Isaiah 3, the Lord directly addressed the immodest women of Judah. In verses 16–18, He described their seductive behavior. In verses 19–24, He was very specific about the various adornments these women wore to attract men. They were advertising themselves as immodest and available, and the men were taking them up on their offer. But the whole thing made God sick.

Mom, you have tremendous positive influence in this area, especially with your daughters. Pray that God will help you make the most of your example.

GIVE GOD SOMETHING
HE CAN BLESS

The plans of the diligent lead surely to advantage,
but everyone who is hasty comes surely to poverty.

PROVERBS 21:5

*G*od concerns Himself with your finances, because everything you have is on loan from Him, and one day He will call you to account for how you handled His resources. He wants to help you make a wise and godly plan now, so that you won't have to be ashamed before Him when He returns.

In fact, God is so big on having a plan that He says if you don't know how to plan, talk to people who do. "Without consultation, plans are frustrated, but with many counselors they succeed" (Proverbs 15:22).

Let me give you one important element. Your plan must always include a surplus. God expects you to plan in such a way that there is always money left over. If you never have money left over at the end of the month, you know you're not in God's plan.

Proverbs 6:6–8 advises us, "Go to the ant, O sluggard, observe her ways and be wise…. [She] prepares her food in the summer and gathers her provision in the harvest." Even an ant knows you need to lay something aside.

Planning that includes a surplus is wise because you don't want to work all your life only to have your creditors take it all away, leaving you with nothing but regret. God has a better idea for His people.

A PERSON, NOT JUST A FORCE

*"The Helper, the Holy Spirit, whom the Father will send
in My name, He will teach you all things."*

JOHN 14:26

How do we know the Holy Spirit is a Person instead of just a force or an "it"? Because He has all the attributes of personality: intellect, emotion, and will.

He knows things (Romans 8:27; 1 Corinthians 2:10–11), He experiences emotions (Ephesians 4:30), and He acts with purpose (1 Corinthians 12:11). Only persons can do these things.

The Bible also uses personal pronouns for the Spirit, as in today's verse. The Spirit refers to Himself in the first person, and also speaks His thoughts to others (Acts 13:2).

When God saves us, He calls us into a personal relationship with the Holy Spirit. But we need to think again about our expectations. We hear people talking about their need for Holy Spirit power. We *do* need Holy Spirit power. But only after we have met the Holy Spirit as a Person.

The Christian life is more than a series of power surges. The Spirit's job is not just to give you a power boost to lift you to the next spiritual level. The Spirit is a Person we need to know and relate to, not just a force to be used.

Is your marriage suffering from a Holy Spirit deficit? If you'll ask Him, He will help you draw closer to one another as you draw closer to the Lord.

LOOKING GOOD

She makes coverings for herself;
her clothing is fine linen and purple.

PROVERBS 31:22

*O*ur culture's message to women today is to take care of your-self, *no matter what.*

Never let a husband or family, we're told, get in the way of your "self-fulfillment." And if other people do get in the way of that quest, just walk away from them!

This "me first" mentality is a far cry from the kind of self-care we see in Proverbs 31. It's obvious that this woman did not neglect her family to lavish attention on herself. But she also understood that to be at her best so she could minister effectively, she needed to take care of the temple of her own body.

Tony often says to husbands, "It's a tragedy if your wife is less beautiful today than she was the day you married her. If you load her down with responsibilities and demands, and then talk about how bad she looks, that's your fault! It's your responsibility to make sure she is so well cared for that all of the beauty she possesses is enhanced."

My sister, God does not expect you to wear yourself to a frazzle doing His will. If you are seeking Him and living for His glory, He will give you the time and energy you need to accomplish your call-ing…as well as keep your own body and spirit in tune.

COMING UNDER GOD'S AUTHORITY AT CHURCH

Obey your leaders and submit to them; for they keep watch over your souls as those who will give an account.

HEBREWS 13:17

*B*rother, if you want to strengthen your marriage and family, here's a tangible way to do that: Make sure you are under the God-ordained authority of your church.

A man under Christ (1 Corinthians 11:3) is in subjection to Christ's authority in the church. The church is to exercise discipline where needed. This was evident in the case of the unrepentant, immoral man of 1 Corinthians 5, and with any man in the church who refuses to work (2 Thessalonians 3:10–15).

If I have a young son in the house, he needs to obey my instructions for one reason: because Papa said so and he's under the authority of my house. Even so, Christian men are under the authority of God's house, the church, and are to submit themselves accordingly.

This is a problem we have with too many Christian men today. They don't want to be married anymore because they don't *feel* like being faithful. They don't *feel* like working. They don't *feel* like raising children.

My response is, "You felt like getting married and having children at the time. It's a moot point to say, 'I don't feel like it anymore.'" What we need is a generation of kingdom men who are responsible under God.

Any man can follow the crowd, but only a kingdom man can follow Jesus Christ.

MAKING THE TRANSFER

Who has known the mind of the Lord,
that he will instruct Him?
But we have the mind of Christ.

1 CORINTHIANS 2:16

*O*ur families, churches, and communities are in dire need of Christian men who think biblically. Who think with the mind of Christ.

In Matthew 19, the Pharisees wanted to trap Jesus in a no-win situation. So they asked Him a trick question about divorce. Our Lord's answer shocked them. "Have you not read…?" (v. 4). And then He quoted the relevant Scripture to them.

Jesus was saying, "You guys aren't thinking correctly. You of all people should know that there is a higher authority here than your sinful desires to get rid of your wives. God has given you His mind on this question."

God has given us His mind, too. We as Christian men need to develop biblically informed minds. God wants us to think like Him as a way of life, so we can transfer biblical values to our wives and children.

That's why Paul said that if a woman has a question in the church, she should ask her husband first (1 Corinthians 14:34–35). He should have some answers because he is a man of the Word.

That's the ideal—but I'm afraid it's not often the reality. To be the spiritual leaders God intended us to be—that our wives and children *need* us to be—we need to devote ourselves to the Book and humble ourselves in prayer.

DESTINY AND DISCIPLINE

*"I have chosen him, so that he may command his children
and his household after him to keep the way of the LORD
by doing righteousness and justice."*

GENESIS 18:19

What does it take to be the kind of husband and father who is able to pass on kingdom values to his wife and children?

We find the answer to that question in today's verse, which God spoke concerning the patriarch Abraham. The transfer of godly values from one generation to the next is never automatic. Born in sin, our children are not going to raise themselves and pick up the right values on their own. Someone has to pass them on.

That's what God called Abraham to do in his generation. Look how God equipped Abraham for his task.

First, the text says that God chose Abraham. This man had a *destiny*. Abraham knew that God's hand was on his life. You need to know that God's hand is on your life, too, if you want to be a kingdom husband and father with something to pass on. That means you need to get close to God and keep that lifeline going.

Abraham also committed himself to *discipline,* so that he could "command his children and his household after him to keep the way of the LORD." In other words, he passed along nonnegotiable standards to his family.

A kingdom man says, "We do things God's way in our home because this is a kingdom home. Under this roof, we obey the King."

GET IT TOGETHER AT HOME

*[An overseer] must be one who manages
his own household well,
keeping his children under control with all dignity.*

1 TIMOTHY 3:4

God wants men to take the lead in managing His kingdom. The Bible leaves no doubt: God's plan is that you and I practice good leadership at home so we can bring it to church.

That's the idea in 1 Timothy 3:4–5, where Paul tells Timothy that a candidate for church leadership must be a man who has it together at home.

Every Christian man is a pastor with a built-in congregation…his family. Paul says if a man can't manage three or four people in his own household, don't let him lead in the church. The home is a man's training ground for kingdom leadership and management.

Take the example of prayer. As a man becomes comfortable and capable leading his family in prayer, he is better equipped to assume a role of prayer leadership at church.

In 1 Timothy 2:8, Paul writes, "I want the men in every place to pray, lifting up holy hands, without wrath and dissension." The word *men* here is the specific term for males. God wants men to step forward and set the pace, to take leadership both at home and in the church. But it starts at home.

A kingdom man leads by loving and serving. Let's get at it, brother!

IRON ON IRON

Iron sharpens iron, so one man sharpens another.

PROVERBS 27:17

If you want to be a kingdom man who hangs in there even when he feels like throwing in the towel, you need two or three "homeys," fellow men of the kingdom, who will hold up your hands when you get weary.

In Exodus 17:8–16, Moses sent Joshua out to lead Israel's army into battle against the Amalekites, while he, Aaron, and Hur went to the top of a nearby hill to oversee the battle.

As Moses raised his hands, Israel prevailed. But after a while Moses got tired, and his arms drooped. When that happened, the Amalekites began winning. So Aaron and Hur lifted up Moses' hands and held them steady. Israel won!

Israel was able to win the fight because even though Moses' hands got tired, he had some brothers around him to hold him up. Too many of us men try to be "Lone Ranger" Christians, trying to make it all by ourselves. But even the Lone Ranger had a partner.

When you feel like you aren't going to make it as a dad or a husband, or when the job is dragging you down, you need some brothers to come alongside, hold up your hands, and say, "We're going to make it together, brother. We're going to hang in there with you. We're going to prevail for God."

HOUSEHOLD SALVATION

*"Believe in the Lord Jesus, and you will be saved,
you and your household."*

ACTS 16:31

When I was ten, my father, Arthur Evans, came to Jesus
Christ.

Before Dad became a Christian, he and Mom didn't get along.
It was violent sometimes. They were headed for divorce court.

But then, at age thirty, Dad was gloriously saved. And he made
a commitment: "By God's grace, I'm going to save my family."
Mom, however, didn't want his religion, and she made life hard for
him.

My father was a longshoreman who worked very hard loading
ships in the Baltimore harbor. He would get up at 3:00 A.M., when
the house was quiet, and pray for his family.

A year after Dad was saved, he was up at three praying as usual.
He heard the steps creak and knew my mother was coming down-
stairs. He thought, *Oh no, here we go again.*

But this morning was different. My mother told him, "I've been
doing everything I know how to discourage you. I've tried to make
your life as miserable as I could. Yet you haven't budged, so whatever
this thing is in your life must be real, and I want it right now."

My father got on his knees with Mom and led her to Jesus
Christ.

Humanly speaking, I'm where I am because one faithful man
wouldn't give up on his family. I pray you will leave your family that
kind of heritage.

A GODLY WOMAN'S PRIORITY

*Women will be preserved through the bearing of
children if they continue in faith and love
and sanctity with self-restraint.*

1 TIMOTHY 2:15

*T*his is a verse Christian wives and mothers have read and wondered about.

What does Paul mean by a woman being preserved by bearing children? He's not talking about salvation, but about a godly woman's devotion to her primary calling: the guiding and management of her home. The reference is to a believing wife and mother fulfilling her kingdom agenda.

What do children have to do with a woman's kingdom agenda? Everything. God is asking His women to reverse the damage Satan did to them and the stigma he laid upon them.

What did Satan do? He induced Eve to act independently of Adam, and as a result the whole world was plunged into sin. Ever since then, woman has borne the stigma of her contribution to the fall of mankind.

But a woman can be preserved or delivered from that stigma by raising up a godly seed. God wants a woman to bear children and raise them in the discipline and instruction of the Lord so that they go out and wreak havoc on Satan's kingdom.

God wants women to bear children who have His mark on them, rather than the mark of Cain. So whenever a kingdom woman produces a righteous child, she is, in a sense, getting back at Satan for what he did in the garden.

Fattening Up Your Soul

"Blessed are those who hunger
and thirst for righteousness,
for they shall be satisfied."

MATTHEW 5:6

When you're really hungry and thirsty for the things of God, you don't have to worry about going away unsatisfied.

How thirsty for righteousness do you have to be to qualify for Jesus' pronouncement of happiness? As thirsty as the deer in Psalm 42:1. David writes, "As the deer pants for the water brooks, so my soul pants for You, O God."

How hungry for God do you have to be to have your spiritual appetite fully satisfied? As hungry as Paul was to know God. It was the consuming passion of his soul. He counted everything else in his life as "rubbish" in order that he might know God intimately (Philippians 3:8–10).

Our society is fixated on being thin. Many of us, however, are too spiritually thin. A good, stiff breeze would blow us down. A fair-sized trial would wipe us out. We're anorexic because we don't eat right. Our spiritual diet is as thin as watery oatmeal.

People who are spiritually skinny are always saying, "Lord, change my circumstances." But the Lord is saying, "No. Fatten up your soul. Develop a deeper hunger and thirst for righteousness. Seek Me with all your heart, and your circumstances will be no problem." Rather than always changing the wind of circumstance, God wants to "fatten" us up so we'll be able to stand up against the wind.

GET OFF YOUR DONKEY

*"Blessed are the merciful,
for they shall receive mercy."*

MATTHEW 5:7

*R*emember the story of the Good Samaritan in Luke 10? The
man who was robbed, beaten, and left for dead needed someone to
care. He needed mercy.

The two "preachers" who passed by were too busy working on
their sermons to stop. But then the Samaritan came along, got off
his donkey, treated the man's wounds, and took him to an inn,
where he picked up the tab.

Tell me… If this Samaritan had been a real person in that day,
and if he himself had been robbed and beaten later on, do you think
God would have sent someone along to take care of *his* needs? I
think God would have sent a merciful person to care for him.

That's the idea behind Jesus' statement, "If you want to be a
receiver of mercy, you must be a giver of mercy."

There will come a time, sooner or later, when each of us will
need mercy. One of the best ways to prepare for your time of need is
to ask God to make you a merciful person today. That He will give
you eyes to see those who need tender attention and care.

Jesus says the mercy-giver is blessed, or happy. If you want a
sense of joy you can't find anywhere else, get off your donkey—stop
to help someone in need.

LIVING WITHOUT MASKS

"Blessed are the pure in heart,
for they shall see God."

MATTHEW 5:8

*J*esus commended people who are without hypocrisy, a term that means to wear a mask or play a role that isn't the real you. God wants us to be authentic men and women, through and through.

That sort of spiritual honesty and purity is only possible when we put our faith in Christ.

Being pure in heart doesn't make a person perfect, of course. But even when people like this blow it, they don't try to hide. You hear, "I was wrong. It was my fault. I'm sorry."

Wouldn't it be great to be married to someone whose heart was pure—a person you could trust, someone whose heart was an open book? I hope you are married to a person like that. Better yet, I hope *you* are becoming a marriage partner like that!

The pure in heart will not only see God themselves, but they will help other people see God because they're not blocking the view with their hypocrisy. It's easy to look good at church, where every-body acts nice and dresses nice. But at home the masks come off. That's one reason married life is so stressful for some people. It forces them to drop the pretense and come clean.

If you want to see God at work in your life, allow Him to purify your heart from sin and pretense.

LOOKING AND ACTING LIKE OUR FATHER

"Blessed are the peacemakers,
for they shall be called sons of God."

MATTHEW 5:9

Jesus had a wonderful commendation for those who pursue peace. He called peacemakers the children of God.

The Bible speaks of several kinds of peace. We have peace *with* God when we are forgiven of our sins and reconciled with Him through the Lord Jesus Christ. We have the peace *of* God, the internal calm that comes when we're walking in fellowship and obedience with the Lord.

God's Word also tells us to pursue peace and unity among our fellow believers. Biblical peacemaking is so highly valued by Jesus because the unity of His people is such a high priority with Him. In His last night on earth, Jesus prayed that His disciples might be one as He and His Father are one (John 17:21).

Jesus then went out from that Passover meal in the upper room to make peace possible by His death on the cross. Biblical peacemaking, you see, isn't easy. It's costly.

It's costly because in order to maintain the unity of the Spirit, people have to give something up. It may be something of value to them, like their ideas or plans.

But if you will pay the price, you'll reap the reward of peace. And you'll have people saying, "He acts like his Father," and "She reminds me of Jesus."

SUFFERING FOR THE RIGHT REASONS

"Blessed are those who have been persecuted for the sake of righteousness, for theirs is the kingdom of heaven."

MATTHEW 5:10

*C*ount on it: When we are serious about our commitment to Jesus, someone isn't going to like it.

This final Beatitude is also the longest, because Jesus explains what it means to be persecuted for the sake of righteousness, and why the person who endures this is blessed.

Notice first the persecution and insults must be "because of [Jesus]" (Matthew 5:11). That is, the suffering comes as a result of your ministry and witness for Christ, not because you were just being hard to get along with.

Second, the believer who suffers in this way can be considered blessed or happy because suffering for Christ brings a great reward in heaven.

Do you want to lay up some treasure in heaven, where nothing can touch your investment? Jesus says if you encounter persecution just because you remind people of Him, then He will credit that to your heavenly account. So whenever someone puts you down for your faith, the bank of heaven logs another reward.

So don't go looking for persecution today. Just live out God's kingdom agenda in your life—and if you encounter somebody who doesn't like what you stand for, smile and stand firm.

Where are you most likely to encounter opposition to your faith? Pray that God will prepare you to stand for Him in that place.

GOING FOR THE CROWNS — 1

*We must all appear before the judgment seat of Christ,
so that each one may be recompensed for his deeds in the body.*

2 CORINTHIANS 5:10

The Bible tells us of a coming day when the children of God will be judged.

"But, Tony," you say, "I thought when we accepted Christ, we passed out from under God's judgment."

Yes, that's true in relation to your eternal status. If your sins have been forgiven, you are under the blood of Christ, your home in heaven is secure. Nothing can separate you from the love of Christ.

The judgment I'm talking about is not to determine whether you are going to make heaven. This is an evaluation of your *service* as a child of God, not your *status* as a child of God.

The Bible calls this evaluation Christ's "judgment seat," and Paul says we must all appear there to be either rewarded or reprimanded, based on the quality of our service to Christ since we have been believers.

Talk about motivation! The prospect of Jesus Christ Himself saying to us, "Well done, good and faithful servant," and bestowing honor on us ought to spur us on every day to be our best and do our best for Him.

And the thought of our works not standing up to the fire of Christ's judgment (1 Corinthians 3:12–15) should make us determined to serve Him with full sincerity of heart.

GOING FOR THE CROWNS — 2

*Everyone who competes in the games exercises
self-control in all things. They then do it to receive
a perishable wreath, but we an imperishable.*

1 CORINTHIANS 9:25

*T*he thought of a future day, standing before the judgment seat
of Christ, filled Paul with a fire of holy desire. The apostle said he
was training like an athlete and disciplining himself so that he might
win the prize—just as athletes in his day competed for the winner's
wreath in the games (1 Corinthians 9:24–27).

This wreath was awarded at the Isthmian Games, something of
a forerunner to the modern Olympics. Athletes in Paul's day competed in these games for an oak wreath, placed on their heads at the
bema, or judge's seat.

This is the very word Paul used in 2 Corinthians 5:10 to refer
to Christ's judgment seat. At the *bema,* the judge handed out
rewards to the winners.

And so it will be with every believer. The New Testament tells
us that Jesus Christ Himself will be the judge on that day, and He
will reward those who competed for victory through the days of
their lives. But these prizes won't be like the fragile, perishable
wreaths of leaves handed out in the ancient games. The rewards
Christ gives out will shine through all eternity, and never, never fade.

The New Testament calls these rewards crowns, and urges us to
seek them.

"O God, purify my heart before You so that my service for You
will be acceptable to You."

GOING FOR THE CROWNS — 3

They then [compete] to receive a perishable wreath,
but we an imperishable.

1 CORINTHIANS 9:25

*I*n 1 Corinthians 9:24–27, Paul makes it clear that he was in the race of his life. This was no 5K "fun run." This was a marathon that took all the energy, endurance, and focus he had within him.

If you belong to Jesus Christ, you're in that race, too. Paul finished his course long ago, but if you're reading these words right now, you're still running! Just as first-century athletes disciplined themselves for competition, we believers must discipline ourselves spiritually, shedding anything that holds us back, weighs us down, or distracts us from our goal.

Believers who make it a pattern of life to discipline themselves for godliness (1 Timothy 4:7) will receive eternal rewards from our Lord's own hand.

"But, Tony," you say, "it's kind of late for me. I'm already forty [or whatever age]. Can I still win this crown?"

You certainly can! The Christian life is like a basketball game. You may be behind at halftime. The score may not look good, and the game is already half over.

But there's another half to play—and no one declares a winner until that final buzzer sounds. So no matter where you are in the game, as long as you're alive, it's not too late for a comeback. God can give you the ability to make a comeback with Him...and with your family.

GOING FOR THE CROWN OF LIFE—1

"Be faithful unto death,
and I will give you the crown of life."

REVELATION 2:10

One of the crowns the Bible tells us to strive for is found in the risen Jesus Christ's message to the church in Smyrna. His message had to do with what this church was about to undergo: "Do not fear what you are about to suffer. Behold, the devil is to cast some of you into prison, so that you will be tested, and you will have tribulation for ten days" (Revelation 2:10). Then Jesus stated the promise quoted at the top of this page.

The crown of life has to do with faithfulness in suffering or enduring trials. Some believers have known intense levels of trial and testing. God says that their suffering will not go unnoticed in heaven, so don't throw in the towel. There is a crown waiting for those who hang in there and suffer by faith, knowing that God always permits suffering for a purpose.

It's hard to suffer, especially when you don't know all the reasons for your pain. But the Bible makes it clear that the Christian life involves hardship as well as glory. And if you are faithful in the hard times, at the judgment seat of Christ you will be rewarded with a crown that represents a higher quality of life in His kingdom.

GOING FOR THE CROWN OF LIFE — 2

Blessed is a man who perseveres under trial;
for once he has been approved, he will receive
the crown of life which the Lord has promised
to those who love Him.

JAMES 1:12

What is the crown of life?

Who can begin to imagine? The Bible doesn't give us any details. But we can be sure that if the Author of life gives you an eternal crown of life, it will be more wonderful than words can explain.

If you run from trials, however, this crown is not for you. If you refuse to seek the wisdom of God to deal with your suffering (James 1:5), this is not your crown. This crown is for those who suffer abuse for the sake of Christ, and stand strong in Him. It's for the person who stays put in a tough situation for the sake of testimony for Christ.

John Mark wanted this crown. He was the young man who deserted Paul on the first missionary journey when things got tough (Acts 13:13). John Mark ran from the suffering, but then he repented, got back in the race, and reached for the crown. He became an author of Scripture and a valued ministry companion of the great apostle (2 Timothy 4:11).

God wants to use trials in your marriage and family life to prepare you for greater usefulness to Him.

We are never told to seek suffering or persecution—but to expect it, and be faithful when it comes, knowing the Lord will use it for our growth.

The Difference Between Needs and Wants

The eye is not satisfied with seeing,
nor is the ear filled with hearing.

ECCLESIASTES 1:8

Every couple needs a financial plan that prioritizes spending and saving. You need a plan that takes care of first things first—which means knowing the difference between a *need* and a *want,* or desire.

Always take care of needs first—those necessities required to survive and function. First Timothy 6:8 lists food and clothing as needs. We could add things like shelter and, in our culture, transportation.

Never skip needs in order to satisfy wants! In Philippians 4:19 Paul writes, "My God will supply all your *needs* according to His riches in glory in Christ Jesus." Whenever you skip needs and go to desires, you're skipping God's priority.

Once you've taken care of your needs, then you can start considering desires. These are choices or preferences you make as you fulfill your needs.

For example, shelter is a need. If you have an apartment, you may want a house, and that's okay. Your need may be a car that runs, but your want may be a new car that runs.

God can help you sort through your desires as you seek His will, but don't shortchange your needs to satisfy your wants!

Look at the things you are doing with your money as a couple, and list each purchase or activity under the category of "need" or "desire." Talk about what your chart reveals.

MADE FOR NURTURE

Fathers, do not provoke your children to anger,
but bring them up in the discipline
and instruction of the Lord.

EPHESIANS 6:4

*R*aising children is really kind of a woman's thing, isn't it? After all, women are made for that nurturing stuff, aren't they?

Yes, Dad, but so are you! When God's Word addresses the issue of raising and nurturing children, *the instruction is given primarily to fathers.* But Christian fathers who would never harm their children physically are discarding them emotionally and spiritually by being the silent partner in their nurture and training.

Dad is too busy out working or playing. And even when he's home, he doesn't really want to be bothered with the details. It's easier to let the kids watch TV, because too often he's watching TV, too.

With this kind of fathering, what we are getting is a generation of children being raised on the world's values. Now, a father may say, "Well, I tell them what to do." That's fine, but it's not enough.

Children are born in sin, just like you and me. Given the opportunity, apart from Jesus Christ they *will* do what they are not supposed to do. Their bent is toward sin. What children need is a father who can guide them in the way of truth and train them in the things of God.

Dear God, thank You today for my children. Help me to love and discipline them the way You love and discipline me.

IT GOES WITHOUT SAYING — OR DOES IT?

[Love] does not act unbecomingly;
it does not seek its own.

1 CORINTHIANS 13:5

The Bible has some powerful and beneficial things to say to Christian husbands.

People used to say a man's home was his castle. That meant he was king of his domain. If you always wanted to be the king of your castle, here's your chance. By living for your heavenly King as a husband, you can bring a royal presence to your home. Not because you sit on your throne and bark out orders to the wife and kids, but because you reflect King Jesus.

One way a husband can reflect a kingdom agenda in his marriage is to love his wife. Unfortunately, a lot of what goes under the name of love has little to do with true, biblical love.

The word *love* has become devalued. People say, "I love my job. I love my home. I love chocolate cake." What they're really saying is that these things make them feel good.

That's fine, but that's not love. Biblical love, God's *agape* love, involves the sacrifice you make for the one loved. You can measure your love for your wife by the degree of your sacrifice for her.

Human love is usually conditional on that love being returned. But biblical love expresses itself even when it is not being reciprocated.

BEING A SAVIOR TO YOUR WIFE — 1

*Walk in love, just as Christ also loved you
and gave Himself up for us.*

EPHESIANS 5:2

What does it mean for a husband to love his wife the way Christ loved the church? One thing it means is for the husband to be a savior for his wife.

Now I know what you're thinking. But my theology is firmly in place. Obviously, I'm not using the term *savior* in any theological sense, but I am using it deliberately. Let me show you what I mean.

In Ephesians 5:25, the apostle Paul says, "Husbands, love your wives, just as Christ also loved the church and gave Himself for her."

How did Jesus give Himself up for the church? He died. As far as God is concerned, to talk about marital love is to talk about a cross. To talk about love is to talk about Calvary. To talk about love is to talk about a Savior.

We have a Savior in Christ. And our wives ought to have a savior in us. We have a Deliverer in Christ. And our wives ought to have a deliverer in us. Loving your wife means carrying a cross. So if you feel like your wife is crucifying you, you have the perfect opportunity to look like Jesus.

BEING A SAVIOR TO YOUR WIFE — 2

Husbands, love your wives,
and do not be harsh with them.

COLOSSIANS 3:19, ESV

*Y*ou may know that nowhere in Scripture is a wife commanded to love her husband. She is commanded to respect him (Ephesians 5:33).

It's not that a woman shouldn't love her husband. But her love is a *response* to his salvation. If you and I are going to be biblical lovers as husbands, we must become biblical saviors.

That means loving as Christ loves. So a husband is called to love his wife no matter what.

This gets very practical. A husband's love cannot say, "She's meeting my needs. Therefore, I will love her." No, you love her even when she's not meeting your needs. You love her until she learns how to meet your needs.

Most men date in order to marry, whereas the biblical principle is marry in order to date. Most men shower a woman with love to get her to say "I do." But the biblical ideal is have her say "I do" so we can spend the rest of our lives showering her with love.

Every man likes to think of himself as a lover. But the measuring rod for a biblical lover is the size of the cross he is carrying. Christ loved the church to death.

SOMEONE HAS TO BLEED

*The LORD God caused a deep sleep to fall upon the man,
and he slept; then He took one of his ribs
and closed up the flesh at that place.*

GENESIS 2:21

God opened Adam's side and took out a rib to create Eve.

Adam had to bleed to get Eve. Christ had to bleed in order to birth the church. If a wife is going to grow from where she is to where she ought to be, her husband has to take a trip to Calvary.

Husband, you need to decide, "I am willing to pay whatever price it takes to bring my wife to fulfillment. I am willing to go the distance to bring her from where she is to where she ought to be—spiritually and every other way."

When a man comes home, he must say, "Things may not be right. I may not like what's happening, but a savior is in the house. I am your deliverer. Whatever is wrong, I am Mr. Fix-It. Whatever price has to be paid, I will pay it."

At the heart of a husband's love is sacrifice. If there is no sacrifice, there is no love. *If I asked your wife what price you are paying to love her, could she tell me?*

A husband who truly loves his wife says, "If this marriage ends, you're going to have to leave me, because I'm not going anywhere. No matter how you treat me or what happens, I want you to know that I will be here."

A SANCTIFIER IN THE HOUSE

*"She is your companion and
your wife by covenant."*

MALACHI 2:14

A husband is his wife's sanctifier, the way Christ is the church's sanctifier (Ephesians 5:26–27). Jesus' purpose is to cleanse the church. In the same way, a husband's love is to be a sanctifying agent to cleanse and heal the things she brings into the marriage that may not be right.

Maybe she was abused by her father, or raised by a domineering mother. That stuff won't disappear just because a woman gets married. Our wives need our sanctifying love.

The result of a husband's sanctifying work is a wife who has "no spot or wrinkle" (v. 27). *Spot* means defilement from outside. If something drops on your shirt, you get a spot. *Wrinkle* has to do with internal aging. Wrinkles are evidence that we're getting older.

The church has spots, external stains from the world; and wrinkles, internal aging and decay. Jesus says, "My job is to wash off the spots and remove the aging." That is the husband's job in his marriage.

This means that when your wife needs strength, you are her strength. When she needs encouragement, you are her encouragement. When she needs joy, you are her joy. When she needs peace, you are her peace.

Husband, when you love your wife like this, she will be eternally young because she's got a sanctifier in the house!

BEING YOUR WIFE'S SATISFIER — 1

"Like an apple tree among the trees of the forest,
So is my beloved among the young men.
In his shade I took great delight and sat down,
And his fruit was sweet to my taste."

SONG OF SOLOMON 2:3

A husband who wants to love his wife according to God's kingdom agenda must be his wife's satisfier.

Solomon and his Shulammite bride celebrated the joy of each other's love. The bride's speeches show how satisfied and protected she felt in Solomon's love—and she was talking about more than just their sexual relationship.

The apostle Paul gives us the New Testament version of this when he says that husbands need "to love their own wives as their own bodies" (Ephesians 5:28). What we need today is a group of Christian men who know how to satisfy their wives.

Now most men think sex when they hear the word *satisfy*. And some men will brag about how many women they can "satisfy." But any man who makes such statements doesn't know what he's talking about.

A real man is one who can commit himself to his wife, remain faithful, and love her with a steady commitment so that after fifteen, twenty, thirty, or fifty years, his wife can still say, "I'm satisfied."

Paul explains this as loving your wife the way you love your own body. So just as a man works out to make his body look good and seeks to satisfy his own needs, he is to help his wife look good externally and feel content internally so that she is fulfilled and satisfied.

BEING YOUR WIFE'S SATISFIER — 2

"He has brought me to his banquet hall,
and his banner over me is love."

SONG OF SOLOMON 2:4

There are too many dissatisfied wives out there because there are too many unsatisfying husbands. Too many husbands and wives look like they were married by the secretary of war rather than the justice of the peace.

They're like Winston Churchill and Lady Astor in England. Lady Astor despised Churchill. She once said angrily, "Winston, if you were my husband, I'd put arsenic in your tea."

Churchill responded, "Lady Astor, if I were your husband, I'd drink it."

That's the way a lot of couples live. Changing that situation begins with you, my fellow husband. And please hear me on this: *It has nothing to do with what your wife does in return.* We're talking about biblical love here, which loves—period.

A man who is determined to satisfy his wife won't stop even if his efforts aren't met with love in return. Praise God that He doesn't reject you and me in those times when we refuse to respond to his overtures of love! The first thing on a husband's kingdom agenda is to love his wife by being her savior, sanctifier, and satisfier.

Ask your wife how you're doing as a satisfier. Encourage her to be specific in pinpointing areas where you're doing well, and areas where you can improve.

SHE MARRIED YOU FOR YOU — 1

"If a man were to give all the riches of his house for love,
it would be utterly despised."

SONG OF SOLOMON 8:7

*T*oday's verse reminds us of a timeless truth: Biblical love cannot be bought.

For us as husbands, this means that no amount of financial provision on our part can substitute for our responsibility to give ourselves to our wives.

Here's what I mean: One way you as a husband can fulfill your calling in marriage is to really *live* with your wife. It's part of what I call loving your wife according to a kingdom agenda.

You may say, "Hey, that's easy. We're in the same house. We're still together." But there's more to it than that. Peter tells us to live with our wives "in an understanding way" (1 Peter 3:7).

The Greek word *live* means to dwell in close harmony, to be closely aligned with someone, to live together with intimacy. When you say to a guest, "Make yourself at home," you mean more than just sit down. You want your guest to be comfortable, to be at peace.

I know we men have the responsibility to provide for our families. My plea to you is, don't let the things you do *for* your wife replace your presence *with* her. She married you to share life with you.

SHE MARRIED YOU FOR YOU — 2

But godliness with contentment is great gain.

1 TIMOTHY 6:6, NIV

*M*any men have the idea, "I'm the husband; I go out and work. You're the wife; you stay home. I do my job; you do your job."

Yes, but the home is the husband's job, too. The wife is to help her husband do his job at home well, but she is not designed to replace him in the home.

It's part of a husband's kingdom agenda to make sure, as much as possible, that his home is a place of peace. That means he has to *be* there! He has to be present to be the leader.

Your wife didn't just marry you for a paycheck, a car, or a job title. She married *you*. Whenever you measure the quality of your marriage by the number and size of the trinkets you own, you've missed it.

If your marriage is typical, your wife loved you when you didn't have a dime. She married you when you were just out of college, up to your ears in student loan debt, and nobody knew your name. That's the man she wants to live with. She doesn't want to trade the relationship for a nice car or a big house.

A husband needs to create an atmosphere of intimacy in his home—and he can do it with his wife's help. But he has to try!

ENJOY LIFE WITH YOUR WIFE — 1

*Enjoy life with the woman whom you love all the days
of your fleeting life which He has given to you.*

ECCLESIASTES 9:9

I'm as guilty as anyone when it comes to being absorbed with my job.

There have been days when I've been so absorbed in ministry pressures at the church that I've left Lois at home with no one to talk to for hours on end. And even when I am home, I'm sometimes so tired and distracted from caring for the flock that I don't have the energy to minister well at home.

I know what it is to work twelve- and fifteen-hour days, then go home and feel like throwing in the towel because I'm so exhausted. But the moment I do that, I have stopped enjoying life with my wife. Instead of living with her, I'm living with my ministry.

For a husband, making a priority commitment to his wife may mean making some hard decisions. But imagine what it would mean to a woman for her husband to tell her, "I'm committed to you. If I have to give some things up or back off at work, I'll do it."

Sometimes a husband's "job" is as simple as calling his wife in the middle of the day to say, "I can't get you off my mind today." Husband, making your wife feel special and cared for will pay better benefits than any job!

ENJOY LIFE WITH YOUR WIFE — 2

May your fountain be blessed,
and may you rejoice in the wife of your youth.

PROVERBS 5:18, NIV

*O*beying God's Word means that when a husband goes home, he goes home to his second job.

Many men expect that when a wife comes home from work, *she's* coming home to her second job. She's supposed to get something on the table and clean and make sure everyone, including hubby, is taken care of. Then she's supposed to have enough energy to meet her husband's physical needs at night.

A wife and mother can't just come home and turn on the TV or pick up the newspaper. She needs a husband whose attitude says, "We're in this together, so when I come home, I come home to work, too. We'll get these chores knocked out and then we can both relax." What kind of chores are we talking about? Whatever kind of help the wife needs at the time.

Your wife was given to you to be your partner, not your slave. God wants you to live in the intimacy of that partnership. When you've got that right, there is nothing on earth more satisfying.

EYEBALL-TO-EYEBALL ATTENTION — 1

He who finds a wife finds a good thing and
obtains favor from the LORD.

PROVERBS 18:22

A husband needs to study two things: the Bible and his wife.

Both are difficult to interpret. Any man will testify that it takes work to understand a woman.

That's why we have to study our wives. Now, you can't study something without giving time to it. When your wife wants to talk, she's giving you the opportunity to know her. She'll tell you all about herself if she knows you really want to hear the answer. Remember, God built a complex circuitry into women. That circuitry includes hormones that are on the move.

So each month, you need to be aware of what is happening to your wife. The week before her menstrual cycle, she is going to be a little bit more sensitive, and perhaps a little more irritable, based on her temperament. During this time she may also be a little bit more frustrated, but after that she may bounce back with new energy.

A husband who really wants to know his wife will have the attitude, "I understand what's going on. So let me be a little more understanding, a little more tender, a little more conversational. I know you're coming into a rough time, but I want you to know that I'm going to be here for you."

Study. Learn. Take time. And be blessed.

Eyeball-to-Eyeball Attention — 2

*Husbands, in the same way be considerate
as you live with your wives, and
treat them with respect as the weaker partner
and as heirs with you of the gracious gift of life.*

1 Peter 3:7, niv

A wife needs her husband to be there when she comes to the
end of her hormonal roller-coaster ride. That doesn't mean it's always
easy to be an understanding husband. But it's worth the effort,
because in the process of knowing your wife, the two of you will
grow closer together.

Knowing your wife means you have to make some adjustments.
You may have to give up some TV programs, or get your news from
somewhere besides the evening newscast.

Why? Because that time of the evening is now your time to say,
"Honey, I'm ready to listen. Tell me anything you want me to know,
because when I learn it, I'm going to use it to love you better. You've
got my undivided attention."

Now that's a big change from reading the newspaper while you
"listen" to your wife, or watching TV while she tries to tell you
something. But if you want to know what makes your wife tick, you
need to give her eyeball-to-eyeball attention.

There are "some things hard to understand" (2 Peter 3:16) in
both your Bible and your wife—but both will richly repay your
careful study.

ROLL OUT THE RED CARPET — 1

A gracious woman attains honor.

PROVERBS 11:16

*O*ne great way a husband can bring God's kingdom agenda to bear on his marriage is to honor his wife.

Peter tells husbands, "Show [your wife] honor as a fellow heir of the grace of life" (1 Peter 3:7). To put it another way, if you want to be a true "kingdom" king, treat her like your queen. She's not just another woman.

The concept of honor has to do with placing your wife in a position of significance, treating her as someone very special. Does your wife feel special? Do you do things for her that let her know she is different from every other woman?

Many of us men do little courtesies for other women we don't do anymore for our wives. But when chivalry dies, a marriage starts to die. Husband, you need to make a commitment that other women may have to get in the car by themselves, but not your wife. Other women may have to open the door for themselves, but not your wife. She is your queen, so roll out the red carpet and pull out the chair and open the door and escort her.

ROLL OUT THE RED CARPET — 2

Give her the reward she has earned.

PROVERBS 31:31, NIV

There are so many ways we can make our wives feel special. A gift for no particular reason is a great way to tell your wife she's special to you. Your time is also a gift to your wife. You don't have to give her a new car. Just the fact that you want to take her somewhere in the old car will do.

Have you ever written your wife a note and put in under her pillow? Talk about how great it is to sleep next to her and wake up to sunshine even when the drapes are closed. Let her know you wouldn't have it any other way.

I know a lot of husbands do something special for their wives on their birthday or anniversary. But if that's the only time we do something, we become too predictable. The key is to be consistent and creative in communicating to your wife how much you love her.

It takes very little time and effort to pick up the phone, call your wife in the middle of the day, and tell her she's on your mind and you can't wait to see her when you get home.

RECAPTURING THE FEELING

Now faith, hope, love, abide these three;
but the greatest of these is love.

1 CORINTHIANS 13:13

I often ask husbands, "When was your last date with your wife?" Now, by a date, I'm not talking about coming home and saying, "What do you want to do tonight?"

That's not a date. A date is "Honey, I've got this evening all planned out. All you need to do is come along. Here's what I have planned. If you want to make some adjustment, that's fine. But I want to let you know I have thought this evening out."

That kind of thing communicates honor and value to your wife. It tells her she's not just an afterthought to you.

Your wife is your equal in terms of her value as a human being and her spiritual value to God. She may be called to be submissive to your leadership, but she deserves honor as your fellow heir (1 Peter 3:7).

She may be not as physically strong as you are, but she is worthy of your honor. God's mandate must be reflected in the way you relate to your wife.

Now don't misunderstand. Honoring your wife doesn't mean you two always see eye-to-eye. You may have to make a decision she doesn't agree with.

But honoring her means you take her thoughts and feelings into account before you make that decision, because God may be showing her some things you need to hear.

DON'T BOTHER GOD

The one who does not love his brother
whom he has seen, cannot love God
whom he has not seen.

1 JOHN 4:20

*P*eter told husbands that if they weren't living with their wives in the way God expected, their prayers wouldn't get any higher than the ceiling.

Let me put it like this: If a husband and wife are out of touch spiritually, and he is not pleasing God by the way he treats his wife, his prayers are a waste of time. In other words, if there is no dynamic spiritual relationship between you and your wife, your relationship with God will lose much of its dynamic, too.

Since this is true, it has to be said that one of the great sins today is that men aren't praying with their wives. Wife, if your husband is trying to pray with you, encourage him! He's calling on the greatest force available to your home. Help him and encourage him, because God is not going to help him apart from you.

Husbands need to pray with their wives, so the two of them can enjoy the spiritual riches of God's kingdom plan and inheritance together.

If your marriage needs to be turned around spiritually, I want to challenge the husband to let the turnaround begin with you.

My brother, if you turn the right way, your wife will follow your lead. And when God sees you turn, He will turn a fresh ear to your prayers.

A WOMAN AND HER FEARS—1

God has not given us a spirit of timidity,
but of power and love and discipline.

2 TIMOTHY 1:7

*F*lying has never been one of my favorite activities. But as I travel with Tony more and more these days, I've had to deal with this fear head-on.

Fear is a valid emotion. It only becomes invalid when it begins to *control* you. Controlling fear, what the Bible calls "a spirit of timidity," can manifest itself in many ways. And if left unchecked, it can grab hold of you and destroy you.

For us women, fear can be destructive to both inner and outer beauty. It can produce tensions which keep us uptight and irritable. It can produce mistrust, so we are always questioning everything. And it can definitely produce unhappiness, since we're always waiting to see "what's going to go wrong next."

This kind of fear is not from God, but directly from Satan. And since Satan comes at us from many directions, his fear hits us in different ways, too.

Whatever form your particular fear may take, there is a solution. I use some very basic, but important, biblical principles to help me overcome my fears whenever they surface. The first is this: Fear is an issue of the will, not just the emotions. Fear arises from a lack of faith in God. We must make a decision of the will to accept God at His Word.

A WOMAN AND HER FEARS — 2

I sought the LORD, and He answered me,
and delivered me from all my fears.

PSALM 34:4

or a woman, the first attack of fear may concern her family. "Is my husband being faithful? Are my children involved in something they shouldn't be? Will they accept Christ as their Savior and live for Him?"

Satan-inspired fear can attack both men and women at work. "Will I ever be promoted? What does the boss really think of my work? Will I be part of the next downsizing?"

The devil knows our fears and preys on us where we are weak. It's his job to keep us defeated and frustrated, to keep us from using our divine resources. But we have all the power of God available to us.

How will you overcome fear? *By yielding yourself to the power of the indwelling Holy Spirit.* He who is in you is greater than he who is in the world (1 John 4:4). If you will walk in the power of the Spirit, you will block Satan from carrying out his will in your life (Galatians 5:16).

Here's a second step. Believe that Jesus Christ can solve your problem, and live like it! Claim victory every minute of every day. Every time you feel you're about to succumb to your fear, remind God of His promise, "I will never desert you, nor will I ever forsake you" (Hebrews 13:5).

A WOMAN AND HER FEARS — 3

I fear no evil, for You are with me.

PSALM 23:4

*J*ust as with other human emotions, fear is a gift of God to be used for His purposes.

The fear of God, for example, is a holy reverence for Him which leads us to obey Him. We are in awe of His power and love for us, and we fear displeasing Him.

This is a healthy form of fear. The Scripture says, "In the fear of the LORD there is strong confidence" (Proverbs 14:26). Again, "The fear of the LORD leads to life, so that one may sleep satisfied, untouched by evil" (Proverbs 19:23).

Unhealthy fear, however, robs us of our witness for Christ. If we're not careful, we can find ourselves denying with our lives what we say with our lips. Since I've been seeking the Lord to help me with my fear of flying, I can't tell you how much more relaxed my life has become.

As I rest in God's provision for me, I can relax. In fact, I am writing these lines in an airplane, waiting to take off from New Mexico to Los Angeles!

Faith activates the Lord. Fear activates the devil. Which do you want to be active in your life? Satan wants to keep you in bondage to fear. Read Romans 8:15 together and thank God that as His children, you are free!

SMILING THROUGH YOUR TEARS

Weeping may last for the night,
but a shout of joy comes in the morning.

PSALM 30:5

*M*y sister in Christ, God can enable you to smile in spite of your tears. To carry on when you feel like giving up. To pray when you're at a loss for words. To love even though your heart has been broken time and again. To be understanding when nothing seems to make sense. To listen when you'd really rather not hear it again. Anything is possible when God is at the center of your life.

God brings trials into our lives as women to show us whether we really believe what we say we believe. He wants us to become so secure in Him that we will apply His truth to our circumstances and obey Him…even when those circumstances seem to contradict His promises.

It's so important that we learn the lesson of obedience in the trials God sends. We're like students in school, who must pass a test on the information given before going on to the next level.

The Christian life is a growth process. Salvation is free, but sanctification—steady growth in Christ—is expensive.

When a trial comes, and you are in your night of weeping, it is natural to ask God why the pressure has come. His answer will always include the testing and perfecting of our faith, and through suffering preparing us for indescribable joy.

FAILURE IS NEVER FINAL

Why are you in despair, O my soul?
And why have you become
disturbed within me? Hope in God,
for I shall yet praise Him.

PSALM 42:11

*K*ay James says the only difference between people who succeed and people who fail is that the ones who succeed get up again
after they fail!

Failure is an inescapable part of our flawed humanity. We all
face setbacks and defeat at times—especially when we're in the midst
of hardships and trials.

Whatever your area of struggle, let today's verse remind you that
discouragement never has to be final for the Christian. Even when
all you can do is cry out to the Lord for the grace to continue in
spite of your feelings, He will answer your cry.

And because He who is in us is greater than he who is in the
world (1 John 4:4), you can get up from any failure or discouragement and live a victorious life—even today!

David's words have encouraged me again and again: "I love You,
O LORD, my strength. The LORD is my rock and my fortress and
my deliverer, my God, my rock, in whom I take refuge; my shield
and the horn of my salvation, my stronghold. I call upon the LORD,
who is worthy to be praised...and I am saved from my enemies"
(Psalm 18:1–3).

God often has to work in us before He can work through us.
Ask Him to help you turn your weaknesses and failures into
strength.

GIVE HIM SOMETHING TO STUDY

You husbands in the same way,
live with your wives in an understanding way...
so that your prayers will not be hindered.

1 PETER 3:7

*P*eter gave us a wonderful insight into marital communication. When he says a husband needs to live with his wife in an "understanding way," he's saying that a man should *study* his wife.

Now that's a great assignment for our husbands. But what about us as wives? We have responsibility here, too. Anyone who wants to study has to have some information. This is where you can help your husband. Feel free to tell him your needs, and how you're feeling. He needs that information to live with you in a knowledge-able way.

Early in our marriage, I struggled with the role of "pastor's wife"—something I'd never wanted to be. During those years, Tony and I spent a lot of time talking and praying about my insecurities. I could not assume he would automatically know how I felt, so I tried to make my fears and feelings clear.

Those days are far behind us now, and our lives are busier than ever. Tony and I have to *plan* to communicate. We have to carve out the time, because it won't "just happen."

Remember, you are raising your children to leave, but as long as God gives the two of you life, you'll be with each other. So invest the time it takes to communicate and stay close. You will never regret it!

IT'S WORTH THE EFFORT!

*Like apples of gold in settings of silver
is a word spoken in right circumstances.*

PROVERBS 25:11

Ephesians 4:25 teaches us to put away lying because as believers, "we are members of one another." If this is true for the church as a whole, think how much more important honesty is in a relationship as intimate as marriage.

Paul goes on to say that we must not let the sun go down on our anger, because when we do, we give the devil an opportunity to wreak havoc in our lives (vv. 26–27).

At our wedding ceremony, the minister spoke on this issue of dealing with anger before the day is over. His comments made a lasting impression on me. I took this biblical exhortation quite literally to heart, and Tony can testify that it has made a real difference.

In verse 29, the Bible urges us to replace our unwholesome communication with words that edify or build up others, so that our speech might "give grace to those who hear."

Our mates are a part of the body of Christ whom God calls us to serve by the way we communicate with them.

Finally, Paul writes: "Be kind to one another, tender-hearted, forgiving each other" (verse 32). Forgiving means letting go of the pain and refusing to bring up an incident again after it has been resolved. That's advice that never, ever grows old.

A Woman's Priorities

"You shall love the Lord your God
with all your heart,
and with all your soul,
and with all your mind."

MATTHEW 22:37

*N*ew opportunities in education and business have opened doors to women not previously available. While on one hand Christian women should enjoy these benefits and opportunities, we must be careful not to allow this world system to rearrange our biblical priorities.

Our first priority is to maintain a vital, personal relationship with God. Proverbs 31:30 reminds us, "Charm is deceitful and beauty is vain, but a women who fears the LORD, she shall be praised."

The holy reverence for God that brings His praise derives from an ongoing relationship with Him. Our degrees and careers must never overrule our daily intimacy and interaction with the Savior. Daily time with Him gives us stability, confidence, and direction.

A second priority for the Christian woman is her obligation to family. The family is quickly being written off the agenda today. But the Bible clearly states that a woman is to make sure her home is properly cared for (Titus 2:5).

Whether you choose to stay home full time or pursue a career, make sure you are a good manager of your home and family. A great career without a strong and loving family that knows God is a hollow success, and will not endure.

In this quickly changing world, there is a need for strong, stable Christian women who demonstrate a divine orientation to life.

WATCH WHERE YOU'RE WALKING

Therefore I...implore you to walk in a manner worthy of the calling with which you have been called.

EPHESIANS 4:1

In the Bible, to walk means to follow a certain course of life, to conduct yourself in a certain way. Ephesians 4:1–2 urges us to *walk worthily*—to make sure that our conduct fits our calling. For example, gentleness and patience are part of the fruit of the Spirit (Galatians 5:22–23), so it's not surprising that God calls us to live out these virtues.

We are to walk *differently* (Ephesians 4:17–18). In other words, "Do not be conformed to this world" (Romans 12:2). Our thinking should be shaped by spiritual and not by secular values (1 John 2:15–17).

We are to walk *lovingly* (Ephesians 5:1–2). Love is truth in action—doing whatever it takes to help others know and experience God's will for their lives. Christ loved us in this sacrificial way, and we are to walk in that love.

We are to walking *knowingly* (Ephesians 5:8–14). This means seeing things as they really are, and understanding what pleases the Lord. Walking in the light of God's Word helps us avoid the stumbling blocks that lurk in the darkness to trip us up.

We are to walk *wisely* (Ephesians 5:15–17). Wisdom means skillful living, which can only be accomplished when we understand God's will for us. We need the daily filling of the Holy Spirit to accomplish this goal (v. 18).

How is your walk today?

THE GIFTS OF A LIFETIME

Children are a gift of the LORD;
the fruit of the womb is a reward.

PSALM 127:3

*C*hildren are special gifts to be valued and treasured. That's what the Lord expects of us as parents, even on those days when we have to say (as my mother used to say), "For the Lord's name's sake, I will continue."

The early years of a child's life require *so* much physical energy—especially for a mother. During a child's teenage years, parenting demands huge amounts of physical *and* emotional energy. You need knee pads during those teenage years!

Children are a gift of the Lord, loaned to us for a short time. But they belong to Him, just as we do. That's why it's important for us to give our children back to the Lord before they're ever born.

Recognizing that our children are "on loan" to us from the Lord helps us as we do the best we can and leave the rest to Him. This isn't a cop-out or a lack of responsibility, but a matter of relying on His sufficiency.

It's also wonderful to know that we are not alone in this process. Relish the help and counsel of extended family and close friends. What you may spend years trying to instill into your children, another person can accomplish in much less time, because that person holds a unique place of authority or respect in your child's life.

A PROMISE FOR A LIFETIME

Love never fails.

1 CORINTHIANS 13:8

I remember my son's question as if it were yesterday.

It happened many years ago, during one of our trips back to Dallas after picking up our children from summer camp.

Anthony Jr. looked up at me and asked, "Mom, are you going to stay married to Dad?"

When I asked him why he was asking me that question, he replied that most of the kids in his cabin had parents who were either separated or divorced. I told Anthony to look me in the eyes. Then and there I promised my son that I was never going to leave his father.

Broken homes and failed marriages are a national disaster we're only beginning to pay the price for. Where do we break this destructive cycle?

A great place to begin is with our own marriages. I was able to promise Anthony Jr. that his mother would never leave his father because of a commitment I made to God and to Tony on June 27, 1970, and also because I loved Tony. Today, I would gladly repeat that promise to any of my four children who might ask.

Your children need the security that comes from knowing their parents are in love with each other and committed to each other for life.

MY WONDERFUL ROLE MODEL

Train up a child in the way he should go,
even when he is old he will not depart from it.

PROVERBS 22:6

My mother has always been my role model.

She had the kind of dedication, tenacity, and strong love for Jesus that it takes to raise eight children to know and follow Him. She's a wonderful example of the truth of today's verse. She stuck it out when life wasn't fun or easy, because she loved God, loved her husband, and loved her children. She did what she did for the sake of God's name and His glory.

I have a feeling that my mother, and other women who raised large families in her day, could tell us twenty-first-century moms a few things about the "pressures of parenting" we hear so much about these days. And they did it without many of the modern conveniences we take for granted today.

Mother drew her strength daily from the Lord. She stayed focused and relied on the God who is sufficient for any need we may have.

This same God is available to you and me today. Every mother needs a source of strength outside of herself. Have you discovered the day-by-day strength God provides to those who will call on Him?

God honored Mom's commitment, since all eight of her children know the Lord. Four are in full-time ministry, and all are involved in the Lord's work.

Whose role model are you? Someone is watching your life!

STAY CLOSE AND GET FED

Draw near to God and He will draw near to you.

JAMES 4:8

A friend of mine and her husband were feeding birds at the beach one afternoon. A large number of birds gathered to receive a bite of food, ate, and then left. Our friends went back to their chairs and blankets to read and relax, then got up to feed the birds again. And again, the birds returned for food, ate what they wanted, and left.

But in between the feedings my friends noticed one little bird that remained behind. They decided to give this little one more food. And the more they gave him, the more he stayed close. This went on all day, because every time they turned around, they saw this little bird, waiting patiently for more food. They didn't disappoint him! He always got more than the other birds who ate and left.

What a wonderful picture of the hunger we should have for God. The psalmist uses the imagery of a timid, thirsty animal to depict the intensity of desire we should have for God: "As the deer pants for the water brooks, so my soul pants for You, O God. My soul thirsts for God, for the living God" (Psalm 42:1–2).

James makes the promise that if we will draw near to God—the way that little bird drew near to my friends—He will draw near to us.

ONE WHO UNDERSTANDS

All of us like sheep have gone astray,
each of us has turned to his own way.

ISAIAH 53:6

One of the hard realities of parenting is that our older children can make potentially life-changing choices that fly in the face of all that we've worked so hard to teach them.

At times like this, it can be comforting to realize that even God, the perfect Parent, has to endure the choices of His children that violate His training. In other words, even perfect parenting doesn't prevent children from making poor decisions…and God understands our grief.

The next time a child's decision or rebellion makes you feel that you've done it all wrong as a parent, remember that you can lead a child to wisdom but you can't make him drink!

Now, I'm not suggesting that we simply feel bad when our children stray from the truth. There may be mistakes and failures on our part that we need to deal with honestly.

But when you've done the best job you know how to do, the best thing you can do is to simply commit your children to the Lord…and keep on praying!

Remember, God has promised that He will not give you more than you can bear (1 Corinthians 10:13). Thank Him today for His sufficient grace to handle any problem He permits to come your way.

FEELING TRULY ALIVE!

For to me, to live is Christ and to die is gain.

PHILIPPIANS 1:21

*W*hat is life?"

Jesus answered that question when He declared, "I am the life." Paul found the same answer when he declared, "For me to live is Christ." In other words, what got Paul going and made him feel truly alive was his relationship with his living Lord and Savior.

What is it that makes you come alive? Different things excite different people. We all know that when a man or woman meets that special person they've been looking for all their lives, the mere mention of their beloved brings them to life. They become animated, start acting a little silly, and begin showing pictures no one really wants to see. They feel alive!

Jesus Christ had that kind of animating effect on Paul. How about you? Do you feel really alive today? If not, maybe the problem is that Jesus is no longer the focus, the heartbeat of your life.

How can you tell when that sense of "aliveness" in Jesus has faded? Most likely, you'll lose interest in His Word, in talking with Him in prayer, and in simply spending time in His presence. When Christ becomes dim in our focus, life gets fuzzy and we no longer feel alive. The cure for that sense of deadness is found in the Lord. Make sure that He has first place in everything (Colossians 1:18).

LETTING THE WORD BE AT HOME

Let the word of Christ richly dwell within you.

COLOSSIANS 3:16

The word *dwell* in today's verse means to make oneself at home. Paul doesn't want you to just hear the Word, but to give it access to every part of you. God's Word must be free to rummage in the hidden corners of your life.

We're really not being truthful when we say to our guests, "Come on in and make yourself at home." We don't mean that literally. They aren't free to go into our bedroom and peer into our closets. They're not welcome to rifle through our personal papers. They shouldn't expect access to the refrigerator.

What we usually mean by "Make yourself at home" is "Come into the room I'm going to lead you to right now, and stay there."

But if Christ is going to be Lord of our lives, we can't place such restrictions on Him. We have to say, "Lord, go anywhere. Check the closets, look under the bed, open the dresser drawers. Show me what doesn't belong."

Now when the Lord God starts making Himself at home, there will be some painful "redecorating" issues before you. The Word will set your house in order, even though the process may hurt. But God hurts only to heal. When His Word truly takes up residence within us, we will find peace and a strong anchor for life's turbulent seasons.

Summer

OVERCOMING SPIRITUAL ANEMIA

Those who wait for the LORD
will gain new strength.

ISAIAH 40:31

*A*nemia is a physical condition brought on by a reduction in the number of red blood cells. The anemic person is left weak and unable to pursue normal physical activity.

Spiritual anemia is a problem, too. And it not only afflicts the so-called layperson, it's also a problem for men and women in full-time ministry—including pastors, pastors' wives, and missionaries.

Spiritual activity is no guarantee of spiritual strength. In fact, sometimes activity detracts from spiritual strength.

The cure for spiritual anemia is the same for everyone. "Those who wait for the Lord" are the ones who experience renewed strength. What does it mean to wait for the Lord?

It means spending time in His presence, in prayer, and in the reading and study of His Word.

Many people want to see the Lord's power in their lives, but aren't willing to follow His "prescription" for overcoming spiritual anemia: waiting in His presence.

An individual with physical anemia won't see miraculous results after just one dose of medicine. The patient needs to follow the pre-scribed treatment, and strength will return in time.

The same is true with devotions. If you're having trouble being consistent, keep at it, because you know that's what God wants. When you are obedient, the power will come. You'll have the strength to lift up and encourage those around you.

HOW MUCH DO YOU DESIRE GOD?

His delight is in the law of the LORD,
and in His law he meditates day and night.

PSALM 1:2

Personal devotions are to the soul what regular meals are to the body: sustenance and nourishment. If you don't eat daily, you'll become physically weak—even sick. The same will happen to us spiritually if we fail to nourish our souls in God's Word and in prayer.

Time with the Lord each day gives us the assurance, comfort, guidance, and strength we need to move through our day with confidence.

People often say, "I just don't have time for devotions." But if Jesus could find the time to pray despite the incredible demands on Him (Mark 1:35), we have no excuse. It's really not a matter of time, it's a matter of priority.

Others say the Bible is too difficult to understand. You might consider a good modern translation, like the New American Standard Bible, the New International Bible, or the English Standard Version. It's amazing, but the more you read and study, the more this Book will open up to you.

If lack of desire is a problem, ask God to give you a hunger for His Word. But while you are asking, *do* something. Start spending time in the Word in obedience to God, and the desire will come.

Make time with God a priority, and He will meet with you!

A FORMULA FOR PEACE

*Let the peace of Christ rule
in your hearts.*

COLOSSIANS 3:15

*M*any verses in the Bible spell out God's will in very clear terms. But in areas where His will isn't specifically stated, there are steps we can take to find His path and experience His peace.

The first step: "Let the word of Christ richly dwell within you" (Colossians 3:16). God's Word is the greatest source for discovering His will and walking in His peace.

A second step: Make sure you're acting in the name of Jesus, for His glory and honor (Colossians 3:17). When Jesus is the motivation for what you do, you won't get too far off the path.

A third step: Pray! The Bible tells us not to worry about anything, but to pray about everything (Philippians 4:6). And then? "The peace of God, which surpasses all comprehension, will guard your hearts and your minds in Christ Jesus" (v. 7). It's that relaxed mental attitude God gives because your focus is on Him and you are moving in the way He wants you to go.

And a final step: "Humble yourselves under the mighty hand of God, that He may exalt you at the proper time" (1 Peter 5:6). When you are exalting Christ, He will lift you up.

Why not commit your greatest need to the Lord in prayer today? It could be the first step toward finding God's peace.

A QUIET PLACE

*"Come away by yourselves to a
secluded place and rest a while."*

MARK 6:31

With four young children underfoot, the Evans home could sometimes be described as "controlled chaos." Does this morning routine sound familiar to you?

Alarm clock goes off in the dark, get the kids up. Fix breakfast, answer questions like "Did you sign my homework?" and "Where's my other sock?" Comb the girls' hair while they eat. Make four lunches in assembly line fashion. Set the lunches out where the kids will see them, get in a circle and pray, send the children off. Start to relax, but look up and discover the lunches still on the counter, all in a row. Have Tony run the lunches to school, then try to begin my day with prayer.

Whew! No wonder it seems so hard sometimes to find time to be alone with the Lord. But the very busyness of our days and the responsibilities that fall upon us are all the more reason that we need those quiet moments of focusing on Him.

Morning, noon, or night, your devotional time should be at that time when you have the best chance for maximum quiet and minimum distractions. The important thing is to set a daily time and stick with it!

We schedule other things like meals, appointments, and recreation, yet all too often neglect the needs of our souls. We *need* that daily appointment with Jesus.

PUT YOUR MASK ON FIRST

Like newborn babes; long for the pure
milk of the word, so that by it you may
grow in respect to salvation.

1 PETER 2:2

When you're in an airplane preparing for takeoff, the flight attendant always tells you to put your own mask on first before you try to help a small child. Obviously, you won't be much good to your child when you're gasping for air yourself.

The same principle is true in the spiritual realm. We can't minister to others when our own souls are gasping for air because we've neglected our personal time in the Word and in prayer.

Over a hundred years ago, George Muller wrote: "I saw more clearly than ever that the first great and primary business to which I ought to attend every day was to have my soul happy in the Lord. The first thing to be concerned about was not how much I might serve the Lord, or how I might glorify the Lord, but how I might get my soul into a happy state, and how my inner man might be nourished."

Again and again, God clearly teaches the necessity for personal, consistent exposure to the Scriptures. Joshua was told not to let God's law depart from his mouth, but to meditate on the Word "day and night" (Joshua 1:8).

Trying to make it without time in God's Word is like trying to exercise while holding your breath!

WHAT DO THESE STONES MEAN?

*"These stones shall become a memorial
to the sons of Israel forever."*

JOSHUA 4:7

After Israel miraculously crossed the flooding Jordan River to enter the Promised Land, God commanded Joshua to send twelve men—one from each tribe—back into the river to gather one stone apiece.

Joshua used the twelve stones to build a memorial to God's care and protection. When future generations of children saw the stones and asked their parents, "What do these stones mean to you?" (Joshua 4:6), the parents could retell the story of God's faithfulness. In this way, a godly heritage would be passed down from generation to generation.

We need "Joshua stones" in our lives, too. As a child, I watched my parents trust God to take care of us—but never really understood what it was to trust God in that way.

Since Tony and I established our own home, we've had many occasions to see God answer prayer and provide for our needs. We have often recounted to the children the ways God answered prayers when we were facing an impossible situation. These times helped build "stones of remembrance" in our children's hearts. We wanted to give them something to hold onto when they faced their own hard places.

Your children need to hear your stories, too. Did God make a way where there was no way? Tell your kids about it, and tell it more than once.

THE PRIORITY OF ENCOURAGEMENT — 1

*Encourage one another day after day,
as long as it is still called "Today."*

HEBREWS 3:13

One of the most important things your children should know about you is that you are always ready to encourage them.

Now, this doesn't mean you have to ignore it when they sin or disobey. Times of disobedience require discipline, and we need not be slow in applying the "rod" when appropriate (Proverbs 13:24).

What I'm talking about is a trap we can easily fall into as parents. This is the trap of becoming too demanding and critical of our children. Much of this tendency comes from a sincere desire to help our kids do the right thing, and make the most of the potential God has given them.

But too much criticism, even when delivered in the right spirit, is still too much.

So although there is a place for constructive criticism, my hope is that when our children put our criticism and encouragement side by side, they will see that what dominated our conversation was encouragement.

Many adults are angry with their parents today because they cannot remember receiving any encouragement as they were growing up. All they ever heard was "Can't you do anything right?" "You'll never make it," or, even worse, "You'll never amount to anything."

God forbid our children should hear this. Instead of exasperating or embittering our children, let's encourage them every chance we get!

THE PRIORITY OF
ENCOURAGEMENT — 2

*For you know that we dealt with each of you as a father deals
with his own children, encouraging, comforting and
urging you to live lives worthy of God.*

1 THESSALONIANS 2:11–12, NIV

We all know that the Scripture commands children to be
obedient to their parents, "for this is well-pleasing to the Lord"
(Colossians 3:20). But with the very next stroke of his pen, the
apostle Paul warned fathers not to exasperate their children, lest
they "lose heart" (v. 21).

I think Paul specifically mentioned fathers here for two reasons.
First, even though mothers are very much a part of a child's
upbringing, in the Bible it is the father who bears primary responsibility to oversee the home.

But there may be another reason for singling out fathers here.
As Tony often points out, in many homes it is the father who tends
to be more critical and demanding of the children. Of course, children need correction. But part of the skill of parenting is balancing
criticism and correction with genuine encouragement and praise.

Paul gives a wonderful pattern for fathers to follow in today's
Scripture: "For you know that we dealt with each of you as a father
deals with his own children, *encouraging, comforting and urging* you
to live lives worthy of God." Dads can be consistent in that "urging"
part of the verse. But they need to be just as consistent with the
"encouraging" and "comforting" responsibilities, too.

Don't let this day end without your kids hearing an encouraging
word.

DON'T JUST SPRINKLE A LITTLE JESUS ON TOP

Pray without ceasing.

1 THESSALONIANS 5:17

I get numerous invitations to pray at this or that function. I turn most of them down, because the people just want a little Jesus sprinkled on top of their secularism. The rest of the program has nothing to do with God. His thoughts are the last thing they will be considering.

We shouldn't be surprised when that happens in the world. But this is also the way many Christians live. We sprinkle a little Jesus on top with a quick prayer, and then go about our business.

In today's verse, Paul calls us to develop the habit and *attitude* of prayer. What is an attitude of prayer? It's a state of heart and mind in which we are constantly aware of the Father's presence—listening, waiting for direction, seeking His will in everything. The idea is to develop a lifestyle of humility and dependence on Him.

And the truth is, God has decided that there are some things He will not do until we pray. The mother of a newborn lies awake in bed at two in the morning, knowing it will soon be time to feed her baby. She is ready, willing, and able, and fully plans to get up. But she waits to hear the baby's cry to signal the need.

When God hears our cry, the response comes!

THE PERSISTENCE OF PRAYER

*[Jesus] was telling them a parable to show that at all times
they ought to pray and not to lose heart.*

LUKE 18:1

One of the lessons Jesus taught repeatedly about prayer is that
we need to stay at it, to hang in there when we pray.

In Luke 18:1–8, Jesus taught this truth through the parable of
an uncaring, unfeeling judge and a widow who needed justice. Now
even though widows were the most powerless people in Jesus' day,
this woman was so persistent in her appeals that she finally wore
him down. He granted her request.

It's obvious that Jesus was not saying God is like an apathetic
judge who has to be badgered to hear and answer our prayers. In
fact, Jesus contrasts the judge and God. He is saying that if persistent asking can wear down an uncaring judge and make him act on a
person's behalf, how much more quickly will a loving, caring God
respond to the heartfelt cries of His people?

The point of the parable, then, is persistence. Notice that Jesus
only gave us two options in prayer: praying faithfully or losing heart.
When you are tempted to lose heart or become discouraged in
prayer, that's your signal that it's time to pray all the harder!

Is there a tough circumstance you are praying for as a couple?
Jesus' word to you today is don't lose heart. Keep praying. Encourage
each other to stay with it in prayer.

YOUR DIVINE PRAYER HELPER — 1

You have not received a spirit of slavery leading to fear again,
but you have received a spirit of adoption as sons by which
we cry out, "Abba! Father!"

ROMANS 8:15

I hope you have a prayer partner, someone with whom you can share your heart and your prayer life.

This is one of the great blessings a husband and wife can confer on each other. Lois and I pray that the two of you are intimate prayer partners as well as life partners.

But there's an even greater prayer partner that each believer has—our prayer Helper, the Holy Spirit. Paul has some wonderful things to teach you in Romans 8 about the Spirit and your prayer life.

For example, it is the Spirit who makes the Fatherhood of God real to your heart, so that when you pray, you can say, "Daddy!" That's exactly what the word *Abba* means. It's a term of endearment, of intimacy.

But the Spirit's prayer help doesn't stop there. He also comes alongside you in those moments when your heart is so heavy or distressed you don't even know what to say (Romans 8:26).

Why do we need that kind of prayer help? Because we don't always know what to pray for, what to ask for, how to articulate the burdens and desires that are on our hearts. When it comes to serious prayer, we're often weak, and we need God's strength.

God the Holy Spirit comes alongside to pray our very heart to the Father who loves us.

YOUR DIVINE PRAYER HELPER—2

In the same way the Spirit also helps our weakness;
for we do not know how to pray as we should,
but the Spirit Himself intercedes for us
with groanings too deep for words.

ROMANS 8:26

*Y*ou've been there, haven't you? Lois and I certainly have. At some point, all of us reach that place where we are too broken in our weakness to communicate with the Father in intelligible words.

The Bible tells us that our Helper is there in those dark moments, ready to shape our shapeless thoughts before the Father.

We never have to worry about our prayers being well spoken or flavored with the right theological language, to reach the heart of God.

The Holy Spirit helps us when all we can do is groan. He takes that heart cry, and here's what He does. He decodes it, puts heaven's dictionary to it, and by the time it reaches the Father, that prayer you couldn't put in words is four paragraphs long!

So don't worry about it when you reach a place in prayer where language fails you. Just say, "Holy Spirit, I don't even know what I'm thinking right now. I need You to make sense of this and talk to Daddy for me, because I don't how to put my feelings into words." He will do it!

The "cord of three strands" (Ecclesiastes 4:12), consisting of you, your mate, and the Holy Spirit, makes for an unbeatable prayer team!

RENEW YOUR FOCUS

"The eye is the lamp of the body; so even if your eye is clear, your whole body will be full of light. But if your eye is bad, your whole body will be full of darkness."

MATTHEW 6:22—23

The only reason you can see where you're going is because your eyes are able to take in light and focus on it. As long as your eyes are working properly, you can walk where you want to walk and drive where you want to drive. But if something gets in your eyes…

In today's verse, Jesus used the eyes to illustrate a spiritual point. He said that when our spiritual eyes go dark, everything else goes dark, too. We lose our spiritual perspective when we allow the stuff of this world to get in our eyes and block our view of God's kingdom.

The problem with losing our spiritual vision is that everything else goes out of focus, too. When we can't see God and His priorities clearly, we can't see to handle our marriage and family relationships properly.

The same can be said for career, financial, or emotional problems. When your spiritual eyesight goes, the rest of you is very dark. And many Christians are living in darkness today because they are failing to look at life from the perspective of God's kingdom.

Have things been a little blurry to you lately? Are you having trouble seeing your spouse through God's eyes? There's a cure. You need to refocus. Fix your eyes on Jesus (Hebrews 12:2).

YOU CAN'T DO BOTH

"No one can serve two masters.
Either he will hate the one and love the other,
or he will be devoted to the one and despise the other.
You cannot serve both God and Money."

MATTHEW 6:24, NIV

The word *master* in today's verse means slave owner. No owner was about to share his slave with anyone else. There can be only one master.

Jesus is saying that when it comes to the material or the spiritual, you have to make a choice about which one you're going to serve.

Now notice what Jesus did *not* say. He did not say you must choose between having or not having material possessions. He did not say you have to give away everything you have to serve Him.

You can have material possessions and still serve Christ. You just can't *serve* these things and still give Christ the priority He deserves in your life.

What does it mean to be someone's servant? It means that person can tell you what to do. It means that when it comes to a choice between what the master wants and what anyone else wants, the master wins.

So who tells you what to do? Do you take your orders for life from God and His Word, or does your material well-being dictate your choices? If it's a struggle between God and money, who wins?

Jesus is interested in our priorities, not the size of our bank account. He didn't say it is difficult to serve two masters. He said it's impossible!

HIGH INTEREST — 1

*Instruct those who are rich in this present world not to be
conceited or to fix their hope on the uncertainty of riches,
but on God, who richly supplies us with all things to enjoy.*

1 TIMOTHY 6:17

If God were totally negative toward material possessions, as
some assume, Paul wouldn't have said what he said in today's verse.

If you have nice things, it's because God has given you these
things to enjoy. Has He given you a house and a wardrobe? Got
some money in the bank? Rejoice in His provision, and enjoy what
He has given. My job as a pastor isn't to make people who are legiti-
mately successful feel guilty because God has blessed them.

But all of us who have things are prone to a two-pronged temptation. The first is to become conceited over what God has given us,
as though we did it ourselves through our own wisdom and shrewd
planning.

The second temptation is to start fixing our hope "on the
uncertainty of riches." In other words, we start trusting the job or
the bank account instead of the God who provided it.

How do we know when we are falling into a selfish orientation
to life? One way is through what we say. Suddenly, we're always talking about what we want, what we need, and what we're going to do.
What God wants and needs from us, what His glory demands, does
not come up in the conversation.

The antidote to these temptations is to fix our hope on God.
And one evidence that we are doing this is when we use our material
blessings to make eternal investments.

HIGH INTEREST — 2

Remember this: Whoever sows sparingly will also reap sparingly,
and whoever sows generously will also reap generously.
And God is able to make all grace abound to you,
so that in all things at all times, having all that you need,
you will abound in every good work.

2 CORINTHIANS 9:6, 8, NIV

Let me give you a practical reason to make eternal investments. They pay higher interest! Eternal investments always appreciate in value. Earthly investments can depreciate in value and even disappear.

Here are five examples of the high interest you reap when you invest in God and His kingdom program: (1) "God will meet all of your needs" (Philippians 4:19, NIV); (2) God will reveal His will to you and give you direction in life, so that you will wind up where you are supposed to be (Romans 12:2); (3) You will have a God-given sense of contentment that no amount of money can buy (1 Timothy 6:6); and (4) God will give you His wisdom in making the decisions of life (James 1:5).

That's high interest, my friends. And it comes only with investments in God's kingdom! The prayer of Proverbs 30:8–9 is also a good antidote to greed. Make it your prayer as a couple today.

STOP WORRYING! — 1

"Do not be worried about your life, as to what you will eat or what you will drink; nor for your body, as to what you will put on."

MATTHEW 6:25

*C*hristians who make God's kingdom their priority no longer need to be controlled by anxiety.

Are either one of you a chronic worrier? In Matthew 6, Jesus gives you a great reason not to worry. Look at verse 25: *"For this reason I say to you...."*

For what reason? Because of what He just got through saying in verses 19–24 about the importance of laying up treasure in heaven and keeping your spiritual focus clear. Not worrying is so important to Jesus that He repeats it two more times in this chapter (vv. 32–34).

In the Greek language, there are two kinds of negative commands. One means "Don't start doing this." The other means "Stop doing this." The command in Matthew 6:25 is the latter type. Jesus is saying, "Stop worrying!"

You can call it whatever you want: a concern, a burden, a weight on your shoulders. But the fact is that worry is a sin for a child of God. If you are a worrying Christian, you are a sinning Christian.

When Jesus tells us not to worry about *anything*, He means it. The Bible makes no allowance for worry at all.

If the Bible tells us not to worry, then why do we worry? Because we don't think kingdom. It is the absence of a kingdom mentality that produces anxiety or worry.

STOP WORRYING! — 2

"Look at the birds of the air, that they do not sow,
nor reap nor gather into barns,
and yet your heavenly Father feeds them.
Are you not worth much more than they?"

MATTHEW 6:26

In Matthew 6:24, Jesus had just told His disciples that they could not serve two masters. They had to choose between God and money.

See, when you try to serve money you do a lot of worrying. And you had *better* worry, because the monkey is on your back! Once you decide to let money be your god, you have to get out there and fight for it harder than everyone else is fighting for it.

But when you commit your life to God, He takes the responsibility for your welfare. The fight is gone. The worry is gone. Your Father, the owner of heaven and earth, steps into the gap and says, "Trust Me with everything, and I will care for all your needs."

A lot of people have the idea that when you give your all to the Lord, you're taking this big risk. After all, everyone knows you have to work hard to get ahead because this is a dog-eat-dog world. But Jesus turned that kind of confused thinking upside down.

It's the pagans who worry about what they're going to eat and drink and wear (Matthew 6:31–32). For believers the only issue is, are we putting God first?

DON'T CHOKE — 1

Be anxious for nothing.

PHILIPPIANS 4:6

When Paul commanded us not to be "anxious" about anything, he used the same word for *worry* that Jesus used in Matthew 6:25. The word means literally "to strangle or choke." That's a pretty accurate picture of what worry does to us, isn't it?

Does that sound like something God wants for His children? Of course not. In fact, worry is a sin to God, for a very good reason. It's an indictment against His character and His ability to care for us.

If my children had worried every day about whether I was going to feed and clothe them, I would have felt pretty bad as a father. I'm glad my kids didn't get up every morning asking, "Dad, are you going to work today so we can have food and clothes?"

They never raised that question, because they knew something about their dad. They knew I would do whatever it took to care for them. Anyone who worried about my commitment to my children didn't understand my heart as a dad.

When you worry, you're really saying, "God, I don't really know about You. I'm not sure You're a caring and providing God. And since I'm not sure about You, I'm anxious. I've got to take care of things myself."

King's kids should never choke on worry.

DON'T CHOKE — 2

*You can throw the whole weight of your anxieties
upon him, for you are his personal concern.*

1 PETER 5:7, PHILLIPS

Jesus asked an important question in Matthew 6:25. "Is not life more than food, and the body more than clothing?"

Do you know what I think Jesus is telling us here? He is saying that if we are going to worry, let's worry about something big, not something small such as food.

We worry about whether we're going to have enough food to eat tomorrow. But the bigger issue is whether we're going to be alive tomorrow to chew! We worry about finding something appropriate to wear, but the bigger issue is having a warm, healthy body to clothe.

Jesus is saying, "If I have the ability to wake you up tomorrow, don't worry about whether I can feed you today. Don't concern yourself about your wardrobe."

Just as our love for our children motivates us to care for them, so our Father's love for us is our assurance that He will meet our needs. The great thing about God is that our need will never, ever be greater than His ability to supply.

Have you thanked God for His faithfulness in meeting your needs today…and for the confidence you have that He will continue doing so?

A "THEOLOGICAL" DRIVE

"Look at the birds of the air, that they do not sow, nor reap nor gather into barns, and yet your heavenly Father feeds them. Are you not worth much more than they?"

MATTHEW 6:26

*Y*ou may not enjoy driving as much as I do, but let me recommend that you take a "theological" drive out into nature someday. I mean a drive in which you take Jesus' advice and look at life from God's perspective.

Take a look at the birds. Birds never worry about how or what they're going to eat tomorrow, because God has built into their little systems a simple assumption. They assume that when they go out looking for food each day, it'll be there.

It's there because *your* heavenly Father cares enough about the birds He made to feed them (notice that Jesus didn't call Him "the birds' heavenly Father").

Jesus' question drives the point home. If God will stop to put a worm in the ground for a bird, what do you think He will do for you? That's like my children worrying about whether I'm going to feed them while they watch me feed the dog. If I'm feeding the dog, I'm going to at least give them some Cheerios!

The day you see a row of emaciated birds sitting on a fence or power line wringing their little feet over what they're going to eat— that's the day you can start worrying about whether God is going to remember to feed you.

But until then, quit worrying!

DON'T SWEAT IT—1

"Which of you by being anxious can add a single cubit to his span of life?"

MATTHEW 6:27, ESV

Here's a medical flash. Worrying won't help you live one day longer! It might shorten your life, but it won't lengthen it.

Let's put this matter of life and worry in perspective. The apostle Paul says that physical exercise is only of limited profit (1 Timothy 4:8). Now it does profit a little, because it helps increase our quality of life, and we're instructed to take care of our bodies as temples of the Holy Spirit.

But I don't care how far you jog or how fat-free, low-carb, or low-cholesterol your diet is, when God's appointed day comes for you, you are exiting this place. It won't matter whether you are up to ten miles a day or eat soybeans three times a day, your life's span has been determined by God.

You may be thinking, *Thanks a lot, Tony. That's a cheerful thought for the day.* Actually, it is. It means that your times are in God's hands. Is there anyone else into whose hands you would rather commit your days and years?

This truth ought to be comforting to a believer for another reason. As long as you're here, God has promised to take care of your needs. He knows the length of your days, and He has the provisions necessary to fill those days. Every one of them.

DON'T SWEAT IT — 2

"Do not be afraid, little flock, for your
Father has chosen gladly to give you the kingdom."

LUKE 12:32

*T*he person who truly understands and leans on the sovereignty and sufficiency of God can pray, "Lord, there may be a downturn in the economy. I may get 'downsized' by my company. I may have a health setback. The price of gasoline may go up another buck.

"But whatever happens, I remember that You are my heavenly Father. You hold my life in Your hands. And You told me in Your Word that as long as You want me around here, You're going to provide for me. So I may not know *how* You're going to do it, and I may not know *when* You're going to do it, but I thank You in advance for the provision I'm going to receive."

I don't know about you, but thinking about my heavenly Father like that just makes my day. And nothing on earth, heaven, or hell can separate me from the love of my Savior, Jesus Christ.

And just in case we need further testimony of God's care, Jesus advises us to go out and observe a field of beautiful wildflowers, bending in the wind (Matthew 6:28–30). If God can fill a field with lilies, don't worry about whether He can fill your table.

A DONE DEAL — 1

Cast your burden upon the LORD and He will sustain you;
He will never allow the righteous to be shaken.

PSALM 55:22

*C*hristians who make God's kingdom a priority reflect a heavenly rather than an earthly perspective.

One place where a heavenly perspective comes into play is in the matter of worry. In today's Scripture, David invites us to "offload" all of our cares on God. But when we do that, we need to *leave them there,* not take them back. Because God cares so much for us, we don't have to worry about whether He will handle the problem.

When one of my children expresses a concern to me and I say, "I'll take care of it," that means they don't have to ask anymore. As far as they're concerned, it's a done deal.

In fact, we often say to our children, "Why are you worrying about that? Didn't I tell you I would take care of it?"

Now, if we as weak, imperfect human parents can care that much for our kids, what does that say about the care of our infinitely powerful and loving God? When He promises to carry our burdens, it's definitely a done deal!

See, there's a tremendous promise at work for kingdom people. When you seek God's kingdom and His righteousness (Matthew 6:33), He promises to add to you all the things you need—all the things that the nonbelievers are knocking themselves out trying to get.

A DONE DEAL — 2

Commit your way to the LORD,
trust also in Him, and He will do it.

PSALM 37:5

*K*ingdom people can be relaxed about earthly needs, because they have a heavenly Father to look after them. They have a God to gladly supply their needs. They have Someone to do their worrying for them, so they don't have to worry themselves.

Let's face it. As Christians we worry by choice, not by necessity. Once you adopt a kingdom perspective, it changes everything.

Now some believers love to worry and get mad at you if you don't worry with them. They say, "Oh, I'm so worried!"

You say, "Well, you don't have to worry. Everything is going to be all right."

They say, "Are you kidding? If you understood what I was going through, you'd be worried, too."

Maybe, but I like what God says better. "Go get some sleep. You don't need to toss and turn in bed tonight. I'm staying up taking care of the problem so you can rest. I said I would care for *all* of your cares, not just some of them" (see 1 Peter 5:7).

When was the last time you lost sleep through worry? Did the worry help, or just wear you out? So what are you going to do the next time?

LOOKING THROUGH
GOD-COLORED GLASSES

*"But if God so clothes the grass of the field,
which is alive today and tomorrow is thrown into the furnace,
will He not much more clothe you? You of little faith!"*

MATTHEW 6:30

*T*oday's Scripture gives us an important question to think about today. Jesus asks it of you and me, and the only acceptable answer is "Yes, Lord, I believe You will look after my needs."

Jesus says that not to trust God for our daily needs is to possess "little faith." Now that's not a compliment. So you may be wondering today, *How do I know if I have little faith?*

One way you can know is by the questions you're asking. In verse 31, Jesus says that "little faith" people wring their hands in worry and ask, "What shall we eat? What shall we drink? With what shall we clothe ourselves?"

Now in our situation today the questions may take a little different form. "How am I going to make the house payment next month? How in the world are we going to make it if I get laid off? Where is the money for these hospital bills going to come from?"

But the effect on our lives is the same. Spending all of our time fretting about our needs takes us out of the realm of faith.

Jesus wants you to understand that the King of the kingdom is also your Abba, your "Daddy," your heavenly Father. Therefore, Jesus wants you to have a perspective that reflects this reality. It sure beats worrying, doesn't it?

JOY WITHIN THE LINES

Enjoy life with your wife, whom you love.

ECCLESIASTES 9:9, NIV

*I*f you want to enjoy the game of tennis, you can't just hit the ball whenever and wherever you feel like hitting the ball. You can't run only when you feel like running. That is not tennis. That is madness.

It's the same with intimacy between a man and a woman. People can't enjoy sex the way God intended them to enjoy it if they refuse to stay within the lines He has drawn.

But society keeps trying to blur those lines, twist them in ways they were never meant to be twisted—or simply erase them altogether. Unrestricted sex is being touted as a shortcut to personal fulfillment and satisfaction. People have given up their virtue for sex, traded their families for it—and now they're getting sick and dying because of it.

Sex dominates popular culture. A lot of people are trying to make sex outside of marriage seem normal and right. But the best counterargument to that is couples like you—a man and woman committed to a lifelong love relationship in the bonds of marriage. Let your marriage be a clear witness to the joy and fulfillment God intended for His sons and daughters.

Sex is a beautiful gift from God. Are you still treating it as a gift in your relationship—or as a right or obligation?

RENEWING YOUR COVENANT

*But immorality or any impurity or greed must
not even be named among you, as is proper among saints.*

EPHESIANS 5:3

*L*ois and I dated for about two years before we married. When
we first started dating, she looked at me and said, "Let's get the rules
straight up front. I am giving myself to one man, and that is the
man I marry. That's it. Before we get this relationship started, if you
have any other ideas, you're not the man I want to marry."

I knew right then that Lois *was* the woman I wanted to marry,
because she was telling me she was too valuable to throw away her
purity. She understood the value God placed on her, and on my
purity, too, and that commitment on her part really attracted me.

This is the attitude of Scripture. Today, however, popular
society makes a joke out of virginity. If you're a virgin, you're
laughed at and scorned and talked about "sho' as you born," as
the old people used to say.

Not so in God's economy. In His view, a commitment to
chastity before marriage is an act of consecration. Then, the act of
marriage is another form of consecration. Every time a husband and
wife engage in sexual intercourse, they are saying afresh to each
other, "All of me belongs to all of you." The sexual act within marriage is a continual recommitment to the covenant.

ALL OF US BELONGS TO CHRIST

*Now you are Christ's body,
and individually members of it.*

1 CORINTHIANS 12:27

We husbands and wives must understand that our bodies belong not only to each other (1 Corinthians 7:4), but to the Lord. Our spirits are His, too. We are whole beings, which means we can't separate our behavior into neat categories. This means that for the Christian, sex is a spiritual issue.

Paul tells us in 1 Corinthians 6:15, "Do you not know that your bodies are members of Christ?" In verse 14, he had just referred to God's resurrection power. What part of us will be raised from the dead someday? Not our spirits, which never die, but our bodies. And since our bodies have significance beyond the grave, what we do with our bodies now has significance beyond the grave.

I think there's also a question implied here: "Do you mean to tell me that God can raise your bodies from the dead, but can't help you control your bodies here on earth?"

Now you may think this doesn't apply quite as much to you since you are already married. But even though you have a legitimate outlet for the expression of your sexual desires, that doesn't mean that you are beyond the problem of sexual temptation, fantasies, or impure desires.

Ask God to help you treat your sexuality and your sexual relationship as a holy thing, which it is!

KEEP THE FIRE IN THE FIREPLACE

Therefore if the Son make you free,
you shall be free indeed.

JOHN 8:36, NKJV

*Y*ou've probably heard preachers say that true freedom is never doing what you want to do, but what you ought to do.

It's true—especially when it comes to sex. Suppose a man stands on top of a tall building and announces, "I want to be free from gravity. I'm going to do my own thing. So let me serve notice on you, gravity. I'm in charge now. I'm free."

He leaps off the building and for a couple of seconds, he is free. But it soon begins to dawn on him that he's not as free as he thought. As they sweep him up off the pavement, it's clear that he wasn't free at all. Gravity was running the show all the time.

It is possible to have sex outside the boundaries God has set. But it is *not* possible to enjoy sex the way God designed it to be enjoyed outside of His rules.

I say this to help you appreciate the wonderful, *freeing* boundary God has set for the expression of our sexuality. It's called marriage.

Sex is like a fire. Contained in the fireplace, a fire keeps everybody warm. Set the fire free, though, and the whole house burns. You don't want fire in your house to be free. You want it contained so it can generate warmth and joy, not destruction.

SATISFYING MARITAL INTIMACY

*Husbands, love your wives, just as Christ also
loved the church and gave Himself for her.*

EPHESIANS 5:25, NKJV

*T*he husband who is serious about meeting his wife's needs will imitate the self-sacrificing love of Christ.

Most of us will never be called on to give our lives for our wives. But you'd think some husbands were being crucified by the way they react when told they need to be more sensitive to their wives—to talk with them more, compliment them more, date them regularly, and show them care and affection.

If the only time your wife knows you're going to compliment, recognize, and value her is right before bedtime—when you want to be intimate—you are not fulfilling your duty to your mate.

This is why the Bible tells us husbands to understand our wives. Most of our wives were attracted to us at least in part because of what we did during the dating period. We made her feel special. We planned little surprises. We opened the car door for her. Now, she's lucky to get in before hubby drives off!

What made your wife want to marry you was not your physical attributes. It was the fact that you met a need in her. A husband is not fulfilling his duty to his wife unless he is providing what she really needs.

When a wife's needs are being met in a marriage, physical intimacy usually isn't a problem.

WHERE INTIMACY BEGINS

Eat, friends; drink and imbibe deeply, O lovers.

SONG OF SOLOMON 5:1, NKJV

Meeting needs and nourishing intimacy in marriage is a two-way street.

If a husband is meeting his wife's needs, her place is to reciprocate, to respond. She does this by coming under her husband's authority or control. This is what the word *authority* means in 1 Corinthians 7:3–4. The wife relinquishes control of her body to the touch, the care, the caress, the love of her husband.

Then as the husband responds to his wife's response, he also relinquishes control of his body. The picture here is of two people who are learning that they belong totally to each other. There is a giving of themselves, a vulnerability, a yielding of control. Sex should be the ultimate act of self-giving rather than a selfish act done to fulfill one's own needs.

Song of Solomon contains the Bible's most unblushing description of sexual intimacy in marriage. Chapter 4 details the buildup to intimacy in great detail, and a beautiful picture of self-giving between Solomon and his wife, the mutual yielding of their bodies.

Read that chapter together and notice that the intimacy begins with Solomon's compliments and words of admiration and appreciation for his bride, not with the physical act of sex. But when the moment of intimacy occurs, God Himself issues the invitation to the lovers to enjoy one another.

"SEXUAL FASTING"

*Stop depriving one another, except by agreement for
a time so that you may devote yourselves to prayer,
and come together again so that Satan will not tempt you.*

1 CORINTHIANS 7:5

The Bible declares sexual intimacy to be the norm within marriage. Just as single people aren't to act married, married people are not to act single.

When Paul wrote, "Stop depriving one another," he was referring to sexual intimacy. Neither partner should act in a way to make the other partner vulnerable to immorality.

Other than uncontrollable things like illness, there is only one situation in which intercourse is not to be regular in a marriage: an agreed-upon period of time so the partners can give themselves to focused prayer.

First, I want to underline the *agreement* part of this. This is not a unilateral decision that one partner is going to take six months off. Paul says it must be by mutual agreement.

Second, the time is to be limited. After a married couple has devoted themselves to prayer, they are to resume normal sexual relations so that Satan doesn't tempt either partner because of a lack of self-control.

I call this commitment to temporary abstinence "sexual fasting." The Bible has something important to teach married couples here about a different kind of intimacy that can be as satisfying as sexual intimacy.

Fasting is giving up a craving of the body because of a greater need of the spirit, and the Bible indicates it can extend to a married couple's sexual life.

A SOLID STRATEGY AGAINST TEMPTATION

*"I have made a covenant with my eyes;
how then could I gaze at a virgin?"*

JOB 31:1

Any believer, man or woman, who is committed to pleasing the Lord knows the reality of temptation. It's all around us, because this world temporarily belongs to Satan.

Let me give you a simple, biblical plan of attack you can use to deal with temptation:

1. Make the same decision Job made. He said he would not allow himself to give in to the lust of his eyes. That's a great place to start. Watch what you watch, so that what you watch doesn't start watching you back!

2. We learn a very practical truth concerning sexual temptation in 1 Corinthians 6:18. Run! Get out of there! If you have to, start running now.

3. Proverbs 5:15–19 urges married people to look for and find their sexual fulfillment at home. Put forth the effort to build intimacy with your mate, and the result will be more than satisfying.

4. Colossians 3:5 says to resist the flesh, because your flesh is pulling at you all day long. Watch the environments in which you place yourself. Examine your spirit to make sure that you're not putting yourself in compromising situations and settings.

5. Romans 12:1 says to present your body as a living sacrifice to God. Present yourself fully to Him. Get busy for the kingdom, and you'll help to squeeze Satan right out of your life.

YOU DON'T GET ALL THE ANSWERS

*[God] has also set eternity in their heart, yet so that
man will not find out the work which God has done
from the beginning even to the end.*

ECCLESIASTES 3:11

On a cruise ship a couple of years ago, I stood on the deck looking out at the vast Pacific Ocean.

All around me was the largest body of water in the world. Here I was, a little speck on a ship that was a little speck in the middle of that huge ocean.

Then I walked to the stern and noticed something that troubled me more. As the ship sliced through the water, it left turbulence in its wake. It made an impression on the sea. But within a couple of seconds, the water closed up and everything returned to normal.

The thought hit me: That's you, Tony. You'll slide through your seventy years and, Lord willing, cause a little stir. But after you're gone, it will be like you were never here. Talk about a sense of insignificance.

What's this life all about? Solomon tells us God has put eternity within our hearts. In other words, we were made for something more than just eating, sleeping, and going to work. God wants us to look up, to seek Him, to connect with Him. You and I will never solve all of life's riddles. And we don't have to.

What He *has* given us, though, is something infinitely better: a clearly marked path to real significance by inviting us to know Him intimately.

A SATISFYING VIEW OF WORK

I hated all the fruit of my labor for which I had labored under
the sun, for I must leave it to the man who will come after me.
And who knows whether he will be a wise man or a fool?

ECCLESIASTES 2:18–19

When King Solomon lost his way, he began searching for happiness in all the wrong places. One place he looked for purpose was in his work (Ecclesiastes 2:18–23).

Now you'd think that being "Your Highness" would be a pretty satisfying job description. Just like some people today think that if they finally land the right job, they'll have a reason to get up in the morning.

But work will never be the place where we find life's deepest meaning. It distressed Solomon to think that when he died, he would have to leave his kingdom to someone who might mess up what he had built up.

Solomon lay awake at night fretting about those things (v. 23). How many sleepless nights have you spent worrying about your work?

You and I want to know all the questions and all the answers, while God says we need to simply see our life and our work as His gifts, to be received and enjoyed, day by day. If God can ever get us to enjoy His gifts without trying to take them all apart, He knows we'll be set free from the futility of seeking purpose in the things of this life.

In other words, we'll be free to pursue Him.

AVOIDING THE LONG DETOUR

"Vanity of vanities," says the Preacher,
"Vanity of vanities! All is vanity."

ECCLESIASTES 1:2

The topic of Solomon's great "sermon" that we know as the book of Ecclesiastes was…nothing. In fact, you could call it the "nothingness of everything."

We say, "Wait a minute, Solomon. What are you talking about? You're the man. You're the guy with all the wealth and power and wisdom. You're the king. What's this vanity stuff?"

Most people think if they had all the stuff Solomon had, they wouldn't have his problem. But that simply isn't true.

Some of us adults remind me of kids tearing open Christmas presents. We get our new toy, maybe that new car we wanted. We drive it, and we're so excited. It has that new car smell. We look good, we have a sense of significance as we drive it. But as the months go by, it becomes just a car. The new smell fades. The significance disappears. We have to find another toy.

This was Solomon as he wrote the book of Ecclesiastes. He started off close to God. But by the time we meet him here, he's lost his way. He finds it again, but not until he's taken a long and painful detour.

God wants us to avoid Solomon's detour. That's why this book is in *The* Book. Spend time reading and absorbing the message of Ecclesiastes, and you'll avoid a lot of pitfalls.

The Solution to Vanity

Wisdom excels folly as light excels darkness.
The wise man's eyes are in his head,
but the fool walks in darkness.
And yet I know that one fate befalls them both.

ECCLESIASTES 2:13–14

One day Solomon looked out his palace window and saw the local kindergarten dropout. This guy had nothing going for himself, but it dawned on the king that one day both he and the dropout were going to die.

Then it hit Solomon. In the grave, wisdom and foolishness won't matter. The wise person and the fool will be equally dead. In fact, the fool may live to be eighty while the wise person dies at sixty. Solomon considered this and said, "There's got to be more to life than this."

When you are lying in bed at night, do you ever think about your life and the prospect of death and say, "There's got to be more to life than this"? Trying to use human wisdom to come up with a satisfying purpose for life will leave you just where it left Solomon: Empty and depressed.

What's the solution to the seeming vanity of life? Well, one day (and who knows *which* day?) you and I are going to step right out of time and into eternity. That's the *real* world. The question then won't be what we left behind, but what we sent ahead. The solution to vanity is to live *for today* with the perspective of *forever* (see Matthew 6:19–21). We must not allow the illusion of time to replace the reality of eternity.

TOO MANY "FEMINIZED" MALES — 1

The man is the head of a woman.

1 CORINTHIANS 11:3

*T*he statement above gives the New Testament equivalent of Genesis 2, where God created the man and then from the man's side created the woman.

The order of creation established what I call God's covenantal chain of authority. This concept has huge implications for how we do everything, including marriage.

Now God established His chain of authority, but what has happened is the equivalent of the old chain letter deal. Chain letters always carried the threat that if you broke the chain, something bad would happen to you. Well, that's the idea here. When you break God's chain, you lose His blessing.

Many of us have already done that. On the whole, we men have done it passively, by abdicating our role of spiritual and marital leadership. A whole generation of women has been taught to seize that role aggressively.

Satan has successfully duped many of us men into pouring most of our energy and attention into areas that feed our maleness (such as our careers) but don't always help us be godly leaders at home. Brother, it's time for us to become loving leaders again!

If Jesus Christ is a man's model for leadership, his wife won't have to worry about having to "knuckle under" to a heavy-handed husband.

TOO MANY "FEMINIZED" MALES — 2

Fathers, do not provoke your children to anger,
but bring them up in the discipline
and instruction of the Lord.

EPHESIANS 6:4

*T*oday's men know little of biblical leadership. As a result, our young boys have no example to follow. At home, Dad is missing in action. At school, boys are in a system dominated mostly by women.

At church, the pulpit may be filled by a man, but the rest of the church program is largely under female leadership. Most of a boy's Sunday school teachers are women. And now that homosexuals have come out of the closet, boys are getting an even fuzzier picture of what it means to be male.

All of this leads to "feminized" men who have relinquished their leadership roles. Now don't misunderstand. I am grateful for every godly, gifted woman God is using in the home, at church, and at school.

But over the last thirty years or so, this role reversal has given rise to a women's liberation movement with many that preach a dominant role for women.

But I believe that if a woman were receiving the right kind of love and leadership, she would not want to be liberated from that.

It's time to step up to the plate, my brother. It may be late in the seventh inning, but the game isn't over until it's over!

"SPEAK, LORD..."

Jesus said to them, "Follow Me,
and I will make you become fishers of men."
Immediately they left their nets and followed Him.

MARK 1:17—18

*I*t's my burden that we as Christian men reject the temptation to excuse ourselves from our responsibility of spiritual leadership. It's just no good to use the excuse that society has taken away our role and won't give it back to us.

If God were to draw a picture of a real man, what would he look like? I want to suggest that the response of Peter, Andrew, James, and John to Jesus' call to discipleship is a great place to start in defining biblical manhood.

Today's verse tells us that Peter and Andrew immediately left their fishing business to follow Jesus. They dropped everything, even the stuff that most men consider the most important, to obey Jesus' call. In verses 19–20, James and John did the same thing.

These four men, and later the other members of the Twelve, left their means of livelihood, their careers, to become Jesus' disciples.

Does that mean you should drop your job to follow Jesus? Not necessarily. What I want you to see is that a biblical man is one who is prepared to obey God no matter what the cost. If your heart attitude is "Speak, Lord, for Your servant is listening," you won't have any problem providing the kind of leadership your wife, your children, your church, and your community need so badly.

TRAITS OF A GODLY MAN — 1

*A good man leaves an inheritance
to his children's children.*

PROVERBS 13:22

In Job 29, we find several qualities or traits from Job's life that help us define a real man.

First, *he has a spiritual legacy to leave behind.* In Job 29:1–5, Job looked back to the days before his awful trials, when he was in his "prime" (v. 4). What man can't identify with that feeling!

Job isn't saying his faith was a thing of the past. He was simply reflecting on happier days. But because God had illumined Job's way in days past, he had a history—a legacy—of God's presence to help him when his world collapsed.

Notice also that Job shared his spiritual pilgrimage with his children while they were still alive (v. 5). Job's kids had footsteps to follow.

If you don't have a history with God, if you can't see the footsteps of grace in your life, a slice of your life is missing. If God didn't do anything for you yesterday, you won't have what you need to hang in there today—so that you can make it to tomorrow. And you won't have a spiritual legacy to pass on to your children.

Imagine your son or daughter asking, "Dad, has God ever done anything really special in your life?" Would you be able to recount stories of God's grace and help? Let's make sure the answer is yes.

TRAITS OF A GODLY MAN — 2

I have been young and now I am old, yet I have not seen the righteous forsaken or his descendants begging bread.

PSALM 37:25

Even in the midst of his suffering, Job could look back on a spiritual legacy he had left for his children.

In Job 1:5, before all the calamities hit, we see Job acting as the family priest. This was in the days before God's priesthood and sacrificial system was established on earth, so the father acted as priest.

Dad, when was the last time you knelt by your child's bed and said, "I want to talk to God about you"? That leaves a lasting impression.

I'll never forget opening my father's bedroom door one night because I heard this noise coming out from the room. It was my father, wailing in prayer for his children. Just wailing in utter spiritual anguish.

It wasn't easy for my father to do that. He was a longshoreman who did back-breaking work on the Baltimore waterfront for thirty-five years. Talk about being tired. My father would come home dragging, but he was never too tired to pray for his kids. I'll never forget that.

If you as a father aren't building a spiritual legacy, you can fret about it, or you can start building one. Bring God to bear on your circumstances now.

Mom, you're a vital part of building that legacy, too. Pray as a couple that God will establish a strong witness in your home. Begin the legacy today.

TRAITS OF A GODLY MAN — 3

*He who pursues righteousness and loyalty finds life,
righteousness and honor.*

PROVERBS 21:21

According to Job 29:7–8, *a godly man earns respect or honor.*
Job says, "When I went out to the gate of the city…the young men
saw me and hid themselves."

That's respect! The young men ran when Job showed up. "Job's
here, let's go. We can't be doing this stuff out here when Job's
around." How many kids do you know who treat adults with this
kind of respect today?

There used to be a time when kids showed some respect for
adults, gave them some room on the sidewalk. Now what happens?
We see a group of teenagers coming, and we cross to the other side
of the street because we're scared of them.

Someone says, "Kids today don't have any respect for anyone."
But why not? Could it be that we haven't earned it, haven't insisted
on it, and so, therefore, they don't have it?

Now don't misunderstand. I'm not talking about a man strut-
ting around acting tough or throwing his influence around,
demanding that people bow to him. I'm talking about a man who
earns the respect of those around him because of his sterling spiritual
character.

You don't have to be wealthy, powerful, or famous to earn this
kind of respect. You just have to be a man of real spiritual depth.

TRAITS OF A GODLY MAN — 4

I delivered the poor who cried for help,
and the orphan who had no helper.

JOB 29:12

*L*et's look at three more traits of a godly man from the life of Job.

First, *a godly man is a person of mercy and justice.* Job said in 29:13, "The blessing of the one ready to perish came upon me, and I made the widow's heart sing for joy."

A godly man hurts with people who hurt, helps people who need help. He investigates things (v. 16) to get at the truth and brings justice to bear on a situation.

Second, *a godly man is a man of stability.* "I shall die in my nest, and I shall multiply my days as the sand. My root is spread out to the waters, and dew lies all night on my branch" (Job 29:18–19). Job was talking about stability. When the world shook around him, he was rock-solid.

Third, *a godly man is a man of wisdom.* "To me they listened and waited, and kept silent for my counsel" (Job 29:21).

People came to Job for advice because of wisdom from his lips *and* his life. A wise man is a man who has been with God, and who knows His Word. Wisdom is the ability to apply truth to the issues of practical, day-to-day life.

Determine to be the man God wants you to be, and your family will respond to your leadership.

RETURNING TO YOUR
FIRST LOVE — 1

"I have this against you, that you have left your first love."

REVELATION 2:4

nything that comes between us and our love for the Savior is a "love-stealer." One of the greatest love-stealers is the spiritual condition the New Testament calls carnality.

God has too many children who aren't really sure whose family they want to be a part of. They're trying to step out with Christ and the world at the same time, which leads to unanswered prayer, emotional and physical weakness, loss of peace, loss of joy, lack of stability, and all manner of other ills.

Now don't misunderstand me. I'm not insinuating that every time a Christian has a problem, it's because he or she is carnal. But I am suggesting that far too many of us are having far too many failures because we are carnal and are half-stepping with Christ, sometimes hanging with Him and sometimes romancing the world.

Carnality is that spiritual state where a Christian knowingly and persistently lives to please and serve self rather than Christ (1 Corinthians 3:1–4).

If Revelation 2:4 warns us that we can leave our first love, the very next verse tells us how to get it back. Jesus says: *"Remember* from where you have fallen, and *repent* and *do* the deeds you did at first."

This is a powerful formula, not only for personal spiritual renewal, but for revival in your marriage and family.

RETURNING TO YOUR
FIRST LOVE — 2

Therefore remember from where you have fallen.

REVELATION 2:5

When Jesus Christ demands our first love, our undivided loyalty, and our total commitment, He is demanding nothing more than what is His right and prerogative.

And His command to us is to *remember* what that first love we had for Him was like.

In 1970, Lois and I stood before a pastor in a church and entered into a lifetime commitment of love and faithfulness.

Any married person can tell you that when you first get married, you're starry-eyed. Beside yourself! The whole world looks wonderful. I mean, life is going to be nothing but bliss.

At some point, however, you wake up to the disturbing reality that being married isn't necessarily all you thought it would be. You discover there's a little bit more to it than you'd anticipated. You're still committed, but as the song says, "The thrill is gone."

Many of us have found this to be true in our Christian lives. We received Christ, and thought it all was going to be bliss. With God in our lives, there'd be no blisters. Just victory after victory, and showers of blessings. But when the hard times came, our love began to cool.

If that's your condition today, don't let your love stay cold.

Pray that God will light a new flame of love in your heart…beginning today.

RETURNING TO YOUR
FIRST LOVE — 3

*"Those whom I love, I reprove and discipline;
therefore be zealous and repent."*

REVELATION 3:19

I would never want to downplay the joy of being a Christian,
or the eternal bliss awaiting us in heaven.

But you know as well as I do that the Christian life is not a tip-
toe through the tulips. Salvation fixed a lot of our problems, but it
also surfaced a whole new set of problems—and left some of the old
ones around for us to deal with.

We discover that sin is as sinful as it ever was. Temptation is as
tempting as it ever was. The reality hits that being a Christian does
not exempt us from the impulses of the flesh. You and I as
Christians can have our fellowship and closeness with God inter-
rupted by sin.

That doesn't cancel the relationship. You're still God's child. But
sin has come between you and Him, and the intimacy is lost. The
only cure is repentance.

God always calls on people who are in relationship with Him,
or who desire a relationship with Him, to change their minds about
sin. That's the basic meaning of the word *repent*. It means changing
your way of thinking…a change of the mind that brings about a
change of direction.

Repentance is crucial if we're going to restore harmony where
there is chaos, if we are going to return to our first love for Christ.

WALKING THE WALK

You were formerly darkness, but now you are
Light in the Lord; walk as children of Light.

EPHESIANS 5:8

To return to our first love for Christ, we must make sure that what is in our minds gets transferred to our feet. It's what the New Testament calls our "walk."

In Ephesians chapter 4, Paul begins by saying: "This I say, and affirm together with the Lord, that you walk no longer just as the Gentiles also walk, in the futility of their mind" (v. 17).

The word *walk* refers to one's course of living, his lifestyle, his orientation. Paul uses this imagery because of the way a person's course is set.

When you walk, you put one foot in front of the other to progress toward a particular destination. It's a process. You don't get where you're going in one giant step, but you walk step-by-step toward your goal.

That's the way it is in the Christian life. It isn't an airplane ride, it's a walk—a step-by-step practice of moving from where you are to where you ought to be going. Nobody "jets" to spiritual maturity.

When a baby gets his mind and his feet functioning together, he starts walking. That's the same challenge we face as believers in returning to our first love for Jesus Christ. We need to get our minds and our spiritual feet working together.

Husband and wife, walk together in Him!

BUILDING ON THE ROCK — 1

*Everyone who hears these words
of Mine and acts on them,
may be compared to a wise man
who built his house on the rock.*

MATTHEW 7:24

In Matthew 7:24–29, Jesus told the story of two men who built houses in the same neighborhood. I'm sure they pulled out all the stops and built their dream houses. The homes probably even looked similar. In the context of today, these guys probably went to the same church, belonged to the same country club, and had many of the same friends.

There was only one difference between these two houses—but a very big difference. Deep down, under the surface, they were built on dramatically different foundations. One man was wise and built "on the rock." The other man was foolish and built on sand.

The Greek word for *rock* here means a large expanse of bedrock. The wise man dug down deep, while the second man built in loose, unstable sand.

The difference in these two houses wasn't apparent until the first big storm hit. Then the tragic difference was exposed, as the second house utterly collapsed.

So what was the rock that held the first house firm? Jesus said the difference was between those who hear *and act* upon His words, and those who hear them but do nothing about them.

In other words, the difference between your house—your family, your marriage—standing or collapsing is your obedience to Jesus Christ in the way you build.

BUILDING ON THE ROCK—2

"The rain fell, and the floods came,
and the winds blew and slammed
against that house; and yet it did not fall,
for it had been founded upon the rock."

MATTHEW 7:25

*T*he power to live an obedient life is not in the Word of God you amen with your lips. It's in the Word you amen with your *feet*. You have to lay a foundation of obedience to Christ if you expect the building you erect to withstand the storms.

Obeying Christ does not mean you won't get rained on! Storms come into every life, hit every family. But the home built on the foundation of obedience stood strong.

What are you going to do with the Word of Christ? Is there something you need to start doing, or something you need to leave alone, in light of what God has revealed to you in His Word?

When you start acting on the Word, you begin to dig a foundation for your life and your family that hits solid rock. And the higher you hope to build your building, the deeper the foundation has to go down. If you want a "skyscraper" kind of family, don't build it on the foundation of a chicken coop.

Remember, it's hard to lay a foundation when it's raining. Workers have to stop pouring concrete when it rains. The foundation has to be poured on sunny days.

So before the next storm hits, get your foundation in. Make sure your life is anchored on the rock of Christ.

THE INTIMATE FELLOWSHIP
OF OBEDIENCE

"If you love Me, you will keep My commandments."

In John 14:21 Jesus said, "He who has My commandments and keeps them is the one who loves Me; and he who loves Me will be loved by My Father, and I will love him and will disclose Myself to him."

Why did Jesus say that? Because if you don't love Him, if you don't obey Him, the Father can't respond to you. The Father always responds to His Son.

If you want to see God do great things in your life, take the risk of obedience. Because when you decide to obey, God moves on your behalf.

And it gets even better. "If anyone loves Me, he will keep My word; and My Father will love him, and We will come to him and make Our abode with him" (John 14:23). So you not only get God's activity in your life, you get God's presence in a relationship of intimate fellowship.

Jesus isn't asking you to be perfect. What He wants to know is that you are moving in the direction of radical obedience to Him.

Many of us get it backward. We say, "Lord, help me to obey." No, our prayer should be, "Lord, I am obeying You. Please help me." Our Helper, the Holy Spirit, enables us *as* we obey. He empowers our feet as we move toward the right place.

CHECK YOUR OBEDIENCE LEVEL

*"He who has My commandments and
keeps them is the one who loves Me;
and he who loves Me will be loved by My Father,
and I will love him and will disclose Myself to him.*

JOHN 14:21

People often say to me, "I want to know God better. How can I draw closer to Him and come to know Him in a deeper way?"

My answer is, check your obedience level. Just like you keep your car filled up with gasoline, obedience is the fuel that powers your relationship with God.

There's something wrong somewhere when we profess to know and love God, yet don't seek to please Him or take His Word seriously.

There are some Christians who have to be jerked and pulled along to get them to obey God. Other Christians seem to obey Him with joy and eagerness. What's the difference? God has revealed Himself to the obedient Christians at a deeper level. Because they obey His commandments, God is free to disclose Himself to them that He might unleash His Word in them.

These are the Christians who are able to experience God at a more intimate level of fellowship and intimacy because they are experiencing the fellowship of obedience. They started with the foundation of obedience, and now they have entered into the intimacy of obedience.

If you are obedient, you will see God at work in your life. You'll see Him answer your prayers and do a new work of power and blessing in your marriage and family.

LET'S GET PRACTICAL

God has not only raised the Lord,
but will also raise us up through His power.

1 CORINTHIANS 6:14

*G*od has made available to us all the power we will ever need
to do anything He asks us to do. We're talking about *His* power.

How powerful is God? According to Paul, God is so powerful
that three days after Jesus died, God the Father said, "Get up." The
stone rolled away from Jesus' tomb, and He walked out into the
early morning light of the first Easter.

But that's not all. Paul says that God is going to exercise that
same resurrection power on our bodies someday. Even though we
may die, one day God is going to say, "Get up." And we're going to
come out of our graves the same way Jesus came out of His, to
spend eternity with Him. That's how powerful God is.

Now, if God can raise Jesus from the dead, and if He's going
to raise you and me up to eternal life someday, giving us the power
to live for Him *today* is no problem at all.

So...do you need to be more understanding with your spouse?
More patience with the children? Is your job getting to you? Draw
near to God and appropriate His incredible power.

The problem is not that we have too much humanity working
within us. It's that we have too little of God working within us.

BECAUSE IT'S SO GOOD

Marriage is to be held in honor among all,
and the marriage bed is to be undefiled;
for fornicators and adulterers God will judge.

HEBREWS 13:4

*G*od takes the highest view possible of the marriage commitment. Anything less than committed, faithful married love is a perversion of His plan.

God created our bodies to be used for His glory, not simply to satisfy our passions. But God also created our sexuality and gave us our sexual desires. He also created a wonderful avenue for the fulfillment of those desires, the "marriage bed," as the author of Corinthians calls it.

The world is constantly telling us that the grass is greener in the next yard, that real excitement and satisfaction are to be found outside the confining boundaries of marriage.

In this perverted view, God is the ultimate killjoy for trying to restrict us sexually to one person for life. God is also accused of withholding pleasure from us because He is against sex.

Don't buy into that mess! God does not condemn sex outside of marriage because He thinks sex is bad. He condemns sex outside of marriage because He knows sex within marriage is so good! In other words, God is not upset just because two warm bodies come together. God is bothered when that which He created to be so valuable and so expensive is used cheaply.

Guard your marriage! Keep your love for each other strong and warm. For your joy…and for His glory.

THE "GUM" OF MARRIAGE

*Flee immorality. Every other sin that a man
commits is outside the body, but the immoral man
sins against his own body.*

1 CORINTHIANS 6:18

Not long ago, Lois and I stepped out of a cab only to discover that some thoughtless soul (bless 'im!) had left chewing gum on the seat, and Lois had sat in it. The gum was stuck to her beautiful dress.

As you know, gum has a way of sticking and not letting go. Lois went into the restroom to try to clean the gum off. But the more she pulled, the more she snagged the threads and fabric of the dress. Finally, she came out and said in frustration, "This isn't working. The harder I try to remove the gum, the more I'm tearing my dress."

This is exactly what happens when a man and a woman come together in sexual intercourse. There is a joining together not only of their bodies, but of their spirits, too. That's the way God designed sex to work.

This is part of what makes the intimacy of marriage so sweet. But when a person commits adultery and then pulls away from that temporary partner, there is a tearing of the spirits that have been joined. He or she leaves part of his or her soul behind.

This is one reason the Bible warns us so against committing sexual immorality! You can't play games with God and come away undamaged. Cultivate and enjoy the union He has given you.

A HOLY GHOST THING

*Do you not know that your body is a
temple of the Holy Spirit who is in you?*

1 CORINTHIANS 6:19

*Y*our body is a Holy Ghost thing!

That's what the apostle Paul told the believers at Corinth as he wrote to instruct them about how to live in moral purity before God.

In the Old Testament, God's Spirit inhabited the temple. That was what made it a holy place. Today, if you know Jesus Christ as your Savior, your *body* is the dwelling place of the Holy Spirit.

Guess what this means? It means that what you do with your body has holy implications. It involves worship. So, for instance, every time you engage in sex, you go to church. For us as Christians, the act of physical intimacy is a worship service because our bodies are His temple. They are God's church house.

Is God being glorified in the worship you are offering Him through your bodies?

God is intensely interested in what goes on in your marriage—even in the bedroom. He wants to be honored and worshiped in every aspect of your marriage.

Is it possible for a married couple to glorify God in their sexual relationship? Absolutely! *"Whatever* you do," Paul says, "do all to the glory of God" (1 Corinthians 10:31).

Therefore, the way you honor your marriage vows, and the way you honor your mate by seeking to meet his or her needs, are nothing less than acts of worship.

THE ULTIMATE IN UNSELFISHNESS

The husband must fulfill his duty to his wife,
and likewise also the wife to her husband.

1 CORINTHIANS 7:3

*F*ulfilling your duty to your mate means more than sexual performance. Sex is only part of the package. For example, one indication that a husband has stopped fulfilling his duty to his wife is when he no longer romances her or makes her feel special.

The only reason she got excited about you in the first place was because you romanced her. You messed with her mind. You told her how pretty she was, how her eyes looked in the moonlight. You seated her at the table. Opened her door. Did all kinds of loving stuff. And because you made her feel loved and cared for, there was the desire to respond.

But after we get married, many of us husbands stop fulfilling our duty. So let me ask you, my brother: When was your last date with your wife? When was the last compliment, the most recent love note?

If you're not doing those kinds of things, you're not fulfilling your duty. Now, I know it works both ways. Christian wife, if your husband is making a sincere effort to do the right things, you need to respond by fulfilling your duty to him.

Loving, committed sex between a husband and wife is the ultimate act of unselfishness—and the more unselfish you are about it, the bigger the benefit to you!

THE SPIRIT'S BENEFITS

*"It is to your advantage that I go away; for if
I do not go away, the Helper will not come to you."*

JOHN 16:7

hen Jesus says a situation is to your advantage, you're in for
something special. He doesn't make promises lightly. What are the
advantages of God's Spirit dwelling within us?

First, Jesus said the Spirit will "guide you into all the truth"
(John 16:13). Do you need guidance? Do you wish you had some-
one wise to advise you about your decisions? Well, you have that
"Someone" in the Holy Spirit.

Jesus also said the Spirit would "bring to your remembrance all
that I said to you" (John 14:26). Jesus had taught the disciples so
much truth. How were they going to remember it all? The Holy
Spirit would recall these things to their minds.

Our responsibility is to study and hide the Word in our hearts.
The Spirit's responsibility is to bring it to mind when we need it.
Another benefit the Holy Spirit gives is peace. "Peace I leave with
you; My peace I give to you; not as the world gives do I give to
you," Jesus said in John 14:27. Therefore, "Do not let your heart be
troubled, nor let it be fearful."

What's your situation today? Whatever it is, if you have the
Holy Spirit, you have the advantage over any circumstance. Jesus
said so! Draw on those benefits. Find help and wisdom (and
courage) for any situation in your marriage and family life.

AN EVER PRESENT HELPER

The Spirit also helps our weakness; for we do not know how to pray as we should, but the Spirit Himself intercedes for us with groanings too deep for words.

ROMANS 8:26

The Holy Spirit is not only our Helper, He is our *ever present* Helper. Jesus told His disciples just before His crucifixion that it was better for them if He went away, so the Spirit could come (John 16:7).

Now this may not sound better at first. After all, what could be better than having Jesus with you? But the truth is that if Jesus Christ were on earth today in His bodily presence, we would be a defeated, decimated people.

Why? Because when Jesus was here on earth, He encased His deity in His humanity. The result was that even though Jesus is God, He chose to be in only one place at a time. His deity functioned always in the same vicinity as His humanity. Jesus never traveled more than a few miles from home.

But because the Holy Spirit indwells each member of the body of Christ, we can all draw on the full power of deity wherever we go.

So in order for Jesus to meet the needs of all saints everywhere, He had to leave the earth so the Holy Spirit could come to be present with us everywhere.

The Holy Spirit is also the ever present Helper in your marriage and family relationships. What is the greatest need you face at home today? Talk to your Helper about it.

A HELPER OF THE SAME KIND AS JESUS

"[The Holy Spirit] will glorify Me,
for He will take of Mine and will disclose it to you."

JOHN 16:14

One reason many hurting Christians don't get the help they need is that they go to the wrong person first.

A pastor is not the Holy Spirit. Neither is a Christian counselor or therapist. Neither is your best friend. If you are more dependent on these people than you are on the Spirit, you're settling for second-class help.

The *first* Person we should go to when we're in need is the Holy Spirit, because His job is to take the things of Christ and make them real in our lives.

The Holy Spirit is in you. If you keep relying on outside helpers while excluding the Helper inside you, you're never going to realize the full power of God in your life.

The Holy Spirit can minister the things of Jesus to you because He is "another Helper" of the exact same kind as Jesus (see John 14:16). That's the full meaning of the word *another* in this verse.

Jesus' words emphasize the Spirit's work in continuing what He had begun while on earth, without any loss of quality, power, or intimacy. Jesus could promise this because the Spirit is of equal divine essence with Jesus Himself.

There's nothing wrong with seeking counsel from your pastor, a Christian counselor, or a godly friend. Just remember to seek out the wisdom of THE Counselor first!

THE REVEALER

"Things which eye has not seen and ear has not heard,
and which have not entered the heart of man…"
To us God revealed them through the Spirit.

1 CORINTHIANS 2:9–10

*G*od has filled the pages of Scripture with promises and guarantees. And He will not fail to deliver on even one of them.

In fact, the apostle Paul wrote that the good things God has prepared "for those who love Him" (v. 9) are so awesome we can't even imagine what they are. And Paul should know, because he was caught up in a vision and got to take a glimpse into heaven (2 Corinthians 12:1–4).

So if the things of God are so wonderful that we can't even start to grasp them, how do we even know anything about them?

Enter the Holy Spirit. (Thank goodness Paul didn't stop writing at verse 9!) One of the Spirit's ministries is as the Revealer of the things of God. In the upper room, Jesus told His disciples that the Helper He was going to send would take the things Jesus wanted to tell them and reveal those things.

Have you ever had the experience of learning something new about the Lord, and then just basking in that new understanding? That's the Holy Spirit doing His job as Revealer.

Do you ever wonder if God has something more for your marriage than you're experiencing—something greater than you could imagine? Then why not get on your knees together and ask the Revealer to reveal it to you!

THE POWER SOURCE — 1

"Apart from Me you can do nothing."

JOHN 15:5

*T*he night before He was crucified, Jesus shared some critical information with His disciples.

He knew they would need supernatural help after His departure, so He spent much of that precious time teaching about the Person and ministry of the Holy Spirit. Four times, Jesus said a divine Helper would be sent after He left (John 14:14, 26; 15:26; 16:7).

Then Jesus dropped the statement above on His men. There was no way they could please the Lord or serve Him effectively by mere human effort.

It's an important truth for us, too. If you have discovered your own spiritual insufficiency, you are a good candidate for the ministry of the Holy Spirit. If not, you are a good candidate for spiritual disaster.

In the original language of Scripture, the word Jesus used for the Holy Spirit, "Helper," is a pregnant term. Some versions translate it "counselor" or "advocate," because it literally means "one called alongside to help," that is, to enable.

As I said, Jesus knew His followers would need divine power to pull off what He wanted them to do. And He knew where they were going to get that power: from the enabling presence of the Spirit.

God never intended us to manage this business of marriage and parenting on our own. We have One who comes alongside to give us strength.

THE POWER SOURCE — 2

*"I am sending forth the promise of My Father
upon you…stay in the city until you are clothed
with power from on high."*

LUKE 24:49

When Jesus walked on this earth, His disciples could always count on Him. Whenever the disciples needed help, He was always there.

When they needed a friend, Jesus was a faithful friend. When they were discouraged, Jesus was there to encourage them. When they were defeated, Jesus was there to pick them up. When they were afraid out on the sea and wondering how they were going to make it, Jesus walked on the water and calmed their fears.

Whatever these men needed, Jesus was there to provide. So when they heard that Jesus was leaving, the question on the floor was "Who is going to help us?" In other words, "Jesus, if we're going to keep on keeping on, who's going to help us when we're down and encourage us when we're discouraged? Who's going to strengthen us when we're weak? Who's going to lead us when we're confused? You did all that for us."

The answer? Jesus will continue ministering to and empowering His people through the Holy Spirit.

All over the world people hunger to know the power and presence of the living God, and go to almost any length to seek it. You and I have the awesome privilege to experience "God with us," every day of our lives. Cultivate that presence!

A UNIQUE PERSON — 1

The fellowship of the Holy Spirit be with you all.

2 CORINTHIANS 13:14

There's a lot wrapped up in the name "Holy Spirit."

The Spirit is holy because He is God, totally separate from all that is unlike who and what God is. This title also focuses attention on His primary work in the life of believers: to progressively conform us to the image of Christ, the process we call sanctification (1 Peter 3:13–16).

The Holy Spirit is spirit because He is nonmaterial. Both the Hebrew and Greek words for *spirit* mean "wind, breath." The Holy Spirit is the very breath or wind of God. And, like the wind, He wields great power even though He's invisible. So you can't relate to Him simply by trying to use your five senses.

Now I don't mean Casper the Friendly Ghost. I mean the invisible reality of almighty God. So the Holy Spirit is not some kind of impersonal "power" or "force." He is a Person, with emotions, personality, and will.

How can we explain such invisible realities? It's like trying to explain electricity. You know electricity is there. You know it's powerful. But how do you describe it in regular language? So it is with the wonderful mysteries of the Holy Spirit. But Jesus made it clear that the Holy Spirit is knowable. We who know Christ can know the One He sent.

As we walk through our day, we need to learn those attitudes and actions that grieve Him—as well as those things that please Him. He is the closest of close friends, and hurting Him should be the last thing we'd ever want to do.

A UNIQUE PERSON — 2

The fellowship of the Holy Spirit be with you all.

2 CORINTHIANS 13:14

Why doesn't the world know the Holy Spirit (John 14:17)? For the same reason you can't pick up radio stations if you don't have a radio. Radio waves are blasting through the air all the time, but you need a receiver to pick up the signal.

The world does not have a spiritual receiver. But if you know Jesus Christ, He has implanted within you a receiver to pick up heaven's signals so you can tune in to the very voice of God. So in the midst of discouragement, fear, loneliness, insecurity, or even sin, we can tune in to the Holy Spirit.

The living truth about this Third Member of the Trinity isn't just some cold, doctrinal formula unrelated to day-to-day living. He is part of our lives because He is a Person who lives within us.

People often say, "I wish Jesus were here so I could talk to Him." He *is* here, and you can talk to Him—if you understand the Holy Spirit's Person and ministry.

If the Holy Spirit lives within each partner in your marriage and within each member of your family, His love and power and holiness ought to be evident in your home life.

STEWARDSHIP BEATS OWNERSHIP

The earth is the LORD's, and all it contains,
the world, and those who dwell in it.

PSALM 24:1

*I*t's my contention that being a steward under God is the best way to live on Planet Earth…and beats ownership every time!

A steward in Bible times was someone who administered or managed another person's property. A steward didn't own anything, but oversaw everything for the owner. He was accountant, foreman, field boss, and office manager all rolled into one.

Stewardship is God's will and plan for His people. When you and your spouse decide to operate your household as a stewardship under God, you are aligning yourselves with His will. That's a decision He can bless.

Tell me….If Congress were to eliminate the tax deductions for home ownership…would it change your mind about being a homeowner? You might be better off to rent. Why? Because when someone else owns the house, he is responsible for it, not you. If the roof leaks, it's his job to get it fixed. All you have to do is live there and keep the yard mowed.

In the same way, stewardship has real advantages. It's the way to live in obedience to God—and as the Owner, He takes the responsibility. A steward owns nothing, but manages everything under God's ownership.

I don't know about you, but I can't think of anyone I'd rather have as the Owner of my life than Jesus Christ!

WHAT'S MY PART?

*Honor the LORD from your wealth
and from the first of all your produce.*

PROVERBS 3:9

As long as we live in God's world, we need to recognize that He owns it. There's only one Boss.

God has given me the privilege of loving Lois, but she belongs to Him. So do the children God is allowing me to raise. And I belong to Him, too.

What's the concept behind a tithe, then, giving God ten percent of what we make?

God established the tithe with Israel in the Old Testament. He told the people, "I want the first ten percent of everything you produce, whether it's the crops in your fields or the animals that are born to your flocks and herds" (see Leviticus 27:30–33).

The tithe was a way of saying, "God, I acknowledge that You own it all, and gave it all to me. I realize the rest is Yours, too."

See, we get it all mixed up. We figure if we give God ten dollars out of our hundred, the other ninety belongs to us. But giving is designed to remind us that the whole hundred bucks belongs to God. He graciously allows us to keep ninety for our needs, but it's all His.

Giving God's portion back to Him off the top of the paycheck—before you pay any bills—is a way of saying you know who the real Owner is!

R-E-S-P-E-C-T

"If I am a father, where is My honor?
And if I am a master, where is My respect?"

MALACHI 1:6

As you see above, God had some pointed questions for Israel. They were dishonoring the Lord by giving Him the worst of their flock for sacrifice rather than the best, as the Law prescribed (Malachi 1:7–8).

The people would look among their sheep, see a nice fat one, and say, "We can't give that one to the Lord. It's worth too much." So they set aside the valuable sheep for themselves. Then they found the sheep that were lame, diseased, or born with defects, and offered these to the Lord, hoping He would accept their sacrifice.

These people were giving God their leftovers, the junk they didn't want, and saying, "Lord, You ought to be happy we're giving You something."

But God said, "Oh, really? If you think that kind of offering is acceptable, try giving it to your governor. Offer him what you're offering Me, and see whether he'll take it."

The point is unmistakable. If an earthly ruler would be insulted by an offering of our leftover junk, how much more would the Ruler of heaven and earth be insulted by such an offering?

One reason many of us aren't seeing God actively at work in our lives is because we're giving Him our leftovers, and expecting Him to be satisfied. What He wants is to be first in everything.

CHOKING ON THE DETAILS

"Do not be worried about your life,
as to what you will eat or what you will drink;
nor for your body, as to what you will put on."

MATTHEW 6:25

Worry is like fog. I'm told that a fog that can cover seven blocks contains less than one glassful of water. Fog is a lot of smoke and mist and almost no substance.

That's what worry is, too. Yet it's choking the life out of some of us. Did you know that the word *worry* is from a word that means to strangle? That's what worry does to us. It gets us by the throat. It cuts off our emotional and spiritual air supply.

So Jesus tells us not to worry about what we're going to eat or drink or wear. Then He closes the verse with this question: "Is not life more than food, and the body more than clothing?" He's saying if you want to worry, worry about whether you're going to get up tomorrow.

Jesus' point is that if God gives you life, He's going to sustain your life. If you wake up alive tomorrow, that means God has obligated Himself to take care of you for at least one more day.

Jesus wants us to focus on loving and serving Him. He wants us to put Him first. When we do that, He'll worry about what is second, third, and fourth.

Check over your mental worry list (don't tell me you don't have one!). Anything there too big for God? Then quit worrying!

DON'T CALL HIM FATHER,
AND THEN WORRY

"Do not worry about tomorrow;
for tomorrow will care for itself.
Each day has enough trouble of its own."

MATTHEW 6:34

know Someone who knows all about tomorrow, and He tells
me not to worry about what's ahead.

When you give Jesus Christ your worries, that really takes the
pressure off. You don't need to be under stress about tomorrow.
Why? Because Jesus says if you will look after His concerns on
earth—His kingdom and righteousness (v. 33)—He will look after
your concerns.

That doesn't mean you can stay in bed tomorrow and forget
about work. We still need to live responsibly. But Jesus' command
not to worry about tomorrow means we can turn the worry over to
the One who has already been to tomorrow and back.

Now I'm not perfect at this because I worry sometimes, just like
you do. But God takes me to task for all my fretting. He says, "Stop
worrying, Evans. It's a sin for you to call me Father and then act like
I'm not going to take care of you."

The last sentence in today's verse means that God is not going
to give you tomorrow's grace today. He's only going to give you
enough grace for today. So if you're worried about tomorrow and
next week and next year, you're in trouble, because God is not helping you with tomorrow yet.

Put God first, and you can stop worrying.

WHAT'S THE BIG SECRET?

*If we have food and covering,
with these we shall be content.*

1 TIMOTHY 6:8

One of the great rewards for faithful stewardship—giving to God the best of our time, talents, and treasure—is contentment.

Contentment is a quality of life so elusive that the world has been chasing it for centuries and still hasn't found it. The apostle Paul did call it a "secret" in Philippians 4:12, but it isn't a secret because God is hiding it from us. It's a secret because contentment can only be found when we do things God's way.

In fact, in the very next verse of Philippians, Paul reveals the secret: "I can do all things through Him who strengthens me" (v. 13). The secret to being a contented steward is to have such a dynamic relationship with Jesus Christ that your circumstances just don't matter. You're just tickled to death to belong to Him.

Now the reason this is a "secret" even to a lot of Christians is because we haven't slowed down long enough to learn it. God can't teach us this lesson when we're knocking ourselves out to get ahead and don't have time to listen.

So Paul says if you have food and clothing, rest in God's good provision. Learning to live contentedly with what God provides frees us up to pursue His will and His kingdom agenda. And that's when life really begins to get exciting.

LEAVING YOUR STUFF BEHIND

We have brought nothing into the world,
so we cannot take anything out of it either.

1 TIMOTHY 6:7

*I*n today's verse, Paul simply tells us an easily observable truth about life: We came into this world materially naked, and we're going out the same way.

This is a great reason to be content with what we have: It's all going to stay on earth when you check out anyway, so why kill yourself trying to accumulate it?

Why break your neck trying to gain stuff that God may give you anyway if you will live as His steward, faithfully giving back to Him and trusting Him to meet your needs?

You say, "But wait a minute. We don't have a house yet. We only have one car. Does God want us to stay where we are right now?"

I can't answer that for you. But let me say that I don't believe Scripture tells us we should never seek to better ourselves or our earnings.

God is saying just be content until He pleases to give them to you. But don't let them become your obsession, or divert your spiritual focus.

"People who want to get rich," Paul writes, "fall into temptation and a trap" (1 Timothy 6:9, NIV). It doesn't have to be that way. Since all your stuff is staying behind when you leave, don't set your heart on it!

WHAT'S YOUR PASSION?

*Those who want to get rich fall into temptation
and a snare and many foolish and harmful desires
which plunge men into ruin and destruction.*

1 TIMOTHY 6:9

*Y*ou know how a snare works. The hunter covers it with
brush and uses bait to lure the animal. Just when the victim thinks
he has a meal, the trap has him!

That's how money works, too. You think you have it, but it has
you.

Today's verse reminds us that God is not trying to hold out on
us, or keep us from something good. An inordinate desire for money
leads to destruction. Does that sound like a route you want to take?

Paul tells us, "The love of money is a root of all sorts of evil"
(v. 10). Don't misread that. Money itself is neutral. The problem is
in the heart, not in the paper.

You know you love money if your passion for it outweighs your
passion for God...when you have to choose between money and
God, and money wins...when your career keeps you off your knees,
out of the Word, and out of fellowship with the saints.

Do you want to free yourself from the snare? Go to God and
say, "You're going to be number one with me. I'm going to
arrange my life by Your priority scale, be Your steward, and give
You my best. And I trust You now to fulfill Your Word and take
responsibility for my needs."

TEARING DOWN FAMILY STRONGHOLDS — 1

Let all bitterness and wrath and anger and clamor and slander be put away from you, along with all malice.

EPHESIANS 4:31

*T*here are a lot of angry people out there—angry at parents, mates, children, or even themselves, for things that have happened in the past. And yes, if a wrong has been committed against you, you have a right to be angry. Anger at sin is valid.

But prolonged anger violates the scriptural command to resolve it quickly, and provides the wedge Satan needs to slip into your life and build that unresolved anger into a stronghold. Paul says it very clearly in Ephesians 4:27.

For some of us, not only has the sun gone down on our anger, but the moon has gone down as well. In other cases, the week has passed and we're still angry.

This kind of situation makes everyone else in the family pay for what one or two people have done. Suppose you were eating with your family at a restaurant, and when you were finished the waiter brought you your bill—and the bills for everyone else who was eating in the restaurant at that time.

You'd say, "It's not fair to make me pay for what everybody else ate!" In the same way, it's not fair for your family members to pay for what someone else did. Don't let anger rob your family of the joy and peace God wants to reign in your home.

TEARING DOWN FAMILY STRONGHOLDS — 2

*Husbands, love your wives and
do not be embittered against them.*

COLOSSIANS 3:19

*I*t's easy to *say* we need to resolve our anger quickly, but it's another thing to do it. How can we put a stop to the cycle of destructive family anger?

One analogy that helps me is to treat unresolved anger the way we treat a videotape in our VCR. When a particular tape has finished playing, we push the eject button and take it out.

Now, the advantage of a VCR is that it allows you to play a tape over and over again, as many times as you want. But even when you get a new tape, you can't play it until you first eject the old tape.

Unresolved anger is like that old videotape. You play it and replay it and keep reliving what it was that made you angry.

You have to quit playing that anger tape. And the only way I know to do that is to hit the eject button of forgiveness and release the offender. Otherwise, Satan will continue using your anger to defeat you in spiritual warfare and infect your family with his poison.

When Satan tries to get you to play that old anger videotape, serve notice on him that in the name of Jesus Christ, that tape has been ejected!

TEARING DOWN FAMILY STRONGHOLDS — 3

Have this attitude in yourselves which was also in Christ Jesus, who, although He existed in the form of God...
emptied Himself, taking the form of a bond-servant.

PHILIPPIANS 2:5—7

*S*elfishness is a big problem in our day because so many people are after "personal fulfillment," no matter what the cost to their marriages or families. We expect children to be selfish because they're born in sin and haven't learned better yet. But it's a lot easier to deal with selfishness in a child than in an adult.

Satan looks for selfishness in a home so he can exploit it for his purposes. Displaying selfishness is like saying, "Satan, you are welcome into our home."

Now, you may be saying, "I'm trying to do this family thing right, but it just isn't working."

The problem may be that you're trying the wrong thing. The issue isn't just that you're trying, but *what* you are trying. Are you using your spiritual weapons to attack family strongholds, or are you using the world's methods and simply sprinkling a little Jesus on top?

That's what a lot of Christian families are doing. They're trying, but they're using the wrong weapons. Check out Ephesians 6:10–17 and you'll read about the spiritual weapons God has given us. They are awesomely powerful and effective against Satan. Use them and take your family back!

It takes spiritual firepower to defeat our spiritual foe. In Christ, we have all the firepower we need!

FIGHT FOR YOUR FAMILY

*Remember the Lord who is great and awesome,
and fight for your brothers, your sons, your daughters,
your wives and your houses.*

NEHEMIAH 4:14

*N*ehemiah has a great word of encouragement and challenge for us as Christian parents.

As Nehemiah and his fellow Israelites were rebuilding Jerusalem, they were threatened by their enemies. So Nehemiah called them to remember the Lord, and fight for their families.

It's the same for us. When you're at war, you can't afford to let the enemy build strongholds right in your backyard.

In the Garden of Eden, Satan won the first round in this warfare. But Jesus has taken it from there. Genesis 3:15 predicted that Jesus Christ would give the enemy a blow to his head, and Satan would never be the same again.

That blow was delivered on the cross of Calvary, so keep on fighting for your marriage and family. Satan does not have any right to build his strongholds under your roof if you are under the blood of Jesus Christ.

God evicted Adam and Eve from Eden, because of their sin at a tree. But they left with the promise of a coming Redeemer ringing in their ears. That Redeemer came and died on another tree, the cross of Calvary.

That means no matter how deeply Satan has infiltrated your family, because of that other tree, the cross, you have hope in God's salvation. Come against Satan's strongholds in the power of Jesus' name!

JUST KEEP SHOVELING!

We ourselves speak proudly of you among the churches
of God for your perseverance and faith in the midst
of all your persecutions and afflictions which you endure.

2 THESSALONIANS 1:4

On a break after a heavy snowstorm, a man went out to shovel his driveway. But just when he had his driveway clear, the storm returned and dumped several more inches—and he had to go out and do it again. This happened several times, and finally, the frustrated man shouted, "That's it! This is a waste of my time, and I'm not going to do it anymore."

Does that sound a little like your relationship with your spouse right about now? Does it seem that every time you get rid of some negative issues between you, something else comes along to test and try your relationship? Does it seem that every time you try to resolve one conflict, another comes along?

Keep shoveling, my friends. Don't allow personality differences and conflicts to keep you from keeping on. Keep fasting, keep praying, keep loving, and keep communicating. Keep pushing closer to your heavenly Father! Remember there is no pit so deep that God can't reach down and rescue you.

One last note on the man shoveling snow. A few days after he decided to give it up, the sun came out and melted the snow. In the same way, if you persevere, God's presence and power will melt away the very things that have afflicted you in your marriage.

REPLAYING THE PAST

*Bear with each other and forgive whatever
grievances you may have against one another.
Forgive as the Lord forgave you.*

COLOSSIANS 3:13, NIV

Remember Friday night dances in high school? And remember how one song seemed to stand out above the rest? When I was in high school, the song we couldn't wait for and couldn't hear too many times was "Stay," by the Dells. It was a nice, slow-moving dance song, and when it was over, we wanted the deejay to play it again.

Replaying your favorite song can bring back pleasant memories of days gone by. But the devil likes to do some "replaying" of his own. He wants to keep us stuck with our negative emotions. He likes to replay episodes from our lives that bring back feelings of sadness, anger, bitterness, and depression. He wants those things in the past to stay with us, and to keep dragging us down. He wants to remind us of those dark hours, even though we may be years removed from them.

And here's something you need to know: He *really* loves doing that to marriages. There is nothing more destructive to a marriage than dwelling on past wounds, disappointments, and wrongs. And trust me, if you're married long enough, you'll face those things!

We need to let go of the past hurts and move forward, knowing God has great things ahead for us as we walk with Him and trust Him.

PRESENT PROBLEMS

Are they servants of Christ?—I speak as if insane—
I more so; in far more labors, in far more imprisonments,
beaten times without number, often in danger of death.

2 CORINTHIANS 11:23

*T*he devil doesn't only try to bring us down emotionally and spiritually by replaying the past. No, he's too smart for that! He also likes to get us to focus on the trials and pains of the present—in hopes of taking our eyes off of the *good* that God is bringing into our lives.

But it doesn't have to be that way. You want an example? Look at the apostle Paul. If anyone had a reason to be depressed over his present circumstances, this was the guy. He'd been imprisoned, beaten, threatened with death, stoned, shipwrecked, bitten by a viper, falsely accused, and deprived of food, water, and sleep. He had more enemies than he could count, all wanting to bring him and his ministry down.

On the surface, Paul's life looked like a train wreck! Every day it seemed that something was going wrong for him. Yet, Paul was never depressed and never wanted to quit. On the contrary, it seemed that his struggles only strengthened his resolve to press on and accomplish what God had called him to do.

The reason? He tells us in 2 Corinthians 12:9: "But [the Lord] said to me, 'My grace is sufficient for you, for my power is made perfect in weakness'" (NIV).

WATCH HOW YOU THINK

For as he thinks within himself, so he is.

PROVERBS 23:7

Maybe you've never thought about it this way, but emotions don't have a mind of their own. They must "borrow" thoughts in order to emote off of them. In other words, emotions respond to what we think.

If emotions are a product of your thought life, then what you do in your thought life will go a long way in determining how you feel. If you allow the devil to control your thinking, then you'll feel like he wants you to feel. But if you allow God to control your thinking, then you will feel the way God wants you to feel. The devil wants you to feel depression, hopelessness, turmoil, and bitterness. God wants you to feel His peace, the deep-down peace that gives you hope and surpasses understanding.

Jesus once told his disciples, "You will know the truth, and the truth will make you free" (John 8:32). That means not just hearing or reading God's truth, but knowing it and internalizing it. And if you know the truth about God and about how He feels about you, then you can be freed from emotional strongholds.

As we learn about our true identity in Christ, when we begin to think and meditate on those truths, the devil no longer has power to hold us hostage to negative emotions.

THE TRUTH OF JESUS

"In the world you have tribulation,
but take courage; I have overcome the world."

JOHN 16:33

*N*othing helps us overcome negative emotions like focusing on the truth, the truth that Jesus gave us. In fact, Jesus gave us two very profound truths that we can cling to when life gets tough.

Here's truth number one: "In the world you have tribulation." Many people make the mistake of thinking that when they accept Christ as their Lord and Savior, all their problems will melt away. The truth is, many of us have experienced our hardest days *after* we become Christians. As Jesus said, we find tribulation and trouble in this world.

But here's the "good" part of our Lord's promise. He tells us that no matter how bad a day we're having, no matter what we go through, we can be of good cheer, because He has overcome the world.

As long as we're on this earth, we're going to have problems, perplexities, and frustrations. We're going to see evil, we're going to hear bad news. But we have a choice in all of this. We can allow all these things to bring us down and make us depressed, or we can focus on the fact that God is in control of everything that happens, and that He has overcome the devices of this world.

When we have that kind of God focus, then we can daily live in the kind of cheer Jesus calls us to live in.

"EDIFYING" SPEECH

*Do not let any unwholesome talk come out of your mouths,
but only what is helpful for building others up
according to their needs, that it may benefit those who listen.*

EPHESIANS 4:29, NIV

*M*any Christians—including husbands and wives—take great pride in speaking their minds, no matter how it affects others. I've had married people tell me, "I speak my mind so my spouse won't miss what I had to say."

I tell people with this attitude that they are halfway there. Yes, you told the truth, but did you do it in a wholesome, constructive way? In other words, did you speak the truth in such a way that it built up and didn't tear down the other person?

Paul tells us to speak the truth in a way that "edifies." The word *edification* means to build up and to bless the other person. He's not talking about sugarcoating the truth so that nobody knows what you're talking about. We need to speak truthfully, but in a way that blesses others and doesn't leave them feeling condemned and defeated.

Sadly, the way a lot of husbands and wives talk to each other— making cutting and demeaning remarks—makes you wonder how they can have a Bible in their house. "Truth" that tears down, demeans, and destroys is no more biblical than a lie.

Yes, tell the truth, but do it in a way that builds up and fixes something. Since the two of you have become one, you'll be building up yourself in the process.

"CHANGE ORDERS"

Instead, you ought to say, "If the Lord wills,
we will live and also do this or that."
But as it is, you boast in your arrogance;
all such boasting is evil.

JAMES 4:15–16

*I*n a recent church building project, we ended up with some "change orders." Change orders are the adjustments we must make when our plans can't be followed the way we originally drew them. They are, in a word, contingencies.

Some of those changes weren't what we would have preferred, but they were necessary and imperative because of construction issues we ran into. Now, we had a detailed plan for that building. But there are also change orders. There are interruptions and changes to that careful plan.

God has "change orders" when it comes to our plans and dreams for life on this side of heaven. And we must give Him the right to issue those change orders—puzzling or painful as they may be to us at the time. Contingencies happen. Events over which you and I have no control.

James tells us we need to have a heart attitude that acknowledges there is something—Someone—bigger operating here than just us. That is what he calls "the will of God."

When we make plans, we need to submit them to the Master Builder for approval. And we need to be willing to accept his "change orders" when our plans don't line up with His.

God's plans are vast and complex beyond imagining. And He knows exactly how and where we fit best.

THE BEST PLAN YOU CAN FOLLOW

"For I know the plans I have for you," declares the LORD,
"plans to prosper you and not to harm you,
plans to give you hope and a future."

JEREMIAH 29:11, NIV

God has a custom-designed plan for you and your spouse.

Sometimes we get angry with God when he doesn't rubber-stamp our plans. But instead of fussing at Him for interrupting or changing our programs, we ought to be asking Him in what new direction He wants us to go, what new plan He wants us to adopt. When God changes and adjusts our plans, He just may be throwing us a faith curve ball. So instead of getting mad, we should rejoice that He has a perfect plan just for us. We should be glad that He cares enough about us to interrupt us, so that He might accomplish something through us that we may have no way of seeing now.

As long as we live on this earth, we're all in the process of God's construction, and He's not finished with any of us yet. That's good news. We need to remember that no matter where we are or how old we are, it's never too late for us to discover and start following God's plan.

Do you feel overwhelmed by past failures? Remember, God can hit a bull's-eye with a crooked stick. But what's even better is that He can give you back the years the locusts have taken away, the years you thought you lost, the years you regret. He is God!

KNOWING YOUR LIMITATIONS

You do not know what your life will be like tomorrow.
You are just a vapor that appears for a
little while and then vanishes away.

JAMES 4:14

The teakettle whistles on the stove, and you see the steam rush out—and vanish just as quickly. *That* is a vapor. And that is our lives.

James wants us to make plans but not to *depend* on those plans, not to chisel them in stone. You and I are finite beings, and our perspective will always be limited by time. But God is an eternal being, above time, who sees the future as easily as He views the past. As our Lord declared, "I am the Alpha and the Omega—the beginning and the end…I am the one who is, who always was, and who is still to come, the Almighty One" (Revelation 1:8, NLT).

If you've lived long enough, you know that much of life is like going through a jungle without a map. Just as soon as you think you've got north separated from south, something comes along and sets the compass dial spinning like a top.

God will forever keep you guessing. And He will never let you get so comfortable in your sufficiency that you lose your need to depend on Him.

No matter how carefully we lay out our plans or calculate all the angles, we have no guarantees in this life, aside from the fact that we have a Savior who loves us and desires our best.

OUT WITH THE OLD

You were taught, with regard to your former way of life,
to put off your old self, which is being corrupted
by its deceitful desires; to be made new in the attitude
of your minds; and to put on the new self,
created to be like God in true righteousness and holiness.

EPHESIANS 4:22—24, NIV

I recently hosted a couple at our home, and they carried their long-running battle right into our living room.

Still arguing and fighting over issues that were now years old in their marriage, they were creating chaos that worsened by the year.

I told them, "You can't fix the old, and I don't have the time to help you try. I can't unravel all that tangled and knotted string that's brought you up to this point. But if you want to discuss creating something new, we can do that."

Many of us make that same mistake in our own marriage. Instead of looking for a fresh start, we keep going back and dredging up old issues.

Paul tells us that when we come to Christ, we need to put on the "new self." When we don't do that, it's like taking a shower, then putting our sweaty, dirty, old clothes back on. In effect, we're canceling out the purity that came as a result of the cleansing.

When we come to Jesus, He gives us a new way of thinking, a new way of walking, a new way of talking, a new way of relating. We can never undo or untangle the mistakes of the past. Only the blood of Jesus Christ can take care of those. Our task is to start anew…today.

STOP STEALING!

He who has been stealing must steal no longer,
but must work, doing something useful with his own hands,
that he may have something to share with those in need.

EPHESIANS 4:28, NIV

*S*tealing means taking something that belongs to another without his or her permission. But today's verse suggests that there may be more to it than that.

Paul has already told us that we're members of one another, so when we fail to give to others what God has designed us to give, we're really stealing from them.

Our physical bodies are examples of that. When my hand fails to do something it was designed to do, then another part of my body gets overloaded with work. If I were to try to lift up a computer monitor using only my right hand, then my left hand has "overloaded" my right hand. So my right hand has ripped off my left hand by leaving it out there by itself.

One of the ways we steal from others is by desiring to be served while refusing to serve. We do that in our churches, but worse yet, we do it at home with our spouses and children. When we come to Christ, we make a commitment to be a part of His body, and that means service. Likewise, when we enter into a marriage relationship, we make a commitment to serve our spouses. When we fail to serve in these kinds of relationships, we steal from the ones to whom we've made a commitment.

KNOWING THE "BAKER"

For the LORD God is a sun and shield;
the LORD gives grace and glory;
no good thing does He withhold from
those who walk uprightly.

PSALM 84:11

A mother once spent several hours baking a birthday cake for her son. It was a beautiful cake, with thick chocolate icing—just the kind he liked. Later, all the little boy's friends showed up for his party. After the boy blew out the candles, his mother sliced the cake.

Problem was, there were too many guests and not enough cake. They ran out before the guest of honor could get a slice.

"Aren't you upset that you didn't get a piece of your own birthday cake?" someone asked the boy.

"Not really," he replied. "I know the baker."

Our attitude about the blessings God gives us should be just like that little boy's. We don't need to worry about our slice of the blessings when we know the One who blesses.

Sometimes in our humanness it's easy for us to get wrapped up in what we want God to do for us. But if you know Jesus Christ, you know the Baker, and you never have to worry about what, when, and how He chooses to bless you.

Are you and your spouse praying with expectation for God to do something for you today? If so, then all you need to do is rest in the fact that your heavenly Father loves you, that He knows your needs, and that His timing is perfect.

MAKING THE CHOICE OF GRACE

"Mary has chosen the good part,
which shall not be taken away from her."

LUKE 10:42

*S*ome marriages operate by performance. The wife says, "I cook and do the laundry because that's my job description."

The husband says, "I go to work and mow the lawn because that's what's expected of me."

Now it's true that marriage involves responsibilities and routine. But the routine was never meant to degenerate into a rut that both partners come to despise.

When you were first married, your relationship was predicated on love and grace, not performance. Even though the performance was still there, it was driven by relationship, not by a sense of duty.

Jesus spoke to that contrast the day He came to Mary and Martha's for dinner. Mary chose the intimacy of devotion to Christ; Martha chose duty over devotion, and wound up getting angry at Mary and fussing at Jesus.

Does your marriage ever sound like the exchange between Martha and Jesus? Do you ever hear, or ever say, "How come I'm doing all this while you aren't holding up your end of the bargain?"

These are the words of a performance marriage. It is predicated on how much each partner does, not on how much the husband and wife love each other.

Here's the good news. You can regain a grace-based marriage in a short time. All it takes is a choice to forgive and to extend grace to each other.

BEING YOUR WIFE'S SANCTIFIER

*We have been sanctified through
the offering of the body of Jesus Christ.*

HEBREWS 10:10

If a husband is going to live out God's kingdom agenda in his marriage, he must be his wife's sanctifier.

This doesn't mean he can make his wife holy. Only God can do that. I'm using the term *sanctifier* in a different sense.

When a man marries a woman, he also marries her history and her family. He has to accept the good parts and the bad parts. The good parts he enjoys. The bad parts he may not discover until after the honeymoon.

The husband doesn't get to see it all before the wedding. You only see your future wife with her makeup on. You only see her on her "party behavior," so you don't get the whole deal until after you're married.

But if you love your wife, you will be her sanctifier. The word *sanctification* means to set apart for special use. That is, to place a person in a unique category, to take her from where she is to where she needs to go…to help her *grow*.

A husband's job is to make his marriage something special, something set apart. What Jesus is to the church, a husband is to be to his mate.

My brother, if that sounds like a task that's too big for you, you've got the idea! Ask God for His strength to be His man today.

Fall

WORRY IS A CHOICE

*In Your book were all written the days that were ordained
for me, when as yet there was not one of them.*

PSALM 139:16

Worry isn't a bad habit. It's a sin.

Did God wake you up this morning? Then it's a sin to worry,
because you're saying that while God may have the ability to keep
you alive, He doesn't have the ability to clothe, feed, or shelter you.
You're saying, "My Daddy doesn't care."

Not only is worry sinful, it's also *useless*. Far from extending
your life, it may actually shorten it (Matthew 6:27). There's one
thing we need to know about our lives. Our days on earth have been
appointed by God.

That's not fatalism. That's biblical reality. God has allotted to all
of us our life span, and when He's ready to take us home, no
amount of jogging or oat bran or anything else will delay it one day.
(Those things will just help you look better on your way out.)

So if God has your days firmly in His hand, worrying about the
next one won't do a thing for you.

You say, "But, Tony, I'm just a worrier. I can't help it." Yes, you
can. Worry is a choice. You can decide *not* to worry. The Bible
wouldn't command it if you weren't able to do it.

The real issue is whether God is first in your life. If He is, you
can trust Him to take care of everything else.

SATAN'S STRONGHOLDS

*The weapons of our warfare are not of the flesh,
but divinely powerful for the destruction of fortresses.*

2 CORINTHIANS 10:4

*Y*ou may not know it, but Satan wants to start a "building boom" today by erecting his fortresses or strongholds in your family.

Let me explain that a fortress (or stronghold) is a way of thinking that Satan seeks to build in our minds, giving him a tremendous advantage in spiritual warfare.

A stronghold is a mindset that accepts as inevitable what we know is contrary to the will of God. Some examples are addictions, a defeatist attitude that says "I can't" do something when God says "you can," a false view of ourselves, or a belief that our marriage or family is so far gone that even God can't save it.

This brief list shows that Satan uses his strongholds to get a grip on a family and keep it from being everything God intended it to be.

Satan has been at this stuff for a long time, and he knows what he is doing. He built his first stronghold right in the middle of the first family—right in the middle of the Garden of Eden—and he's been after more ever since.

This is serious stuff, but read today's verse again. We have powerful weapons to tear down strongholds. Pray that God will show you how to use the spiritual authority you already have in Him.

Prayers That Get Delivered

*He who searches the hearts knows what the mind
of the Spirit is, because He intercedes for the
saints according to the will of God.*

ROMANS 8:27

$\mathcal{D}$o you know why so many of our prayers hit the ceiling?
Because they're not from the heart. The only prayers the Holy Spirit
delivers to the Father are *heart* prayers.

If we're just repeating words we learned or mouthing formula
prayers without engaging our spirit, there's no heart in that. And if
there is nothing in the heart when we pray, the Holy Spirit has nothing to deliver to the Father, because the Father searches the heart.

Since this is true, it follows that God will respond even to a
confused, inarticulate prayer when it comes from the heart.
Sometimes we are in such need that all we can do is call out like
Peter when he began to sink in the water, "Save me, Lord!"

That wasn't much of a prayer, but it definitely came from Peter's
heart! And the Lord reached out and rescued His man.

Too many times we worry about getting the words right when
we pray. But God isn't searching for articulate prayers. The reason
Jesus condemned many of the Pharisees who prayed nice prayers in
public was that there was nothing behind those beautiful words. It
was all for show.

God is more interested in two sentences from our hearts than
He is in two hours from our lips, because only heart prayers get
delivered.

WORTH THE EFFORT

*No one ever hated his own flesh,
but nourishes and cherishes it.*

EPHESIANS 5:29

One of the best ways a husband can nourish his wife and find out what she needs is...to ask.

Wives tell us they need affection, a sense of security, communication, and a sense of being cared for and esteemed. When these are absent, it's no mystery that a wife's passion for sex dies.

We men have a long way to go in learning the art of intimacy with our wives. We need to learn that for a woman, intimacy involves the whole person and the whole house. It involves the compliment you make about the meal, how you come in the door from work, or how you treat her when *she* comes home from work.

Many couples who tell me they have a physical problem really have an intimacy problem, a relational blockage. Because of this, they can't get the physical part of their marriage on track.

Husband, to nourish and cherish your wife means your duty is to her, not to yourself. When some men say, "I want to meet her needs," what they really mean is, "I want her to meet *my* needs."

Until you are willing to take the time and make the investment to understand your wife and her needs, you will never be able to meet them.

And just a final word here. It's *worth* taking that time!

LOOKING IN THE RIGHT DIRECTION

If you have been raised up with Christ,
keep seeking the things above, where Christ is,
seated at the right hand of God.

COLOSSIANS 3:1

*Y*ou can't drive a car without looking ahead. It's okay to glance in the rearview mirror once in a while, but you have to get your focus right in order to drive. You have to be looking in the direction you need to go.

Many of us are getting lost and veering off the path in our spiritual lives because we're trying to move forward while looking in the wrong direction. We are looking at ourselves, at other people, at our circumstances, or even looking backward at the past.

But the only way you and I can move forward in our Christian lives is by fixing our focus firmly above, on the exalted Christ. He is to be the object of our focus.

Paul urges us to seek the things that are above because that's where Christ is, and because we have been raised with Christ and seated with Him in the heavenly places (Ephesians 2:6).

Paul is telling us to view earthly things through heavenly glasses. We need to use the lens of heaven to draw our conclusions about earth.

Therefore, since we are seated with Christ in heaven, we can stand strong on earth because we are linked to the ruling authority of the universe.

Lean on that link today. Find the strength you need in your connection with Him.

TRANSMITTING GODLY VALUES

My son, observe the commandment of your father.

PROVERBS 6:20

One reason God created family was to give us a system for perpetuating and transferring values.

Now our children won't always *buy* our values. In fact, they may rebel against them. But that's a lot different from what we have today, which is children who don't have to rebel against parental values…because there's nothing there.

If you grew up in a home with values, even if you rebelled against those values, you had to work at it. You had to climb over mother whispering in your ear, even if you were many miles away from home at college, because that godly influence was there.

Proverbs 22:6 tells us: "Train up a child in the way he should go, even when he is old he will not depart from it." But this verse assumes a body of biblical data is being transmitted to our children, which God can use to touch their spirits.

I believe the future of our children and our nation still lies primarily in the hands of fathers. Yes, mothers are crucial to the process.

But I'm calling Christian men to stop making excuses and step up to the plate, ready to own and *fix* the problem of a lost, valueless society. Step one is to show your sons and daughters—and your wife—what it means to be a godly man.

A SAFE PLACE IN TROUBLED TIMES

The LORD's lovingkindnesses indeed never cease,
for His compassions never fail.

LAMENTATIONS 3:22

The book of Lamentations reads like a dirge for the city of Jerusalem, which—just as God told Jeremiah—had been overrun by its enemies.

Jeremiah looks around him and sees death and destruction on a nightmare scale. His world has fallen apart before his very eyes. He is alone and horrified and grieving at all he sees. But in the midst of the shock and sorrow, Jeremiah remembers God. He remembers that He is a loving and compassionate God.

These are the words of a man who knew God intimately. I can imagine that it was only Jeremiah's intimate relationship with the Lord that kept him from going completely over the edge in all his grief.

I believe we can follow Jeremiah's example in dealing with emotional upheaval. I believe that we can maintain such a close and intimate relationship with God that our circumstances—no matter how much they hurt and grieve us—can never take us to a point of utter hopelessness.

In short, we can overcome seasons of emotional upheaval by clinging to an intimate relationship with Christ. When we do that, we can know that our circumstances—and our wounded emotions—will never have the last word.

That word goes to our mighty Lord, who will love and care for us even when our world turns upside down.

REMEMBER HIS MERCIES

As the deer pants for the water brooks,
so my soul pants for You, O God.

PSALM 42:1

Where do you turn when the situations in your life threaten to drive you to despair, hopelessness, and depression? Today's verse tells us we're to turn to the same God we praised during the "good times."

As Psalm 42 opens, it sounds like a wonderful song of trust and worship. But it's also an urgent cry for deliverance in a very difficult time. Nothing is going right for the psalmist. He needs God's help, and he needs it fast!

This is a man who has been weeping bitterly (verse 3), who is depressed to the point of absolute despair (verses 5–6), and who wonders if God has forgotten him (verse 9). But at the same time, he finds hope in his memories of how God has worked in his life in days past. He remembers to praise God in the midst of his despair, and to turn to God for help (verses 4–5).

This is a great psalm of faith. For in the midst of all this man's discouragement, he looked at what God was going to do, even though he couldn't see it.

Days of heartache and trouble in your marriage and family aren't times to throw in the towel. They are times to remember God's mercy and provision in days past, and His strong helping hand today.

WE NEED EACH OTHER

*...not forsaking our own assembling together,
as is the habit of some, but encouraging one another.*

HEBREWS 10:25

*I*f you are suffering through negative emotions, Satan wants more than anything to keep you down, to keep you isolated, to keep you away from anyone who might encourage you and help you out of your depression. Your enemy knows and fears the power of true fellowship with other believers.

Church isn't just a place where you come to hear preaching and music, but a place where you come to find the encouragement—oftentimes from people who are going through some of the same kinds of things you are—to keep your eyes on the Lord, and not on your difficult circumstances.

We *need* that contact. God never intended us to wallow through our problems alone. We need to find people who have been through the same murky waters that we have, but have overcome through the power of Christ.

Someone with thoughts of suicide shouldn't hang out with others who want to end their own lives, and someone who is struggling in his or her marriage shouldn't spend time with those contemplating divorce. And someone who is trying to climb out of depression shouldn't hang out with depressing people. We need people in our lives who have seen the power of God to lift up wounded people.

And where do we find such people? In places of fellowship for the body of Christ!

THE LOOK OF FORGIVENESS

Be kind and compassionate to one another,
forgiving each other, just as in Christ God forgave you.

EPHESIANS 4:32, NIV

What is forgiveness? Forgiveness means canceling the debt, zeroing out the account. For example, if MasterCard writes you a letter telling you that your debt is canceled, but keeps sending you a bill, then the debt has never really gone away, has it? The company is sending you mixed signals!

Many married couples do that kind of thing. They say they forgive, but they keep sending one another the bills. Somehow, the old debt stays on the spouse's account, and keeps popping up again and again.

We need to forgive as our Father forgives! He keeps no record of our old bills and debts. Because of what Jesus accomplished on the cross for us, our account has been cleared and the debt is canceled forever. He will never send you a bill. Instead, He sends constant reminders of His kindness and compassion, His forgiveness and love.

When you say "I forgive you," you've gone halfway on the road to forgiveness. The next step is to demonstrate kindness and compassion to the one who has hurt or offended you. No matter how tempting it may be in an argument, never resend an old bill. The Bible tells us that love covers a multitude of sins.

So let it.

UPROOTING BITTERNESS

See to it that no one comes short of the grace of God;
that no root of bitterness springing up causes trouble,
and by it many be defiled.

HEBREWS 12:15

I once spoke with a woman who had been deeply hurt by her husband.

She told me, "He ought to spend every day of the rest of his life seeking my forgiveness."

This woman had allowed a root of bitterness to spread its poison through her heart...and her home. A root of bitterness means that the anger and rage over a past hurt has gone so deep and become so established that it controls, even defines, one's very existence. It means that you're going to hold on to that anger, no matter what.

"Your husband will never win," I told her. "He'll never say enough or do enough. He can't give you enough flowers, enough notes, enough apologies—because you'll never release him."

I've come to see the relationship between God's love and forgiveness as being like an ATM card and its personal identification number (PIN). When you put your debit card in the machine, you have to enter your PIN before you can access your money. In the Christian life, you've got a debit card called redemption, and it's your ticket to heaven. But when it comes to fully experiencing God's love in this world, He wants to see your pin number. He wants to see that you are willing to forgive and love others the way He forgives and loves you.

WORDS OF WISDOM AND KINDNESS

She opens her mouth in wisdom,
and the teaching of kindness is on her tongue.

PROVERBS 31:26

A man with a vile tongue is certainly bad enough, but there's nothing more offensive than being around a foul-mouthed woman. When she opens her mouth, you want to walk in the opposite direction.

What a contrast to the woman of honor described in today's verse. When this excellent wife speaks, *wisdom* comes out of her mouth. But what does this wisdom look like? It isn't something you acquire at college, and it doesn't come with a degree. Biblical wisdom is the ability to apply God's truth to life, communicating it in such a way that people can understand, enabling them to make good choices.

This kind of wisdom means having both knowledge of God and knowledge of life...and being able to connect the two.

An excellent, honorable wife is marked not only by her ability to teach through her words, but to teach through her words *at the right time*. That's because God has given her an innate ability to *feel* things. For that reason, an excellent wife knows what to say, how to say it, and when to say it. This kind of gracious wisdom comes when a woman is yielded to Christ, immersed in the Scriptures, and allows herself to be filled with the Holy Spirit.

When she speaks, people listen. Before she's said two words they'll know she's worth hearing.

A DISCIPLER

*But I want you to understand that Christ
is the head of every man,
and the man is the head of a woman,
and God is the head of Christ.*

1 CORINTHIANS 11:3

There are men who like today's verses because they think it gives them the God-ordained right to order others around. And there are women who are offended by today's verse, because they don't believe they should follow.

Both of those approaches to marital leadership are dead wrong.

Satan's tactic since the Garden of Eden has been to get men and women to reverse their God-given roles. Satan got Eve to become the leader, and Eve got Adam to become the follower, and all hell broke loose. It's been breaking loose ever since. When a woman looks around and can't find a leader, she'll become one herself.

But that's not how God ordained it. Even Jesus, when it comes to fulfilling God's purpose, does not operate independently, but under the headship of the Father. And if Jesus gladly submitted to authority, so can we.

Every Christian man is to place himself under the lordship of Jesus Christ. In other words, *if you want your wife to follow you, she must see you following the Lord.* If she sees you submit to Him, she will respond and follow you.

When a man refuses to submit to the lordship of Jesus Christ, when he says to his family, "This is my house, and I'm in charge here!" there will be conflict.

And he will have only himself to blame.

Demolition Is Easy

Therefore encourage one another
and build each other up,
just as in fact you are doing.

1 Thessalonians 5:11, NIV

Not long ago, a construction crew erected a new drug store near my church. It was built on the same lot where a grocery store once stood. As I drove by that site one day, I noticed something: After several weeks of work, the drugstore hadn't been finished. But it took only three days to knock down the grocery store.

You see, it takes a lot more time to build something up than it does to tear something down. That's especially true in marriage.

It's hard to build a strong marriage. Sometimes it takes years of hard work to bring a marriage to a point where both the husband and wife are happy and content. But it takes no time at all to tear a marriage down—to smash all the work it took to bring it to a place of strength.

I have known people who have been married six months or less, and they're already wanting to bail. The sad truth is that too many people are great at demolition—demeaning, destroying, and tearing one another down. They focus on their differences—and forget about those things that brought them together.

That's nothing. That's easy. Any fool can tear something down. But it takes patience, grace, years of work, and the very wisdom of God to build a love that will last.

THE FIRST BIG STEP

I acknowledged my sin to You,
and my iniquity I did not hide; I said,
"I will confess my transgressions to the LORD";
and You forgave the guilt of my sin.

PSALM 32:5

*M*any times, when a family is hurting, even in chaos, the call of God for the leader of the home is to take that first big step and humble himself before God.

Humility has a way of disarming even the most tense situations. And when the head of the house takes that first big step, making confession before God and before his family, asking for heaven's help to be the kind of leader God wants him to be, it has a powerful effect.

Maybe you're there right now. Maybe you're feeling discouraged and defeated, aching inside over where you've come up short as the head of your family.

If that sounds like you, it's time for you to pray something like this: "Okay, Lord, here I am. I will now swallow my pride and come under Your lordship, beginning today. I'm tired of trying to do this alone, and with Your help, I'm going to be the kind of husband and father You've called me to be."

Now comes the second step: talking first to your wife, then your children, and confessing where you've fallen short, where you need to do things better. It's time to promise your family that starting today, you'll make the changes God wants you to make.

Then pray! Pray with your family and ask them to continue praying for you.

WHY YOU'RE HERE

*"For David, after he had served the purpose of
God in his own generation, fell asleep…"*

ACTS 13:36

*I*n one particular at bat in the 1958 World Series, home-run king Hank Aaron stepped up to the plate. The catcher for the opposition was the New York Yankees' Yogi Berra, a notorious talker behind the plate. Berra tried to get in Aaron's head, throwing off his focus. When he saw Aaron feeling for the right grip on his bat, Yogi remarked, "Make sure you hit with the label up on the bat."

Aaron's response? "Yogi, I came up here to hit, not to read."

If you're going to be successful in any area of life—including marriage and parenthood—you need to know your purpose for being here. If you aren't sure of that purpose, anyone can get in your ear and distract you from your divinely ordained reason for being.

King David knew why God had put him on earth, and he fulfilled those purposes. There's nothing more sad than living seventy-five years not knowing why God has put you here in the first place.

God has given you a purpose, a calling with your own name on it. When you know that purpose and do what it takes to live it out, you're well on your way to being the man or woman God has called you to be.

Seek His purpose with all your heart…and watch as He begins to lead you.

REAL PEACE

And the peace of God,
which surpasses all comprehension,
will guard your hearts and your
minds in Christ Jesus.

PHILIPPIANS 4:7

*T*wo painters had a contest to see who could paint a better picture of peace.

One of them painted a sunset, with a red-gold sun sliding down over a calm sea. The other artist painted what I consider a better picture of God's peace. His painting portrayed a huge storm on a beach: dark clouds, wind, lightning, thunder, rain, and waves crashing against the rocks. But in the corner of his painting, he depicted a little bird, resting and singing between two huge stones.

You see, real peace is not happy feelings and calmness all around you. No, peace is when God gives you the ability to sing right in the middle of life's toughest storms. It's when you know that God is in control of all things and that, in the words of the apostle Paul, He "causes all things to work together for good to those who love God."

God's peace isn't just feeling better about things. It's a peace that makes no logical sense at all. It's a peace we can't understand or comprehend, a peace that overwhelms us no matter what life circumstances we face. It's a peace that no tranquilizer, no good night's sleep, and no vacation can come close to matching. It's God's peace! And it is yours *today* in Jesus.

OUR PLANS...AND HIS

*You do not know what your
life will be like tomorrow....
Instead, you ought to say,
"If the Lord wills, we will live
and also do this or that."*

JAMES 4:14—15

God is not against planning.

As you work your way through the book of Proverbs, you'll be assured in your heart that God approves of prudent, thoughtful preparation. In fact, He frankly tells us that only a fool fails to plan.

It's one thing to make plans, but quite another to *depend* on them. It's one thing to lay out what you hope to do, but it is another to think you're sovereign over those choices. It doesn't take most of us too many years to discover that a single day—a single hour or moment—can change the course of our entire lives.

God's plans, on the other hand, will be fulfilled, because they're all in the present tense to Him. Besides that, He is the only One who has the absolute power to pull off any plan He comes up with.

He is also all-knowing. We say He is omniscient. In other words, God has all of human history mapped out, and He has already taken into account all the "human" elements that come into His planning.

The best chance we have to see our plans succeed is when we carefully and deliberately link them up with His plans—when we seek His mind and His purposes in our daily lives.

Have you done that today?

THE VALUE OF A WOMAN

Older women likewise are to be
reverent in their behavior...
that they may encourage the young
women to love their husbands,
to love their children, to be sensible,
pure, workers at home.

TITUS 2:3–5

A woman who understands her value in God's eyes can fulfill her role by looking at herself through the lens of Scripture. Genesis 1:26–28 tells us that the woman bears equality of essence with the man as a corecipient of God's image. Then the Gospels reveal the great value our Lord gave to women during His earthly ministry. And as Paul traveled throughout the Mediterranean, many of the believers who labored with him to spread the message of Christ were women. In fact, Paul literally owed his life to some of these female coworkers.

God's Word leaves no doubt that there is positional equality between men and women in terms of their creation and value to God. But the Bible is also clear that there is a differentiation of roles between the sexes (Ephesians 5:22–23).

Many women don't care for the command to "be subject to your own husbands." However, that is what God requires of us. It is the responsibility of women to place themselves under the biblical leadership of their husbands, using all of their gifts and abilities to further the family and the testimony of Christ.

You might not agree with everything your husband does and asks you to do, but you must respect his position. When you do that, God will honor you.

THE PRIORITIES OF A GODLY WOMAN

*She looks for wool and flax and works
with her hands in delight.
She is like merchant ships;
she brings her food from afar.*

PROVERBS 31:13—14

Many modern women build their own careers in relative isolation from their husbands. They have their own money in their own bank accounts on which they write their own checks. But the godly woman uses her skills and gifts for the establishment of her home and the enhancement of her husband, because she is kingdom-oriented, not self-oriented. Her husband knows that every dollar she makes and every dime she spends will make their home a better place to live.

If a wife loves her career so much that her husband never benefits from the career she enjoys, then she is not being a godly wife. She has bought the lie that she's her own woman doing her own thing—and that her man is an inconvenience at best. That's hell's agenda for a home.

God did not give a woman a husband so she could continue living as an independent, single woman. He gave her a husband so she can partner with him, using her gifts, skills, and abilities to the full, so her home is thrust forward and her husband is better off. Because he needs that help.

We're not saying a wife is supposed to help and better her husband while she suffers. No, when a wife enhances her husband, she reaps the benefits, too.

THE SEASONS OF A WOMAN'S LIFE

"Who knows whether you have…
attained royalty for such a time as this?"

ESTHER 4:14

Mordecai's statement to Esther reminds me that there are various seasons in a woman's life.

During my season of staying home with my children, I sometimes struggled to persevere, as many young mothers do. Especially since I longed to use my gifts and abilities outside the home. But my staying home was a decision Tony and I made before the Lord, and I soon realized that I could use my gifts inside the home to *manage*, rather than just maintain my household. Then, as the kids reached school age, I was able to begin using those skills outside the home part-time.

Paul spoke of the seasons in a woman's life when he instructed the older women to teach the younger women how to care for their families. All women need the encouragement and motivation of other women—especially if they're new to the faith and weren't raised according to biblical principles. All of this can be very foreign to them.

Women need the fellowship and support of other women who are in the same season of life. This is where the body of Christ becomes so important. When a woman becomes isolated, she is more vulnerable to the enemy's attacks. Your husband can be a great help here if he understands where you are in your life.

Give him a window into your heart!

DECISION AT THE PUMP

*"Give, and it will be given to you. Good measure,
pressed down, shaken together, running over…
For with the measure you use it
will be measured back to you."*

LUKE 6:38, ESV

A thirsty man staggering through the desert came upon a little shack. Inside the shack—wonder of wonders!—he saw a water pump. The happy man worked the pump vigorously, but no water came out. He slumped down by the pump, totally defeated.

Then his eye happened to spot a bottle propped up in the corner. The bottle was full of water, and beside it was this note: "If you want more water, you must pour the contents of this bottle into the pump to prime it. Then you will get all the water you need. Please refill the bottle before you leave."

The man was on the horns of a dilemma. Should he go ahead and drink the bottle of water, or should he risk pouring that precious, life-giving water into the pump?

This is the kind of choice we must make every day. In our marriages, each of us has the choice of satisfying our immediate needs—perhaps at the expense of our partner—or working toward long-term joy.

The thirsty man in the desert poured the water into the pump and started pumping. At first, nothing happened, but after a minute, water started gushing out. The man drank deeply, filled his canteen, and then refilled the bottle, writing at the bottom of the note, "Believe!"

WHAT DID YOU SAY?

Let your speech always be with grace,
as though seasoned with salt.

COLOSSIANS 4:6

good percentage of marital problems and breakdowns can be traced to the absence of good communication. This need shows up in a lot of ways, but people often see the symptoms instead of the problem.

For instance, a husband may say, "My wife and I can't get along," when he means, "We can't communicate."

Or a wife may say, "We don't know how to be intimate with one another," without realizing that intimacy starts with communication, not the physical act of sex.

You might say, "But we didn't have this kind of conflict when we were dating." Of course not. You were covering up the negative stuff, trying to impress and win the other person.

But when you got married, you found out the real deal. And that jolt of reality can often lead to a jamming of the lines in marital communication. You talk past each other instead of to each other.

One of the greatest challenges and joys of marriage is learning to speak the language of love. Paul gave us a great way to practice: He said we should bathe our words in grace.

Are your words bathed in grace...or soaked in sarcasm?

FOUR ABSOLUTE NECESSITIES

*"All authority has been given to Me in heaven
and on earth. Go therefore and make
disciples of all the nations."*

MATTHEW 28:18–19

We don't have to wonder what was uppermost on the heart and mind of Jesus before He left this earth. Just before His ascension into heaven, Jesus told us what was most important to Him. Those last words, at the top of this page, became known as the Great Commission.

Christ's mandate for the church is to *make* disciples. This is the only command in the passage. Therefore, if Jesus' all-encompassing will for the church is to make disciples, it follows that His will for individual believers is to *become* disciples.

A disciple is a learner, a student. To become a disciple of Christ means that we become like Him (see Matthew 10:25). Working toward this goal consists of what I call the four absolute necessities of discipleship: worship, fellowship, Scripture, and evangelism.

We can see these four essentials in action in the first church ever established, the church at Jerusalem (see Acts 2). One reason this church was so dynamic was because it got off to a great start. Jesus had told the disciples in Acts 1:8, "Don't have church until the Holy Ghost shows up" (Evans paraphrase). They obeyed Him, and the Spirit showed up in great power at Pentecost.

Then those men and women got moving—in the strength, wisdom, and boldness of the Holy Spirit—living out the reality of being Jesus' disciples.

THE ISSUE IS TRUTH

*Preach the word; be ready in season and
out of season; reprove, rebuke, exhort,
with great patience and instruction.*

2 TIMOTHY 4:2

If you're going to worship God in spirit and truth, you must be
willing to accept the absolute authority of His Word. This makes
some people uncomfortable, because they don't want anybody—not
even God—messing in their business.

God wants to get into your business because He's into truth!
My commitment as a pastor is to tell it like it is. Sometimes the
people at our church will like it and applaud. Other times, they
won't like it. They may even get mad. But that's all right, because the
issue is truth.

In the course of teaching on worship in John 4, Jesus made one
of the most awesome statements ever recorded. He said God is *looking* for worshipers (v. 23)! The great God of the universe is hunting
for folks who want to worship Him. Volunteers ought to be lining
up by the millions!

Are you ready to volunteer? Do you understand that the essence
of worship is coming to God on the basis of His truth, with your
spirit communing with His Holy Spirit? (See John 4:24.) If so,
you're ready for some great worship! And it doesn't have to be limited to church. You can engage in God-pleasing worship at home
with your mate and family.

THE HEART OF A SERVANT

*"Even the Son of Man did not
come to be served, but to serve."*

MARK 10:45

The Lord Jesus Christ, our supreme example, left the glory of heaven, laid aside the independent exercise of His deity, and took on the form of a "bond-servant" (Philippians 2:7).

What does this mean for us as Christian women today? It means that as we are willing to exhibit a servant's attitude, we can expect God's blessing on our homes and families.

To illustrate this, I go back to one of our earlier sisters in the faith, the woman of Proverbs 31. Verse 15 of this passage says that she had servants, but she also had a servant's heart.

How do we know this? Because the Bible says she prepared breakfast for her servant girls as well as her family. This isn't normal procedure, is it? Servants usually do the serving, with the family doing the receiving. But evidently this woman valued people so much that she invested her service in the lives of her household helpers.

How can a godly woman serve her husband and family without becoming overworked and underappreciated? One key is her husband's attitude. The husband of Proverbs 31 honored his wife and praised her, and his attitude filtered down to the children.

He made it easier, not harder, for his wife to fulfill her calling. And because he invested in her, he found everything he could ever want in his wife.

THE NEW ENVIRONMENT OF GRACE

By the grace of God I am what I am,
and His grace toward me did not prove vain.

1 CORINTHIANS 15:10

A friend of mine, born and raised in India, came to America for graduate studies. In India, my friend had driven on the left side of the road. Here he had to start driving on the right. Everything in America was so different!

This is how many believers feel when they enter the environment—the new country—of God's grace. Since we are saved by grace, we enter this country the moment we become a Christian.

But even though we are full citizens of our new country, we bring with us a lot of mental and spiritual baggage from the "old country." This means that living by grace will take some getting used to for many of us.

Most of us brought with us the old standard of being accepted on the basis of how well *we* perform, not on the basis of how well someone else—Jesus Christ—performed. Grace says we serve and please Christ, not to earn His love and favor, but because we already have His love and favor.

There's a tremendous, liberating principle here for marriage. Sometimes one partner in a marriage will put the other on a performance basis. But God's grace extends to marriage! Spouses need to love, serve, and accept each other by grace, not because one spouse meets the other's performance criteria.

A NETWORK OF SUPPORT

Her children rise up and bless her;
her husband also, and he praises her.

PROVERBS 31:28

We've talked at length about the wife of Proverbs 31, but we also need to talk about her husband. He was so well-supported at home that he was able to take his place at the city gate among the elders of his city (see Proverbs 31:23). In other words, one reason this man was able to exercise leadership was because he had the strong support of an excellent wife.

But the support flowed both ways. This husband let everyone know that he had an excellent wife. His praise and encouragement of her was also reflected in the love his children expressed for their mother. She was well-supported herself.

All of us need words and actions that express support. Whenever Tony preaches on Proverbs 31, some man always asks him afterward, "How can I get my wife to be a Proverbs 31 wife?" Tony always points him to verse 28 and tells him, "If you want a Proverbs 31 wife, you need to be a Proverbs 31 husband."

I suspect there are legions of my Christian sisters who are starving for a little attention and praise from their husbands. Wives want to hear their husbands affirm them and lift them up the way the Proverbs 31 husband affirmed his wife (see v. 29).

Most women would grow and flourish under that kind of genuine praise.

WHAT GOD IS AFTER IN YOUR WORK

*There is nothing better for a man than to eat
and drink and tell himself that his labor is good.*

ECCLESIASTES 2:24

God wants you to find meaning in your work, but the thing that makes it meaningful is your relationship with God in the task, not the task itself.

Even if you're assigned to a project you're not excited about, if your attitude is that you are participating with God in the project, He can add the meaning of His presence and blessing to any task.

As a couple, the two of you have relatively few years to live and do productive work. In the book of Ecclesiastes, Solomon advised that you make the most of those work opportunities. In other words, don't make it your goal just to warm a spot for eight hours each day. Ask God to give you the ability to enjoy your work—to do it to the full for His glory.

The goal of work is not for you to put in your forty hours a week for forty years so you can retire in Florida. The goal of work is the joy and sense of achievement you get after you accomplish a God-given task. That's what God is after.

And when you think about your job and your chosen field, remember this: It is better to make less money and be eager to get up in the morning than it is to make more money but long to stay in bed.

SEEKING GOD: A WOMAN'S DEVOTIONAL LIFE

*Mary...was seated at the Lord's feet,
listening to His word.*

LUKE 10:39

Mary of Bethany was one sister in the Lord who knew how to keep her life in spiritual balance. A willing worshiper, she would rather sit at Jesus' feet and hear from Him than eat or do anything else. She understood something that we women need to keep coming back to today: A woman's *spiritual* life is the anchor that holds all of life in place and keeps her from drifting away.

When a woman fears the Lord—when her spiritual priorities are in place and she integrates God into every area of her life—she discovers within herself a well of strength, joy, and peace that will never run dry. When a woman is vitally connected to Christ, He renews her strength and her spirit day by day.

What must we do to keep our "first love" (Revelation 2:4) for the Lord fresh? We must guard against anything taking the place of our daily time in His presence.

It's so easy to let life's demands slip between us and the Savior. Before long, we are like Martha, sweating and fuming over our tasks while Jesus Himself is in the next room, waiting to meet with us.

Remember what Jesus told Martha. It is better to do less *for* Him if that's what it takes to have more intimacy *with* Him.

TAKING A SABBATH REST

By the seventh day God completed His
work which He had done,
and He rested on the seventh day
from all His work.

GENESIS 2:2

*G*od says there should be a day in every week when we let work go. He didn't create us as workaholics. We do that to ourselves. I'm guilty here, because I love what I do. So I tend to neglect adhering to Scripture that relates to this area of overworking.

But even God rested from His work of creation. To enjoy His accomplishments, He stepped back and looked at them. He was finished, so He rested. Now, He didn't rest because He was tired. His rest was the rest of accomplishment, of a job well done. It was the rest of reflection on and enjoyment of His work.

God thought it was such a good idea to rest one day in seven that He commanded His people to do the same. The seventh day became known as the Sabbath. This was a big deal with God. In the Old Testament, breaking the Sabbath carried the death penalty.

We're not under law, but as Christians we are to cease our work and take a day to worship the God who provided for us all week long.

Taking our "Sabbath rest" is similar in spirit to giving God His tithe. It's a way of recognizing that we can do more in six days with God's blessing than we can do in seven days without it.

GRACE UPON GRACE

Of His fullness we have all received,
and grace upon grace. For the Law was given
through Moses; grace and truth
were realized through Jesus Christ.

JOHN 1:16–17

The apostle John, who was as close as anyone to Jesus while He was on earth, said that Christ is the full expression of God's grace.

But notice that God's grace doesn't begin and end at salvation, as wonderful as that is. Jesus keeps showering us with "grace upon grace." James calls it "greater grace" (James 4:6).

So how do we make sure we are tapping into the endless flow of God's grace? By drawing closer to the Person of grace. The more intimate your fellowship with Christ, the more you will grow in His grace.

Grace doesn't give us permission to sin, but it deals with the one issue we could never, ever handle: our sin. Once you understand what God's grace has done for you, you can't help but want to draw closer to Christ in loving, intimate fellowship.

It's the same for you and your spouse, as a Christian couple. The relationship between intimacy and a greater enjoyment of God's grace also applies to marriage. The more the two of you draw together in genuine spiritual and emotional intimacy, the more your individual spiritual lives will feel the benefit. We're convinced you can't be in intimate, growing fellowship with Christ unless your marriage is also growing in grace…showering each other with undeserved favor and kindness…grace upon grace upon grace.

PROFOUNDLY SIMPLE ADVICE

Remember also your Creator
in the days of your youth,
before the evil days come.

ECCLESIASTES 12:1

When we want to know the real deal on the purpose of life, we need to find someone who can speak from experience. We need to hear from somebody who has "been there and back again."

King Solomon fills that bill like no one else.

His book of Ecclesiastes addresses our need to grasp a compelling reason for our existence. It was penned by a man who had everything he needed to pursue every possible avenue that might provide an answer.

Solomon had more gold and silver than most national treasuries. And just in case he got bored with all that money, he also had seven hundred wives and three hundred concubines. He could soak himself in any pleasure a man could imagine.

And talk about a career! If you make it to king, you can't go any higher. And beyond these things, Solomon was also given a depth of wisdom beyond anyone before or since.

That's what makes his simple advice so profound. After all he had experienced, he came up with a two-word key to life: *Remember God.* Don't leave God out of the picture as you plan your life.

You may not consider yourself to be "in the days of your youth." But as long as you're still here, you can turn it around and discover God's purpose for you.

FOLLOWING HIS CALL

We also have as our ambition...
to be pleasing to Him.

2 CORINTHIANS 5:9

As a Christian woman, you need to make sure you are following God's call on your life...and not simply trying to fulfill the expectations of others.

Yes, of course we need to be sensitive to others. Your husband and children have legitimate needs. So does your extended family, your church, and your community. But remember, at the judgment seat of Christ, when we stand before Him to give an account of our lives, the issue will be how well we pleased Him, not how well we pleased others.

When gaining the Lord's "well done" is the dominating concern of our lives, we will not so easily succumb to the demands and expectations that people may try to place upon us. Too many women are living stress-filled, shallow lives because they're too busy doing too many things—things God never asked or expected them to do.

One of Tony's mentors in seminary used to tell his students to practice saying "no" every day in front of a mirror. Then, with all that practice, they could say no to things that would distract them from their primary goal.

The truth is, if you don't plan your days according to what you believe is God's will and calling for you, there will be plenty of well-meaning people who will try to plan your days for you.

MAINTAINING YOUR PRIORITIES

"Well done, good and faithful servant.
You have been faithful over a little;
I will set you over much."

MATTHEW 25:21, ESV

Here's another way for a woman to keep God first in her life: maintain her biblical priorities.

For us women, that means that anything outside the home that conflicts with God's priority of our family must either be readjusted or released. It's amazing how many Christian men and women want to fix the world, but aren't willing to fix their marriage or family first.

After family, our priority should be our ministry in the local church. Tony often says there is no such thing as "Lone Ranger" Christians, and I agree. We were never meant to try to make it on our own in the Christian life.

A third priority is our service to others outside the family and the church. Such service not only contributes to the well-being of the community, but also gives us opportunities to share our faith.

A woman whose priorities are in line with God's purposes will experience His joy and empowerment.

I believe that a woman who is walking closely with the Lord, pleasing Him in her daily life, and living according to His priorities can say to even the most rigorous feminist: "I have a family, fulfilling work, satisfaction, and peace of heart. I have confidence in the present, and know where I'm going in the future. Now…what are *you* offering me?"

TEACHING YOUR CHILDREN HONOR — 1

*Children, obey your parents
in the Lord, for this is right.
Honor your father and mother
(this is the first commandment with a promise).*

EPHESIANS 6:1–2

*C*hristian parents love to quote these verses to their children. And rightly so. God does want children to be obedient. But notice the qualifying phrase "in the Lord." That means you have to instruct them in the things of God if they're going to know *how* to obey. In other words, your children need the right biblical information and the right application. You can't leave them to themselves, thinking "someone else" will teach them these things.

Now, you as a parent can't know what is right until you know what God has said about it. So you need to be hanging around where the Bible is being taught, and be in the Word yourself. Dad, it is primarily your assignment to instruct your children in how they ought to live under God's authority. The best way to do that is to make sure *you* are submitted to the Lord's authority yourself.

Children need their parents, especially their fathers, to help them understand that *we* are the adults, *they* are the children, and children are to respect adults. In time, they're going to get that right. But in the meantime, we parents need to be consistent in teaching honor, encouraging honor, and *expecting* honor.

TEACHING YOUR CHILDREN HONOR — 2

These commandments that I give you today are to be upon your hearts. Impress them on your children.

DEUTERONOMY 6:6—7, NIV

*G*od knows that the children in a home become the fiber of a society. If honor and respect for authority don't start in the home, they will never hit the street. And if they don't hit the street, they will have no impact on the community, the state, or the nation.

The fifth commandment reminds us that honor isn't just some nice, polite little concept to help polish our kids' manners. *It has the power of life and death.*

Deuteronomy 6 teaches that a nation's destiny is determined in large measure by the quality of spiritual instruction in its homes. Verses 6–9 speaks directly to dads and moms, showing them how to keep godly values before the eyes of their growing children.

Let me summarize it: "Dad and Mom, go home and train your children in My truth. Train them when they wake up, train them when they lie down, and at all points in between. Train them formally. Train them informally. I want My truth tied on their foreheads and on their wrists. I want them to bump into My truth when they come into the house and when they leave the house."

Teaching God's truth as a lifestyle is a huge responsibility for parents, but the payoff is great. What you do today to teach your children God's truth can impact your family for generations!

A SPECIAL WORD TO DADS—1

Fathers, do not embitter your children,
or they will become discouraged.

COLOSSIANS 3:21, NIV

*D*iligent fathers understand that a dad can't exasperate and frustrate his children, and still expect them to come out right.

What are some of the ways we dads provoke or anger our kids?

One way is by smothering, or over-parenting, them. Fathers can stifle their sons and daughters by trying to do everything for them, never letting the kids try—and sometimes fail—on their own.

Favoritism is another spirit killer. This can be a real temptation if, for example, you have one son who is athletic and another who is more artistic. Depending on your preference, you can end up frustrating the son who doesn't meet your idea of what a man should be and do.

A father can also frustrate his children by forcing his unfulfilled dreams upon them. ("I didn't get to be a doctor, son, but *you* are going to be a doctor.")

Discouragement, criticism, perfectionism, and the withholding of approval are several other prime ways we dads can embitter our children. And here's a biggie: failure to sacrifice. By that I mean fathers who send this message to their boys and girls: "I need my own fulfillment now. You are in my way."

Are any of these on your list? All of us dads have messed up, but when we do, we need to ask for forgiveness and move on.

A SPECIAL WORD TO DADS — 2

*Fathers...bring [your children] up in the
discipline and instruction of the Lord.*

EPHESIANS 6:4

*G*od wants our families to be built on His truth and righteousness. He left us in the world to show what happens when a family
worships and serves God as opposed to simply being like everyone
else.

But that's not what we have today. We have too many Christian
children who act just like all the other kids in the neighborhood. We
have Christian parents saying, "I love Johnny, so I don't spank him."

Excuse me, but if this is your attitude, you *hate* Johnny. Do you
know what the Bible says about God? "Whom the Lord loveth, He
skins alive." (That's an Evans paraphrase of Hebrews 12:6.) In other
words, God disciplines His kids—for their good.

To discipline children means more than just correcting them
when they mess up. It means to *train* them. To show them the right
way. Sure, it includes laying down the rules with the rewards and
punishments attached to the rules. But it also means creating an
environment in which your kids are set up for success, not failure.

How do you help set your children up to succeed? By instruct-
ing them in God's Word. Teaching your children the Scriptures will
help them avoid a thousand pitfalls in life, and learn to walk in the
safe path of God's will.

RESTING ON THE SABBATH

*Then God blessed the seventh day and sanctified it,
because in it He rested from all His work.*

GENESIS 2:3

The Sabbath was serious stuff in Israel. It was the day to cease from work and worship God. It was a time to enjoy the God of work, rather than the work itself.

Today resting on the Sabbath also means you're working in the will of God, and trusting Him for next week's work, next week's opportunities, next week's promotion, next week's challenges and blessings. So instead of knocking yourself out, on the Sabbath you say, "God, this is it. I'm done. I'm going to stop working and trust You."

For the Christian, workaholism often reflects a lack of trust in God. It's that silly, arrogant idea that we've got to do it all ourselves, or it won't get done. It's too important to leave up to anyone else…even God.

Another problem with workaholism is that it kills relationships—with God and with each other. The reason so many of us men are workaholics is because we're scared of relationships. See, if we're not working on Sunday, we might have to sit down and talk with our spouse or our kids. And we just might discover we have a problem or two needing attention.

If you're working so hard that you never get time with God or your loved ones, you're working too hard. Your work was never meant to replace God in your life.

STAY IN THE VICINITY

"I will never desert you,
nor will I ever forsake you."

HEBREWS 13:5

I once saw a lady walking through a park, throwing bread crumbs to a flock of pigeons.

But as the birds were eating, a boy approached. He had no crumbs to give the birds. Instead, with a wave of the hand, he ran among the pigeons to frighten and scatter them. Some of the birds flew away, while some lingered in the vicinity.

That scene made me think of how our heavenly Father provides for us in abundance (see Matthew 6:26). But Satan tries to scare us away from the Father, while offering nothing good himself.

Here's the point: When Satan shows up to make you fearful, don't run too far from the source of your blessing and strength. Stay in the vicinity of your Father, and Satan will flee. Then you can return to enjoy what the Lord has freely provided for you.

In my own life, for instance, I have a strong fear of flying. Before a flight, I am very nervous and indecisive. But God is teaching me to trust in His promises, and realize that everything He brings into my life is for my best.

In such times, I've decided to make a conscious decision to yield to Christ. I claim victory by praising God for His promise never to leave me, no matter where I am…even miles above the earth!

LIVING WATER FOR THE
"DRY ZONE"—1

*"Whoever drinks of the water that
I will give him shall never thirst."*

JOHN 4:14

*T*he setting for John 4 couldn't be more appropriate.

Jesus meets a Samaritan woman at a well...to talk about worship. Worship is the pump that keeps the living water flowing when our hearts feel dry.

Many of us go through the motions and rhetoric of worship. We know the hymns and choruses and the right phrases to say at the right times. But far too many believers harbor a "dry zone" deep down inside.

No matter where you are on the continuum, the way to get the inner spring of your life flowing is by pursuing an intimate relationship with Jesus Christ...and by learning to worship Him.

That's what Jesus told the Samaritan woman, who thought she was just going outside of town for a bucket of water. Jesus told her about a water that would quench her thirst forever, and she asked Him for some. The fact that she thought this water would quench her physical thirst shows she wasn't really tuned in to what Jesus was saying (yet).

Are you tuned in to what Jesus is trying to tell you? In spite of her lack of understanding, the woman at the well was open to what Jesus had to offer (John 4:14)—and we can imitate that. Real worship begins with an open, honest heart before God.

LIVING WATER FOR THE "DRY ZONE" — 2

"Give me this water, so I will not be thirsty."

JOHN 4:15

*J*esus and the Samaritan woman had been discussing water, when suddenly He asked her to go get her husband.

This request uncovered the truth of the woman's adulterous life. Perhaps in an attempt to change the subject, she threw out a remark about worship. Jesus was willing to pick up the topic, since the only way she could get things right at home was to get things right with God. That's true in our families, too!

The woman brought up two places of worship—one favored by the Samaritans, and one by the Jews. In other words, she wanted to know "which church was the right one." Jesus didn't choose either of her options (see v. 21). Instead, He said a new "hour" was coming.

In other words, Jesus was saying, "I'm going to inaugurate a new basis for worship that has nothing to do with family heritage or the location of the worship center."

What she would soon learn, to her wonder and joy, was that worship wasn't as much about a place as it was a Person. And that Person had sought her out, and opened His arms to her.

Beyond all the forms and traditions and procedures the church has developed through its two thousand years, the bottom line of worship is still the Person of Jesus, with His arms open wide.

LIVING WATER FOR THE
"DRY ZONE" — 3

*"God is spirit, and those who worship
Him must worship in spirit and truth."*

JOHN 4:24

*J*esus told the Samaritan woman that the old system of worship would soon be canceled. Under that system, worship was tied to where you were. You had to be part of Israel, gathered around the tabernacle or temple. But in the future, Jesus said, worship would not be tied to where you are, but *who* you are.

Worship has less to do with "where you go" on Sunday morning than *Whom* you are in touch with all week long. Paul later spelled that out in 1 Corinthians 6:19: "Do you not know that your body is a temple of the Holy Spirit?" God's presence is no longer centered in a temple or a city or a mountain. He now lives inside of His people.

So where can you worship? Anywhere! *You* are the temple of the living God. He now lives within you. This doesn't mean we give up worshiping in church. Instead, the overflow of individual worship should lead to corporate worship. The Bible commands us not to forsake the assembly of the church (Hebrews 10:25).

But if you go to church thinking you are now entering *the* place of worship, you've missed the message. If you limit worship to where you are, the minute you leave that place of worship you'll leave your *attitude* of worship behind. And that should never be.

LIVING WATER FOR THE
"DRY ZONE"—4

Let us not give up meeting together,
as some are in the habit of doing,
but let us encourage one another—
and all the more as you see the Day approaching.

HEBREWS 10:25, NIV

*T*hose who think worship only happens in a place—a "worship center"—don't understand that they carry worship around with them.

Hebrews 10 has some powerful things to say about this new way of worship that Jesus inaugurated through His death and resurrection.

"Therefore, brethren, since we have confidence to enter the holy place by the blood of Jesus, by a new and living way which He inaugurated for us through the veil, that is, His flesh…let us draw near with a sincere heart" (vv. 19–22).

Where can you go to worship today? Directly into the presence of God! You don't need a confessional booth. You don't need a preacher or a priest.

Even so, the Bible does not leave this thing on an individual level. People who ask, "Do I have to go to church to worship God?" aren't really interested in worship. Private worship *always* leads to corporate worship. If you are worshiping in private, you can't wait to worship in public. If you don't care about private worship, you'll debate whether you even need church.

Some people will argue, "I don't have to go to church to worship God. I can worship right here in my bed." Maybe—but the issue is, *do* they worship God when they kill the alarm and pull the covers back over their heads? I doubt it!

LIVING WATER FOR THE
"DRY ZONE"—5

Jesus cried out again...and yielded up His spirit.
And behold, the veil of the temple was
torn in two from top to bottom.

MATTHEW 27:50–51

They killed the Lord Jesus on the cross, and then went back to the temple. And guess what they found? The huge, heavy veil covering the holy place had been torn in two.

This veil, which separated the people from the presence of God, was ripped in half—from top to bottom—at the moment of Christ's death, because His sacrifice on the cross gave His people permission to walk right on inside. The living God now invites you to worship Him in spirit—to step into His immediate presence.

Sometimes, when you're distracted or bored, you might try to worship with your body alone—just going through the motions. But that won't work. You cannot worship properly with your body only. If all God has of you on Sunday morning or in your devotional time is your body, you aren't worshiping. If you don't want to be there, if you're thinking about work, if you're in a hurry, you've just wasted your time.

Jesus said those who worship the Father must worship Him "in spirit" (John 4:24). Fellowship occurs when God's invisible Spirit and your invisible spirit get together, when they commune and communicate.

You can clap to the songs. You can sing with the choir. You can say "Amen" to the words. But unless your spirit has kicked into gear, you cannot worship.

LIVING WATER FOR THE "DRY ZONE" — 6

The Spirit searches all things,
even the depths of God...
The thoughts of God no one knows
except the Spirit of God.

1 CORINTHIANS 2:10–11

*I*f you want to worship God you must be yielded to His Spirit. You must come before Him with the attitude, "Lord, I am depending on the Holy Spirit to bring me in contact with You."

In addition, your mind must be centered on God. If you sit in church worrying about your problems (or even counting your blessings), you're not worshiping. If you stay up late every Saturday night and go to church so tired you wish you were home, you're in no condition to worship God.

And in your devotion time, if all you do is read a passage of Scripture and rattle off a few prayer items, that is not worship. Worship includes yieldedness to the Holy Spirit, and a fixation on God.

The key to true worship is "spirit and truth" (John 4:24). It's not either/or but both. Some groups really get high on spirited worship. They shout praises and sing and clap and feel good. There's nothing wrong with spirited worship. But it is not true worship unless it is combined with truth. The people may be shouting, but what is the truth God wants you to learn? True worship is when our innermost beings, having received the proper information about God, explode with joy at the very thought of such a God being ours!

ENTERING INTO GOD'S REST

It is vain for you to rise up early, to retire late,
to eat the bread of painful labors;
for He gives to His beloved even in his sleep.

PSALM 127:2

In the Old Testament, the Israelites entered into God's rest in Canaan, a land flowing with milk and honey, a land already stocked with everything they needed. All they had to do was trust Him and enter into His rest.

Now this doesn't mean that the people didn't have to work or cultivate the land. Don't mistake this "rest" for the "folding of the hands to rest" that marks the lazy person (Proverbs 6:10).

God didn't tell the Israelites to just sling their hammocks and kick back when they entered Canaan. Entering His rest was an acknowledgement that God was their provider, and they could trust Him for their needs.

Today's verse speaks of how endless work and worry are futile. Why? Because "unless the LORD builds the house, they labor in vain who build it; unless the LORD guards the city, the watchman keeps awake in vain" (Psalm 127:1).

These verses mean that when you're sleeping, God is cutting a deal. He's arranging things. He's fixing the system. In other words, when you place limitations on your work by entering into God's day of rest, you put yourself in line for His supernatural provision.

Sometimes the most productive thing we can ever do is to rest in God and let Him work on our behalf.

DESTINY AND DISCIPLINE

*"I have chosen him, so that he may
command his children and his household after him
to keep the way of the LORD
by doing righteousness and justice."*

GENESIS 18:19

*T*oday's verse, which God spoke concerning the patriarch Abraham, tells us the transfer of godly values from generation to generation is not automatic. Our children are born in sin. They're not going to raise themselves and pick up the right values on their own. Someone has to pass them on.

That's what God called Abraham to do in his generation. Look how God equipped Abraham for his task.

First, God chose Abraham and gave him a *destiny*. Abraham knew that God's hand was on his life. You need to know that God's hand is on your life, too, if you want to be a kingdom husband and father with something to pass on. That means you need to get close to God and keep that lifeline going.

Abraham also committed himself to *discipline*, so that he could command his children and his household after him to keep the way of the Lord. My father never asked me, "Son, do you feel like going to church today?" He got me up and took me to church, no matter how dog-tired he was. There was no negotiation. A kingdom man says to his family, "We do things God's way in our home, because this is a kingdom home. The King rules here, and I am the leader under the king."

THE ULTIMATE IN UNSELFISHNESS

*The husband must fulfill his duty to his wife,
and likewise also the wife to her husband.*

1 CORINTHIANS 7:3

When it comes to sex, the world asks, "What can you do for me? How can you make me feel good?" The Christian marriage partner should ask, "What can I do for you? How can I meet your needs?" True sexual satisfaction in marriage comes when we say to our mate, "I want to fulfill my duty to you."

Fulfilling your duty to your mate means more than sexual performance. Sex is just part of a larger package. For example, one indication that a husband is not fulfilling his duty to his wife is when he stops romancing her and making her feel special.

My brother, when you stop romancing your mate, you can pretty much forget about having a passionate wife. The only reason she got excited about you in the first place was because you romanced her! If you're not seeking to meet her emotional needs, you're not fulfilling your duty. When you romance your wife and make her feel special, she feels the desire to respond.

Christian wives, remember this principle works both ways. If your husband is making a sincere effort to do the right stuff, you need to respond by fulfilling your duty to him.

WORTH THE EFFORT!

*Like apples of gold in settings of silver
is a word spoken in right circumstances.*

PROVERBS 25:11

The fourth chapter of Ephesians teaches us to put away lying because, as believers, "we are members of one another" (v. 25). If this is true for the body of Christ as a whole, think how much more important honesty is in a relationship as intimate as marriage.

Paul went on to say that we must not let the sun go down on our anger, because when we do, we give the devil an opportunity to wreak havoc in our lives (v. 26–27).

And Ephesians 4:29 urges us to replace our unwholesome communication with words that edify or build up others so that our speech might "give grace to those who hear."

We read these verses and see them applying to our communication with fellow believers, but sometimes fail to remember that our spouse is one of those fellow believers! We need to walk in the Spirit at home, too. Our mates are a part of the body of Christ whom God calls us to serve by the way we communicate with them.

This great chapter closes with a verse married couples need to apply every single day through their lives: "Be kind to one another, tender-hearted, forgiving each other" (v. 32).

A thousand times over, it is worth the effort to communicate!

MEN: GET IT TOGETHER AT HOME

*[An overseer] must be one who manages his own household
well, keeping his children under control with all dignity.*

1 TIMOTHY 3:4

*T*he Bible leaves no doubt that men are responsible to take the
lead in the management of God's kingdom. His plan is that you and
I practice good leadership at home so we can bring it to church.
That's the idea in 1 Timothy 3:4–5, where Paul told Timothy that a
candidate for church leadership must be a man who has it together
at home.

Do you know why God desires this? One reason, of course, is
because He wants to see godly young men and women growing up
in godly homes. But another reason is that God is preparing men for
a bigger agenda than just their families.

Jesus said there is no marriage in heaven (see Matthew 22:30).
The reason is because once the reality has come, we don't need the
picture anymore. We're not going to heaven as family units, but as
individual believers. So a man needs to look at his family as his
training ground for kingdom leadership and management.

Take the example of prayer. As a man becomes comfortable and
capable in leading his family in prayer, he is better equipped to
assume a role of prayer leadership at church. God wants men to step
forward and set the pace, to take the leadership, both at home and
in the church.

But it starts at home.

A GUIDING PRINCIPLE FOR GODLY WOMEN

Giver her the reward she has earned,
and let her works bring her praise at the city gate.

PROVERBS 31:31, NIV

This closing verse from the description of the "excellent wife" (Proverbs 31:10–31) highlights a basic principle that should guide the decisions of a Christian wife and mother concerning work outside the home.

The principle is this: Whenever a woman's work outside the home compromises her ministry *inside* the home, she's in the wrong job. It's time for her and her husband to sit down, examine their priorities, and do whatever is necessary.

Today's verse says that the Proverbs 31 woman received the reward for her labor. But her "works"—the things she did to care for her family and those in need—brought her praise as well.

A person's role and calling in the kingdom is a spiritual issue. For a woman, putting her home and family first is not just a matter of economics or scheduling. It's a matter of obeying God.

A woman may say, "But we need the money I bring home." Obviously, no one can judge to what extent that may be true in every home. There are certainly homes in which the mother has to work to make ends meet. In that situation, the creative woman may be able to find ways to produce income from within the home. But either way, she can still order her priorities in a way that God can smile on and bless.

HERITAGE AND PRIORITIES

The rich rules over the poor,
and the borrower becomes the lender's slave.

PROVERBS 22:7

*B*iblical counselors warn young couples against the trap of developing a lifestyle that demands two paychecks just to make ends meet. When that happens and children come along, Mom is trapped into working just to keep the house and cars.

Too often, the need for a wife's income is the result of pressure couples put on themselves to acquire too much stuff too soon. But God never called Christian husbands and wives to keep up with the Joneses. He called them to save the Joneses.

It's all right to get what money can buy as long as you don't lose what money cannot buy in the process! Nothing can replace the value of a strong Christian heritage.

A woman's primary assignment is to manage her home. The blessing that she creates when she fulfills God's agenda reaches even further than her own family's well-being and the next generation. When her own children are grown and gone, she can share the blessing with still another generation—younger wives and mothers who are coming along behind her (see Titus 2:3–5).

If two incomes seem necessary to keep your home running, perhaps you and your mate don't need more money, but new priorities. Ask God to guide you in developing financial goals that are in keeping with His will for your family's spiritual health.

HELPER OR COMPETITOR?

Her husband is known in the gates,
when he sits among the elders of the land.

PROVERBS 31:23

One reason marriages fail is because the wife isn't out to help her husband; she's using the marriage to help herself. A wife who thinks like this has become his competitor. She's not cooperating with God's kingdom agenda for the family.

Now if God expects a wife to help her husband, the assumption is that he *needs* help. I'll be the first to admit it. We men are not complete in and of ourselves. That's the reason God created woman in the first place.

So wives, when your husband's faults show up, they are opportunities for you to fulfill your biblical job description. If you are the complete opposite—or counterpart—of your husband, that's wonderful. That means you can fill in all the blank spots where your husband needs help. You can cooperate with God in molding and shaping him into what God wants him to be.

In Proverbs 31:12, this kind of wife is described as someone who "does [her husband] good and not evil all the days of her life." Here's a woman who is perpetually, ferociously, and determinedly looking out for the good of her man.

The reason the husband in today's verse was able to take his place among the leaders of his community was because he had a wife, friend, businesswoman—a helper—at home.

A WIFE'S KINGDOM AGENDA

A wife of noble character who can find?
She is worth far more than rubies.

PROVERBS 31:10, NIV

One of the worst statements a wife can make is, "My mama told me." Now, I don't have a thing against your mama, but you need to know that her opinion is no longer the reigning voice in your life.

Some women grew up in homes where Mama ran the show. Perhaps she had to, given the nature of the father in the home. Even so, that dominant attitude may have gotten transferred to her daughter, who then brings a domineering spirit into her own marriage.

A wife may say, "Yes, but you don't know my husband." Well, your husband can't be that bad. He chose you! He had sense enough to know whom to marry.

If something has gone wrong, it may very well be on his side of the fence. But in these devotions, our burden has been to help you be the wife God wants you to be.

There are plenty of things a husband needs to do to accomplish a kingdom agenda in his marriage. But as I examine the biblical data, I think we can narrow the wife's primary tasks down to two areas. She needs to *help* her husband (see Genesis 2:8) and *reverence*, or respect, her husband (see Ephesians 5:33; 1 Peter 3:2).

Wife, if these two qualities mark your life, you're in line for blessing from God.

THE DIGNITY OF WORK

"I glorified You on the earth, having accomplished the work which You have given Me to do."

JOHN 17:4

*T*he person who works gains a sense of dignity that nothing else can bring.

We know there is inherent dignity in work because God Himself worked at creation—and continues to work. Jesus had important work to do also. On the cross He said, "It is finished" (John 19:30). In other words, "I have accomplished what I came to accomplish."

If you take away a man's ability to work, you damage his sense of purpose and worth. Obviously our work doesn't determine our ultimate worth in God's sight, but it fulfills our built-in need for a feeling of dignity.

Sometimes my father would take me out to the Baltimore waterfront when he picked up his paycheck on his day off, and he'd show me the other longshoremen at work. They didn't have all the fancy equipment they have today for loading and unloading ships. I remember watching them and thinking of my father, *This man really works.*

That did something for me. I saw my father work, as you probably saw your father work, and it helped to teach me the dignity of honest, hard labor.

The task may be difficult at times, and the load might be heavy. But when we put our shoulder into jobs and do our best as a sacrifice of praise to our Lord Jesus, we gain the smile of heaven.

GOING FOR THE CROWN OF RIGHTEOUSNESS

*I have fought the good fight, I have finished the course,
I have kept the faith; in the future there is
laid up for me the crown of righteousness.*

2 TIMOTHY 4:7–8

The crown of righteousness is one of the rewards the New Testament urges us to seek through faithful service to Christ. The rest of this passage tells us that the apostle Paul expected to be given this reward by Jesus Himself, the "righteous Judge."

And the prize wasn't for Paul alone. Jesus will award it "to all who have loved His appearing." That includes the two of you—and your children, we pray.

Besides the awarding of crowns, something else will happen when we stand before the judgment seat of Christ (see 2 Corinthians 5:10). In that awesome moment, we will present to Him everything we have done since we became Christians.

Then He will put the fire of His judgment to our works, and at that point all the stuff we did for our own glory—or for any reason other than to bring glory to God—will go up in smoke. When that happens, there will be a loss of rewards for those lost works.

But when we are faithful in our service for Christ, when our works consist of "gold, silver [and] precious stones" (see 1 Corinthians 3:12), those works will stand the test of fire, and we will receive a reward, the crown of righteousness. Those good works include a faithful, committed marriage and a family raised for God's glory.

THE QUIETNESS OF
GODLY SUBMISSION — 1

You wives, be submissive to your own husbands
so that even if any of them are disobedient to the word,
they may be won without a word by the behavior of their wives.

1 PETER 3:1

The apostle Peter raised an issue faced by many Christian women today. *"What am I supposed to do? My husband isn't even a believer."*

Peter's advice actually takes a burden off the wife; it reminds her that God didn't call her to be her husband's pastor. She doesn't have to turn up the gospel radio station so her husband can hear the preaching. She doesn't have to pin Bible verses to his pillow or slip Christian tapes into his car's tape player. Peter said the way a messed-up husband is won to the Lord is not by his wife's preaching, but by her humility.

As most women can attest, the more a wife tries to change her husband by badgering him, the worse he usually becomes.

Why? Because when a woman does that, she's messing with the one thing a man will not compromise on, which is his ego. Now, I'm not saying this is right, I'm just telling you that's the way it is. This is the way men are built.

Men have egos, and those egos need to come under the lordship of Christ. God can work on a man's ego better than his wife can. What she needs to do is get out of the way so He can get to her husband. Her quiet, godly behavior makes that possible.

THE QUIETNESS OF
GODLY SUBMISSION—2

If you suffer for doing good and you endure it,
this is commendable before God.

1 PETER 2:20, NIV

*G*od can't get a husband's full attention when his wife is in the way. This doesn't mean that a Christian wife is to be speechless in her home. It does mean she is to honor her husband's position, even when she disagrees with him.

God says to the wife, "Be like Jesus in your home." The wife's example is the way Jesus bore up under His suffering. Peter wrote, "While being reviled, He did not revile in return; while suffering, He uttered no threats, but kept entrusting Himself to Him who judges righteously" (1 Peter 2:23).

Jesus didn't threaten. He didn't manipulate. When Jesus was mistreated, He committed Himself to God the Father. He took the suffering.

When you do it God's way, He makes it work. Christian wife, have you tried God's way to change your husband, or have you been complaining and nagging at him? If you've been pushing him, you're telling God, "Don't bother trying to change my husband. I'll take care of it myself."

Instead of preaching, God wants "chaste and respectful behavior" (1 Peter 3:2) from a wife. That word *behavior* means to stare at, to take a close look at. In other words, a Christian wife should make her husband stare at her in wonder by her loving, submissive attitude and reaction to him.

THE QUIETNESS OF
GODLY SUBMISSION — 3

Your adornment must not be merely external...
but let it be the hidden person of the heart,
with the imperishable quality of a gentle and quiet spirit.

1 PETER 3:3—4

*I*nstead of giving her husband the leftovers of her energy, emotions, and attention (after serving and looking good for the boss all day), a Christian wife looks for ways to help her man.

The idea is to make him stare, to shock him with your support and submission, to make him say, "We're going to church next week" because he likes what he sees and wants to find out what's going on.

Now, I realize some women can say, "You don't know my husband. He'll just take advantage of me if I do that." God says, "Leave that to Me." The issue once again is, do you trust God, or do you follow what your mind and your emotions are telling you?

One thing women can do to please their husbands is to keep themselves as attractive as possible. When Peter wrote about "braiding the hair, and wearing gold jewelry, or putting on dresses" (v. 3), he wasn't telling women it's wrong to look their best. He was urging them to keep those things in proper perspective.

Fixing up the outer person is good. But the Bible says women are to give that same meticulous attention to their inner person as well. A gentle and quiet spirit isn't just attractive to your husband. It is "precious in the sight of God" (v.4).

THE QUIETNESS OF
GODLY SUBMISSION — 4

*In former times the holy women also,
who hoped in God, used to adorn themselves,
being submissive to their own husbands.*

1 PETER 3:5

The most misunderstood verse in 1 Peter 3:1–6 may be the last one: "Just as Sarah obeyed Abraham, calling him lord, and you have become her children if you do what is right without being frightened by any fear." This doesn't mean that Sarah was Abraham's slave. It means she reverenced him. And by calling him "lord," a term of deep respect and honor, Sarah took her submission public.

Now, the context in which Sarah called Abraham "lord" is very interesting (Genesis 18:1–15). God came to Sarah and Abraham and told them they were going to have a baby the next year.

Sarah wondered about the promise, because at ninety, pregnancy was an impossible situation for her. Abe was one hundred, and there was no hope in sight. But when God saw that Sarah reverenced Abraham, suddenly Abraham could do things no hundred-year-old man was supposed to do. As a result, Sarah got pregnant. When she called Abraham "lord," God gave her a miracle.

The lesson, my sister in Christ, is that when you reverence your husband, God can make him do things he couldn't do before. God can turn his attitude and his life around. If you do your part and get out of the way, God can reach your husband.

LOOK FOR WORK, NOT EXCUSES

If any would not work,
neither should he eat.

2 THESSALONIANS 3:10, KJV

*P*aul's directive to the Thessalonian church is some of the best advice ever given on the importance of work. In effect, Paul was saying if a man can't work, you help him. But if he won't work, you don't help him.

When he gets hungry enough, he'll change his mind. That's why the church is not like the welfare system, which pays people not to work.

Throughout history, lazy people's excuses for not working could be pretty humorous. In Bible times, for example, a lazy man might have said, "There is a lion in the road! A lion is in the open square!" (Proverbs 26:13). In other words, "Hey, I can't go to work; I might get eaten."

In today's world, a sluggard says, "There are no jobs out there." No, there may not be any openings in your *field,* but a man who understands his responsibility before God does whatever it takes to provide for his family—even if it means flipping hamburgers for a time. Granted, it's not the best job. And it certainly isn't the best income. But it can be done with integrity—even joy—to God's glory.

You are working for the Lord, not just for "the man." Work for the Lord's approval, trust Him to provide, and the other stuff will take care of itself.

HELPING YOUR HUSBAND
AS A PARENT

*She rises while it is still night and gives food to her
household and portions to her maidens.
She is not afraid of the snow...
for all her household are clothed with scarlet.*

PROVERBS 31:15, 21

A Christian woman has to take care that the pull of the out-side world doesn't keep her from being an effective wife and mother.

In other words, don't let your job interfere with your duties at home. If somebody has to work overtime, let it be the husband.

A Christian wife helps her husband, not only by helping him parent their children, but also by taking care of herself, her person (see Proverbs 31:17, 22). She takes pains to look good, both for herself and for him. Her man is excited to come home. This is what happens when the wife's priorities follow the guidelines of Proverbs 31.

Instead, here's what often happens: The woman dresses up every morning because she wants to look good on the job. She knows the boss doesn't want haggard-looking people walking around the office. And when she gets to the office, she takes care of the boss, because he has her money in his pocket. Meanwhile, her husband comes home and has to fend for himself.

It's okay for the office to get in on what a woman does to enhance herself for her husband, but that's secondary. A wife who wants to help her husband strives to make him look good by taking care of herself.

WAITING FOR THE REAL THING

"How beautiful is your love, my sister, my bride!
How much better is your love than wine."

SONG OF SOLOMON 4:10

*A*nything God creates is intended to produce ecstasy and not guilt. When Adam and Eve came together sexually they had no remorseful memories that made them think, *I shouldn't have been there. I shouldn't have thought that. I shouldn't have done that.* Obviously, they were virgins before their marriage, so they had no reason to feel shame.

The entrance of sin into the world didn't change God's sexual standards. Men and women are still expected to be virgins before marriage.

But today, men in particular make excuses for their sin by saying, "Well, I'm a man, and you know how men are." No, you don't set the standard; God does. I'm really concerned about this, because America is producing a generation of young men who are like my dog. When my dog wants to satisfy his sexual desires, he goes looking for a female dog. His standards aren't very high. All he's concerned about is that his partner is a female.

You may be saying, "Tony, we're concerned too, but what can we do about it?" We can begin, of course, in our own homes with our sons and daughters, teaching them God's standards for love and sex.

For the sake of your children, and *their* children…for the future of our nation…step into the gap and use every ounce of influence God gives you!

DON'T REVERSE THE PROCESS

*"Seek first His kingdom and His righteousness,
and all these things will be added to you."*

MATTHEW 6:33

*C*hristians who prioritize God's kingdom each day will have their needs met. That's what Jesus said.

You can't improve on a promise like that! Why, then, do we reverse the process so often? So many times we say by our actions, "Lord, I'm going after all the things I need and want in life, and whatever is left over of my time, talent, and treasure, I'll use to seek Your kingdom and Your righteousness."

At other times, we say, "Lord, I'm going to worry about all these things because frankly, I'm not sure I can trust You to provide for me and my family."

That orientation to life is characteristic of people who don't know Him (see Matthew 6:32). Jesus asks you to put Him first in each decision and commitment of your marriage and family life...and then relax.

You have a heavenly Father who says, "If you will put Me first, you can leave your daily needs in My hands."

How can we learn to seek God's kingdom today and not worry about tomorrow? The secret is to live life one day at a time. God only gives you the help you need for today. So you don't worry about how you're going to make it tomorrow, because when you get there, God's grace and provision will be there to meet you.

GOING FOR THE CROWN OF GLORY

When the Chief Shepherd appears,
you will receive the unfading crown of glory.

1 PETER 5:4

*J*esus Christ has an indescribably wonderful reward waiting for those who guide and care for others in His love and in His name.

Peter urged leaders in Christ's body to carry out their ministry as shepherds under the leadership of Jesus Christ, the "Chief Shepherd." Those who shepherded God's flock in the right spirit and for the right reasons could expect to be rewarded by Christ for their faithful service.

What is the attitude and motive Christ wants from His servants? We're to "Be shepherds of God's flock that is under your care, serving as overseers—not because you must, but because you are willing, as God wants you to be; not greedy for money, but eager to serve; lording it over those entrusted to you, but being examples to the flock" (1 Peter 5:2–3, NIV).

Any Christian can win this crown by helping new believers grow up in Jesus Christ. The church should not only be a place where new believers grow up, it should be a maternity ward where new Christians are born, and a nursery where those babies begin growing.

Have you ever considered your role as a discipler and shepherd to your mate? With the help of the Chief Shepherd, set an example for each other and urge each other on to maturity in Christ.

HOW TO MAKE YOUR HUSBAND SECURE

*She does [her husband] good and
not evil all the days of her life.*

PROVERBS 31:12

One of the marks of a godly woman's home is her husband's feeling of confidence. Deep in his heart, he knows his wife will do what is right for him and for her family. And that brings rest to his spirit.

Many women groan when someone teaches on Proverbs 31. How could all of those wonderful traits and practices be wrapped up in one woman? How could anyone live up to such a role model?

There's one thing for certain: A solid, growing, and spiritually mature marriage takes time. But you have vowed, "Till death do us part." So relax and enjoy your mate because, as the Lord wills, you have a lifetime to lovingly work on the various adjustments and challenges in your relationship. You may not fully hit your stride until you're in your eighties!

My sister in Christ, the best way I know to make today's verse a reality in your home is to remember that you are your husband's helpmate. You are his completer, not his competitor. A wife is functionally subordinate to her husband, although she is equal with her mate in essence and spiritual value.

A woman who honors her marriage commitment and knows how to accept God-given authority in her life will do her husband and her family good.

A DECLARATION OF WAR

Our struggle is…against the rulers, against the powers,
against the world forces of this darkness,
against the spiritual forces of wickedness in the heavenly places.

EPHESIANS 6:12

*Y*ou are at war! In fact, no war in history can compare with the battle that you, your mate, and your family are fighting. And this war can either be the cause of your greatest joy as a Christian or the source of your deepest pain.

The war we're talking about is the spiritual warfare that became part of your life the moment you trusted Jesus Christ as your Savior. This war affects your relationship with your spouse and your children, and there is no way you can avoid the conflict. There is no bunker or foxhole you can crawl into that will shield you from the effects of this cosmic battle between the forces of God and the forces of Satan.

This is a war between invisible, angelic forces—a battle that impacts you and me. It's hard enough to fight an enemy we can see. It's much harder to fight what we can't see—but this is exactly the kind of enemy our marriages face. A spiritual battle requires spiritual armor. That's why Paul followed his classic statement on the nature of spiritual warfare with a description of the Christian's armor (see Ephesians 6:10–17).

Paul follows his discussion of the armor by exhorting us to "pray at all times" (v. 18). Why don't you and your spouse arm yourselves with prayer right now?

HONORING YOUR HUSBAND

Sarah obeyed Abraham, calling him lord,
and you have become her children if you do
what is right without being frightened by any fear.

1 PETER 3:6

If you know anything about the story of Sarah in the book of Genesis, then you know she was not a passive, "wallflower" saint. She was a woman of strength and dignity. Even so, she understood that God had assigned Abraham the role of leadership in their family, and she honored him for that.

Sarah honored him even though he had weaknesses. In fact, Abraham made a number of serious—potentially tragic—mistakes. Yet despite Abraham's shortcomings, the Bible says Sarah honored his headship in the family. The term *lord* was a word of respect for the husband, not a term of humiliation for the wife.

And here's the best part. When Sarah obeyed God by honoring Abraham, she received a miracle. God gave her the desires of her heart (see Psalm 37:4), and when she was ninety years old and childless, she had a baby.

What miracle are you asking God for in your marriage or family? Perhaps God wants you to begin honoring your husband's position before He will give you that miracle.

Some wives may say, "But if I honor my husband in this way, he'll take advantage of me." Go back to the last part of the verse above. If you do what is right, you need not be frightened by any fear.

AN UNBEATABLE TEAM FOR GOD

She extends her hand to the poor,
and she stretches out her hands to the needy.
She opens her mouth in wisdom,
and the teaching of kindness is on her tongue.

PROVERBS 31:20, 26

*O*ne result of a wife's helping hand in her husband's life is that he acquires a solid reputation. The husband in this chapter was one of the elders at the city gates (see Proverbs 31:23), where officials conducted business and governed the land. In other words, the guys at the office should know that a Christian man is where he is and is able to do what he does because he has a wife who helps him get it all together.

Just before I go to the office or to the church to preach, Lois checks me over and make a few adjustments. If I'm looking good when I arrive, it's because she helped me look good.

Now, I know that some women are at this point thinking, "But what about me? I don't always want to be in the background." The woman in our text wasn't an invisible person. Verse 28 says her children and her husband blessed her and praised her.

My brother, if you have a wife like this, you should "talk her up" all day long: "Thank you. Can't live without you. Need you. Enjoy you. Don't want to go to sleep without looking at you one more time. You're the first person I want to see in the morning."

Go public with this woman! You've got someone to brag about!

READY FOR BATTLE

...so that we would not be outwitted by Satan; for we are not ignorant of his designs.

2 CORINTHIANS 2:11, ESV

*Y*our five senses are not the limit of reality. If you are going to wage successful spiritual battle, you need a "sixth sense"—a keen awareness of the invisible, spiritual realm. This awareness begins with your worldview.

Your worldview is simply the lens through which you perceive reality. It has to do with the presuppositions that determine what you believe and the way you look at life.

There are really only two worldviews. One is called the natural, materialistic, or scientific worldview. It says that mankind, by his own reasoning, can figure out how the world works. This view leads quite naturally to agnosticism and atheism because it believes you don't need God as long as you have test tubes, microscopes, and telescopes.

The second worldview is the spiritual worldview, which says there is a realm outside of the physical. This view is very popular today, but unfortunately it is often not a biblically based, theistic view that believes in the one true God. Instead, too often it involves horoscopes, palm readers, and all sorts of New Age teaching. This is not the worldview of the Bible.

We need to keep our heads and our hearts in the Word, asking the Holy Spirit to reveal the truth to us. Then we'll be ready for spiritual battle.

SATISFYING MARITAL INTIMACY

Rejoice in the wife of your youth,
a lovely deer, a graceful doe.
Let her breasts fill you at all times with delight.

PROVERBS 5:18–19, ESV

*S*ome people think the apostle Paul was a self-righteous single person who looked down on those who could not control their passions. It's possible, however, that Paul was married at one time. He had been a member of the Sanhedrin, the Jewish ruling council, whose members were required to be married.

We do know that he spoke very forthrightly about the subject of marital intimacy.

In 1 Corinthians 7:3, a passage we've encountered before, Paul wrote, "The husband must fulfill his duty to his wife, and likewise also the wife to her husband." This word *duty* can cause great consternation. What did Paul mean? Is marital intimacy supposed to be a *job?*

We believe Paul was talking about the distinction between sexual intimacy between Christian couples and sexual intimacy between non-Christian couples. To generalize, intimacy between nonbelievers is primarily self-generated, by individuals thinking, *This is what I want.* But intimacy between two Christians is designed to be *other*-generated, by individuals who say, *This is what my mate needs.*

One challenge in building true physical intimacy is understanding those needs. What a woman needs starts in the morning, not at night. It starts in the kitchen and not in the bedroom. It begins with her emotions and not with her body. We husbands need to relearn that constantly.